Bringing Climate Change Into Natural Resource Management

Proceedings of a Workshop
June 28-30, 2005
Portland, Oregon

Technical Coordinators:

Linda Joyce, Richard Haynes,

Rachel White, and R. James Barbour

Olympic National Park

Abstract

Joyce, Linda; Haynes, Richard; White, Rachel; Barbour, R. James, tech. coords. 2006. Bringing climate change into natural resource management: proceedings. Gen. Tech. Rep. PNW-GTR-706. Portland, OR: U.S. Department of Agriculture, Forest Service, Pacific Northwest Research Station. 150 p.

These are the proceedings of the 2005 workshop titled implications of bringing climate into natural resource management in the Western United States. This workshop was an attempt to further the dialogue among scientists, land managers, landowners, interested stakeholders and the public about how individuals are addressing climate change in natural resource management. Discussions illustrated the complexity of global climate change and the need for managers to consider how the impacts of climate change will unfold across regional and local landscapes. The workshop offered examples of how managers are already responding to those aspects of the global climate change that they can see or perceive. While no comprehensive solutions emerged, there was an appreciation that policy complexity may exceed the science complexity but that eventually the accumulation of local actions will shape the future.

Keywords: Climate change, forest and range management.

Contents

Introduction

Agenda

Extended Abstracts

Poster Persentation Abstracts

— Introduction —

Rachel White[1] and Jamie Barbour[2]

Erik Ackerson, EarthDesign, Ink

Tom Iraci, USDA Forest Service

Tom Iraci, USDA Forest Service

[1] Science Writer-Editor, USDA Forest Service, Pacific Northwest Research Station, P.O. Box 3890, Portland, OR 97208. Email: rachelwhite@fs.fed.us

[2] Program Manager, USDA Forest Service, Pacific Northwest Research Station, P.O. Box 3890, Portland, OR 97208. Email: jbarbour01@fs.fed.us

1

A few unusually big tropical storms and hurricanes don't "prove" global warming is happening. But the hurricane season of 2005, which included monsters Katrina and Rita, has at least pointed anecdotally toward the predictions of extreme weather that have accompanied most climate change scenarios. Scientists around the globe have been making these predictions and warnings about climate change for decades. The Intergovernmental Panel on Climate Change (IPCC), created in 1988 by the United Nations, has issued strong statements about the changing climate and has written a comprehensive study of it and its potential effects (IPCC 2001). This team, which includes more than 2000 scientists from 100 countries, represents the largest scientific collaboration in history. Public understanding of the issue varies. Many in the science community recognize climate change as a serious matter where the consequences are likely to continue for many centuries. In the land management community, some managers are starting to adapt management strategies for changing climatic conditions.

> Many in the science community recognize climate change as a serious matter where the consequences are likely to continue for many centuries.

The issue of global climate change is highly complex and the spatial and temporal natures of its impacts are highly uncertain. First, there is the scientific complexity of a global issue and its relation to specific localities relevant to land managers. Second, there is uncertainty about the speed and extent of its occurrence that complicates human responses. Third, there is great market and policy complexity since it is an issue that crosses national and ownership boundaries.

Integrating (let alone locating) scientific information is sometimes a task easier said than done. Recognizing this, in 2003 then Pacific Northwest Research Station Director Tom Mills launched the Focused Science Delivery (FSD) program as one way to help address what he saw as a flaw in the way that scientific information is adopted and used by policy makers and natural resource managers. The purpose of the FSD program is to conduct syntheses of existing scientific information, perform analyses that will make this information more useful to natural resource practitioners, identify gaps in current knowledge, frame problems so that original research is more efficient, and deliver information in innovative ways that will quickly bring it into use. The "Bringing Climate Change into Natural Resource Management" conference is an example of a recent FSD effort—one intended to create a venue for scientists and managers to explore together problems and potential strategies for bringing climate change into natural resource planning.

It is the manager's response to the complicated aspects of the global climate change issue that motivated this workshop. How are they adapting their local actions and how do these actions contribute to mitigation of either climate change or its impacts? The workshop was an attempt to have a dialogue on the kinds of information (mostly at the local scale) managers need to address climate change in natural resource management. Through civic engagement, we can help increase the understanding both of the complexity of the issue and ways in which land managers can modify their actions to increase the certainty of outcomes in the face of changing climate.

> It is the manager's response to the complicated aspects of the global climate change issue that motivated this workshop.

The Workshop

In late June 2005, the USDA Forest Service (Pacific Northwest and Rocky Mountain Research Stations) and the Western Forestry and Conservation Association hosted a conference in Portland, Oregon on climate change. The conference presented some of the latest developments in climate change research related to natural resource management, covering topics like the climate of the West, fire dynamics in the future, western water resources, invasive plants, western bark beetle management, native vegetation responses to increasing carbon dioxide, and carbon sequestration. Panels explored western ecological responses to climate change, socioeconomic impacts, and what the future may hold for natural resource management under climate change. The presentations and panels provided excellent coverage of information, using the traditional "lecture-style" conference format, and successfully raised awareness on some very timely topics.

These proceedings are not the usual workshop documentation. Instead they contain four essays (three topical and one synthetic), the results of a series of roundtable discussions, and selected papers including several that are context setting.

The conference presented some of the latest developments in climate change research related to natural resource management...

References

Intergovernmental Panel on Climate Change [IPCC]. 2001. Third IPCC assessment report: summary for policymakers. Geneva: Switzerland: IPCC Secretariat.

— Agenda —

Climate Variability and Change as a Backdrop for Western Resource Management

Kelly T. Redmond[1]

Tom Iraci, USDA Forest Service

Mark Reid, USDA Forest Service

[1] Regional Climatologist/Deputy Director at Western Regional Climate Center, Desert Research Institute, 2215 Raggio Parkway, Reno, NV 89512-1095. Email: Kelly.redmond@dri.edu

Abstract

Climate and its variations constitute a dominant driver of natural systems. Effective management of the natural resources of the West requires knowledge of the spatial and temporal characteristics of climate, and of ways of utilizing that knowledge. The topographic diversity of the West leads to similar diversity and structure in its climates. Climate varies naturally for many reasons, encompassing external forcings and internal dynamics. Human activities are increasingly an additional source of spatial and temporal variability in climate, at global, regional and local scales. Greenhouse gasses and aerosols are two well-known factors, but there are many others as well. The response of environmental systems varies from simple and straightforward to exceedingly complex. The Western United States has been warming during the past three decades, much more than the Eastern states, and more in winter than in summer. Evidence for this comes from many independent sources. Precipitation is much more variable and there are no discernible overall trends in this element for the West as a whole. In broad measure these findings do not appear to contradict theoretical expectations. There is more confidence in temperature than in precipitation projections. Temperature increases, by themselves, have significant hydrological implications. Snow and snow melt are critical factors in western water supplies, and there are numerous indications of reductions in snow over the past 2-3 decades. The U.S. vulnerability of snow-driven hydrology to temperature increase is much greater in the mountainous Western states, and greatest along the west coast. These changes, and apparent connections to temperature, may require societal adjustments and therefore must be more fully characterized and understood. Several teleconnections to global climate exist, the most important being to El Niño, La Niña, and the Southern Oscillation (ENSO), and furnish an important source of interannual variability. Persistent drought episodes in the region are linked to tropical ocean conditions. The region is monitored unevenly, favoring lower elevations and population concentrations. Conditions where important resources are located are not as well monitored. Many opportunities exist for improved monitoring, but they require persistence, dedication, and a strong commitment to coordination. Methods and structures are present to provide access to the large volume of data and information that does exist, but need further improvement. Variations and trends in climate are taking place in a region where many other factors are likewise changing, especially demographics, lifestyles, attitudes, and economics, and these relationships must be understood and accommodated in making good management decisions.

Keywords: Climate, variability, monitoring, temperature, precipitation, snowpack, data.

Introduction

Climate and its variations constitute an important driver of natural systems. This discussion is predicated on the assumption that improved awareness and utilization of climate knowledge will result in improved management of natural resources. Variability is an inherent property of climate, driven by constant fluctuations in flows of energy and mass throughout the system. These flows are seldom in full equilibrium across important system interfaces, and fluctuations in stored energy and mass make up the difference. External drivers and internal dynamics operate on many different time scales, from microseconds to eons, to produce the variations we observe. The mixture of climate drivers is itself not constant, and in recent decades factors of human origin have increasingly been adding a new source of climate variability. No matter what humans do, or how much role they play in affecting climate, the existing natural sources of climate variability will continue to exert their influences as before. (In this article, the term "variability" is generally intended to connote temporal rather than spatial variability.) Fluctuation has been a constant accompaniment to climate and this is not going to stop.

Through their technology and their sheer numbers, humans have acquired the ability to modify climate in many ways. Most of these ways involve the manner in which energy moves through the system, particularly in the form of radiation. Others involve the microphysical processes that produce precipitation, operating at tiny scales. Still others involve chemical and biological pathways, and the vegetation that covers most landscapes. Climate changes associated with humans involve more than just greenhouse gasses, although the latter receive much of our current attention.

Examples of these human modes of influence include greenhouse gasses (carbon dioxide, ozone, nitrous oxide, methane, chlorofluorocarbons, water vapor) and aerosols (particles suspended in a gas: dust from volcanoes, lakebeds, and disturbed soil; soot, ash, and pollution; and gasses transformed through photochemistry to particles), all of which affect the flow of radiant energy through air. Changes in land surface properties all affect the absorption and emission of solar and infrared energy, the partitioning of energy transfer between sensible heat and evaporation, the speed of the wind, and the flow of energy to/from the substrate. These properties include reflectivity or "albedo," wetland fraction, permeability to water, presence or absence of reservoirs, and substrate properties, brought about by activities such as deforestation, irrigation, agricultural practices, paving, or other kinds of development. Cloud droplets and ice crystals form around small nuclei, and recent findings indicate that changes in atmospheric particle concentration can greatly alter cloud properties and reduce precipitation efficiency and amount, and affect its type (rain or snow). Changes in atmospheric CO_2, ozone and other gaseous and aerosol constituents have direct but differential physiological effects on vegetation, species competitiveness, amount and quality of light, which in turn affect soil moisture and recharge budgets, plant species composition and community properties.

Through their technology and their sheer numbers, humans have acquired the ability to modify climate in many ways.

All of the above mechanisms are primary, acting as physical drivers to modify climate. Secondary mechanisms, acting in response to climate, are even more diverse, and include hydrological and biological responses to the original source of climate variation, and feedback effects that act to amplify or dampen climatic responses. Although certain processes and constituents dominate the discussion, climate change is not a single-issue problem and has numerous dimensions, many interacting synergistically.

In some cases the effects of particular changes act on climate to reinforce the original effect (positive feedback) or to dampen the original effect (negative feedback). A multitude of both kinds of feedback processes are at work, although ultimately it is negative feedbacks that keep our climate from wildly fluctuating from one time period to the next or running off to some extreme equilibrium state (Rial et al. 2004).

Observed Variability and Trends

The West is a land of juxtapositions and sharp contrasts, a salient characteristic of its climate and of other attributes. Basic climate categories can change over short distances, as does precipitation seasonality, annual amount, and phase (rain/snow). Temporal variability properties can vary over short spatial distances (Redmond 2003). Elevation plays a key role, and mountain ranges greatly modify and sometimes cause their own weather. Mountain time series of climatic elements can be very different from those in the adjoining valleys. Large scale "teleconnections" with other parts of the globe lead to spatially different responses in reaction to far-away phenomena such as El Niño and La Niña. Much of western hydrology is snowmelt driven ($^2/_3$ to $^3/_4$ by most accounts), so that winter conditions are extremely important to the annual water budget of the entire region. Precipitation and streamflow show much greater relative (normalized) interannual variability in the Southwest than the Northwest (Cayan et al. 2003), with the greatest variability seen along the West Coast (Andrews et al. 2004).

For purposes here we focus primarily on the 11 westernmost continental (mountain) states, although many comments apply to Alaska and Hawaii as well. The 11 states occupy 1.20 million square miles, 38 percent of the lower 48. With Alaska/Hawaii, the 1.87 million square mile total is 49 percent of the U.S. 50-state area. The 11 conterminous states show significant and different variability properties in temperature compared with precipitation. Winter (October-March) temperatures from 1895-96 through 2004-05 are shown in figure 1 for the entire region. They show considerable winter-to-winter variability, and in later decades exhibit a trend that began in the late 1970s/early 1980s. Annual (calendar year) temperatures are shown in figure 2 from 1895-2004. The rising trend over the past 30 years is again evident.

Although attribution is not a main goal here, shown in figure 3 are a series of temperature projections from 6 models and 2 greenhouse gas emission scenarios compiled by Dettinger (2004), for a location between Reno, Nevada and Susanville, California (representative of most of the West). These show that a general rise out of the inherent variability

Much of western hydrology is snowmelt driven ($^2/_3$ to $^3/_4$ by most accounts), so that winter conditions are extremely important to the annual water budget of the entire region.

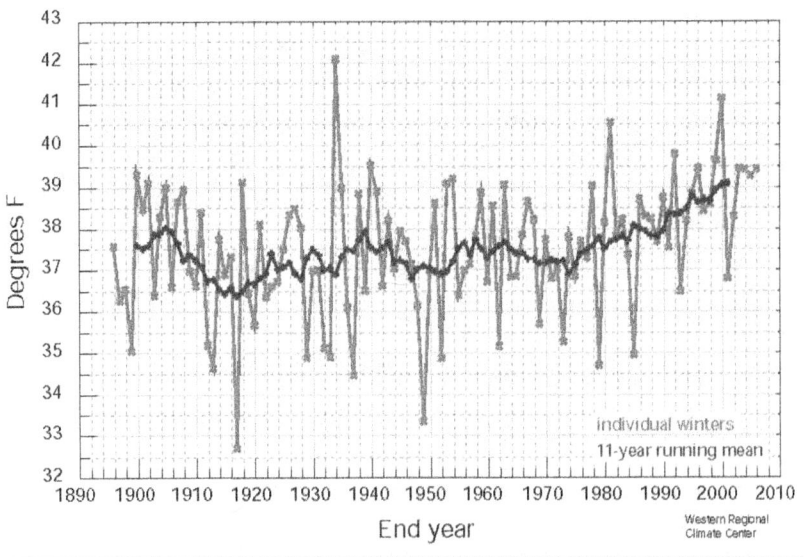

Figure 1—Mean cold-season temperature (October-March) for the 11 westernmost continental states, area-weighted from divisional data, 1895-2006. Data source: National Climatic Data Center.

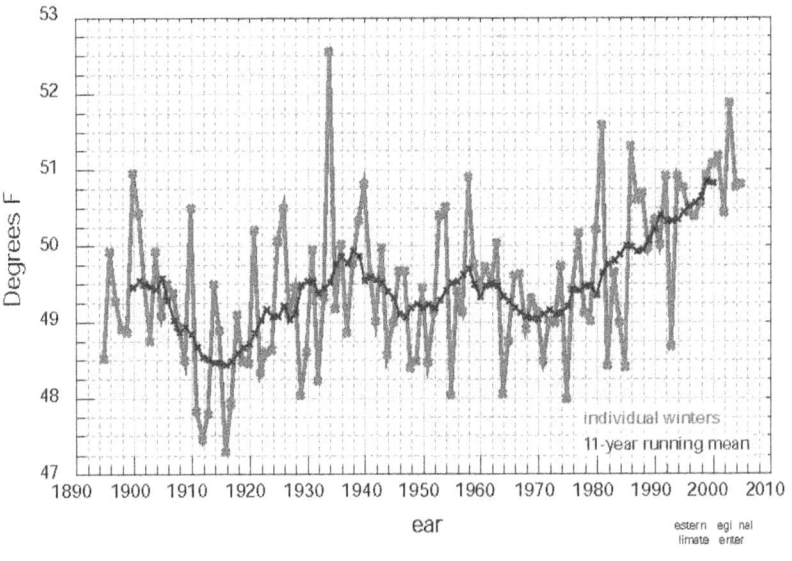

Figure 2—Mean annual calendar-year temperature for the 11 westernmost continental states, area-weighted from divisional data, 1895-2005. Data source: National Climatic Data Center.

should have begun sometime around 1980, and also show fairly close agreement between models during the first half of the 21st Century. There is a strong suggestion in these figures that climate change has already been underway in the Western states, escaping our notice for the last 25 years until this signal began to rise above the background variability. Seasonal temperature trends are shown in figure 4. Winter and spring have the strongest trends in later years.

By contrast, western winter precipitation since 1895 has rather different properties, as shown in figure 5. There is little trend, but great variability, and furthermore there is a change in the properties of variability after the mid 1970s. Water-year precipitation from 1895-96 through 2004-05 is shown in figure 6. After a period of relatively

There is a strong suggestion in these figures that climate change has already been underway in the western states, escaping our notice for the last 25 years...

9

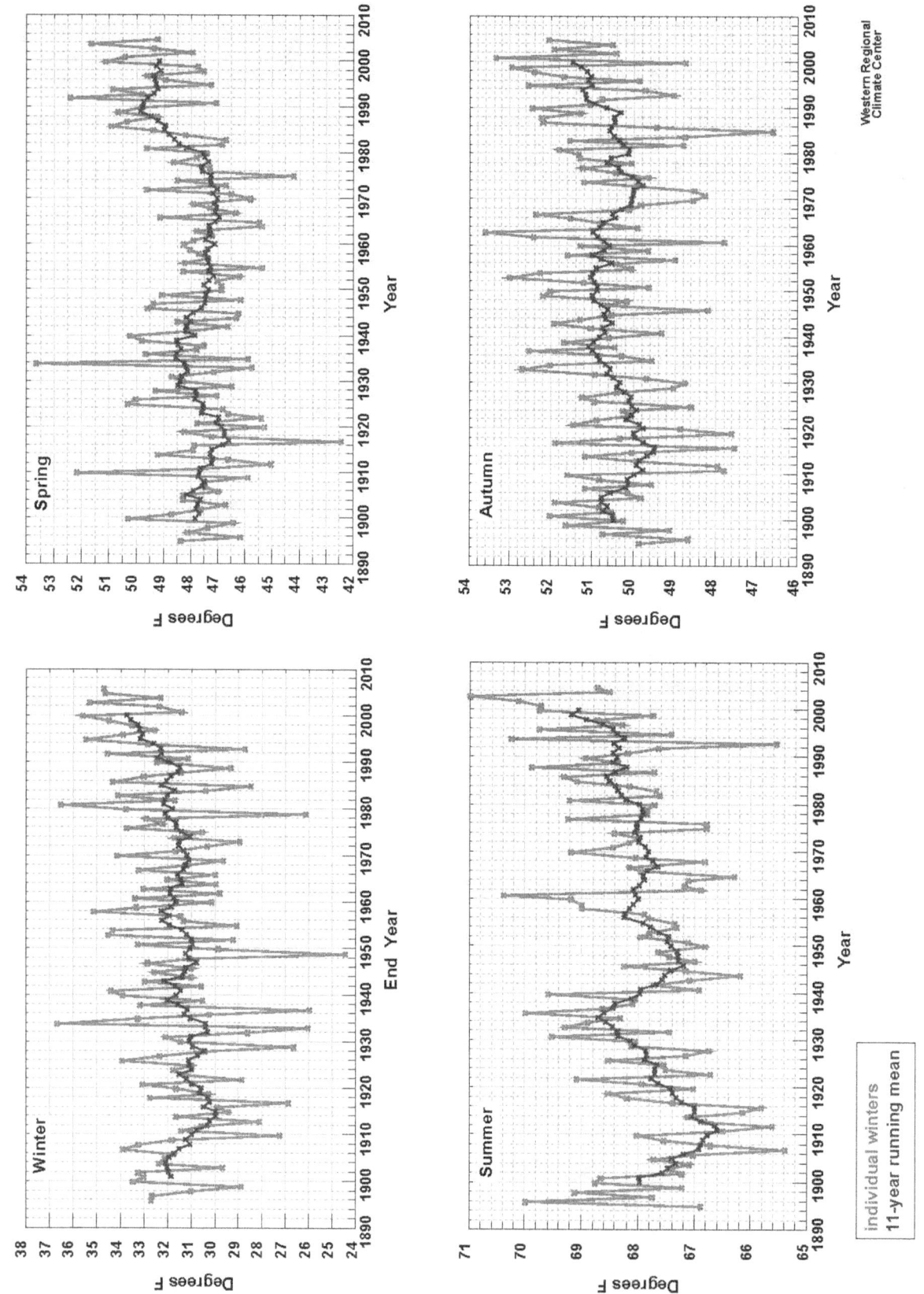

Figure 3—Mean seasonal temperature for the 11 westernmost continental states, area-weighted from divisional data, Jan 1895 through Mar 2006. Upper left: Dec-Jan-Feb. Upper right: Mar-Apr-May. Lower left: Jun-Jul-Aug. Lower right: Sep-Oct-Nov. Data source: National Climatic Data Center.

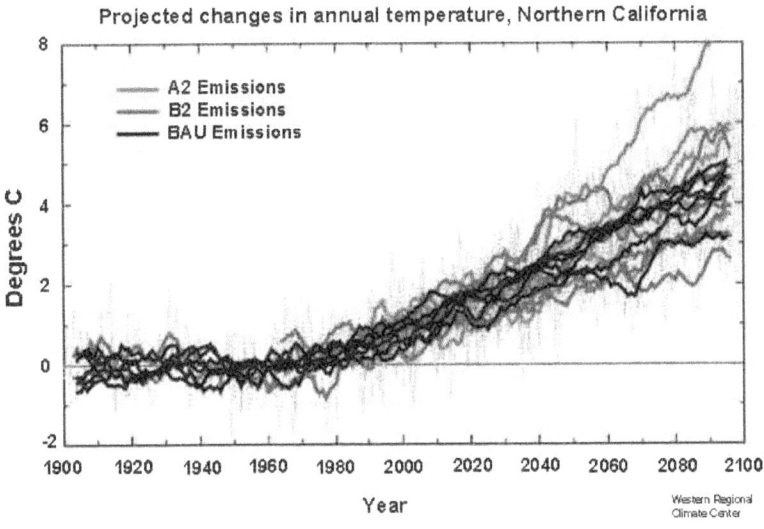

Projected changes in annual temperature, Northern California

Figure 4—Simulated and projected temperature changes, between Reno, Nevada and Susanville, California, 1900-2100, from six climate models using three emissions scenarios, compared with baseline case. (1 C = 1.8 F). From Dettinger (2004).

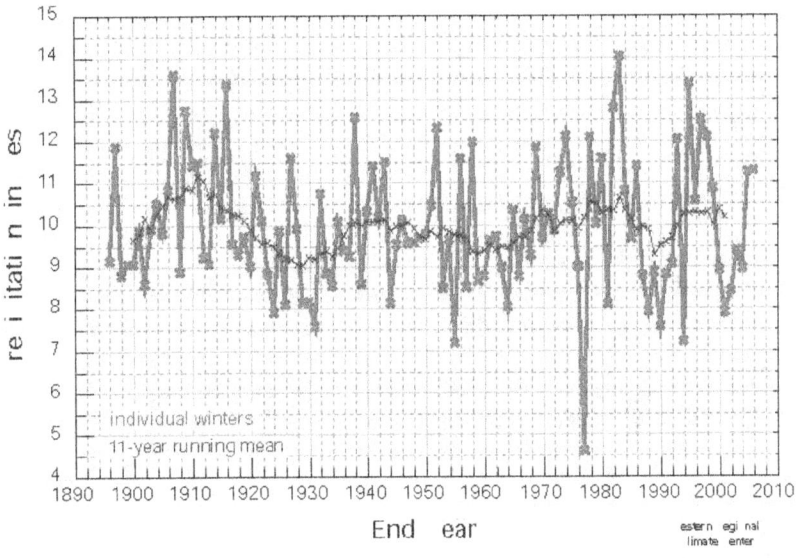

Figure 5—Total cold-season precipitation (October-March) for the 11 westernmost continental states, area-weighted from divisional data, 1895-2006. Data source: National Climatic Data Center.

little variability for several prior decades, the West has seen pronounced variability in precipitation since the standout drought winter of 1976-77, followed a few years later by the wettest winter on record in 1982-83. Not only has there been significant variation from year to year, but also over the past 30 years the West has experienced several extended periods that were wet (early 1980s), dry (1987-1994 excepting 1992-93), wet again (mid to late 1990s), and dry again with very severe drought from 1999-2004 (not known at this writing if 2004-05 marked the end). A portion of this variability appears related to the "1976 shift" in Pacific climate (Ebbesmeyer et al. 1991; Trenberth and Hurrell 1994) and the changed frequency of El Niño and La Niña, but likely not entirely so.

The precipitation projections from the same set of models employed by Dettinger (2004) are shown in figure 7. Collectively they show

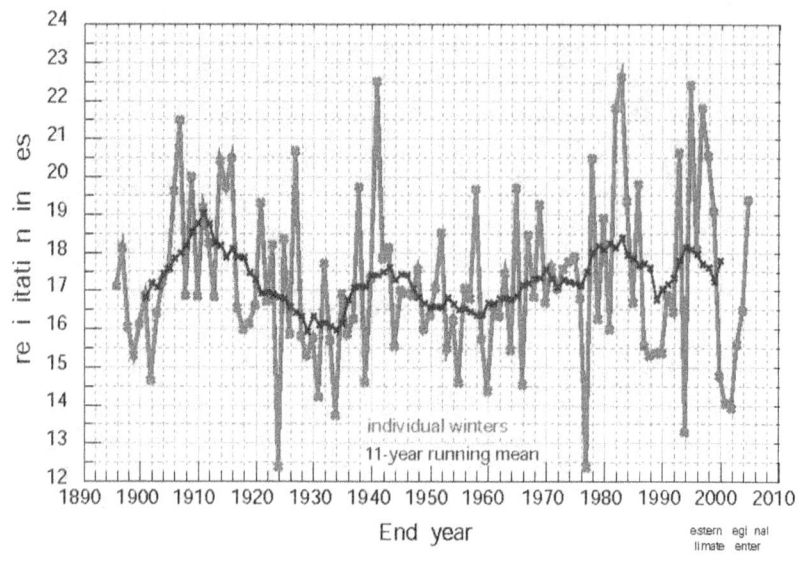

Figure 6—Mean annual water-year precipitation (October-September) for the 11 westernmost continental states, area-weighted from divisional data, 1895-2005. Data source: National Climatic Data Center.

The general expectation is that Earth's climate will warm from greenhouse gasses, and that the hydrological cycle will speed up (more evaporation, more rain).

Whatever the reason, warming of the West appears to be a fact of life.

little trend, and exhibit more scatter among themselves later in the 21st Century, with also a suggestion of greater interannual and multi-year variability.

Global average effects of climate change will not be identical at each and every location.

The general expectation is that Earth's climate will warm from greenhouse gasses, and that the hydrological cycle will speed up (more evaporation, more rain). However, the spatial and seasonal distribution of any such changes will vary regionally and locally. This is especially the case for precipitation. In the West such changes may also vary with elevation, because the ways in which mountains enhance precipitation are dependent on temperature, moisture, vertical stability, and trajectory.

In addition, the projections shown in figures 4 and 7 show more commonality for temperature than for precipitation, with tighter clustering among models and scenarios. At this point there is much more confidence in projections of temperature than in projections of precipitation. The question of whether precipitation will increase or decrease or stay the same, or in what seasons or locations or elevations, is not likely to be answered definitively very soon. Our response and adaptation mechanisms should be prepared to accept this state of affairs.

In terms of regional differences, the era since the turn of the new Millennium has brought warm conditions much more frequently to the West. Figure 8 shows the 72-month anomaly from the period mean, for the interval January-December 2000-2005. These and other studies have shown that most of the warming seen in the United States has been in the 11 Western states and the northern High Plains, with relatively little warming seen in the Eastern and particularly Southeastern United States (fig. 8). Whatever the reason, warming of the West appears to be a fact of life.

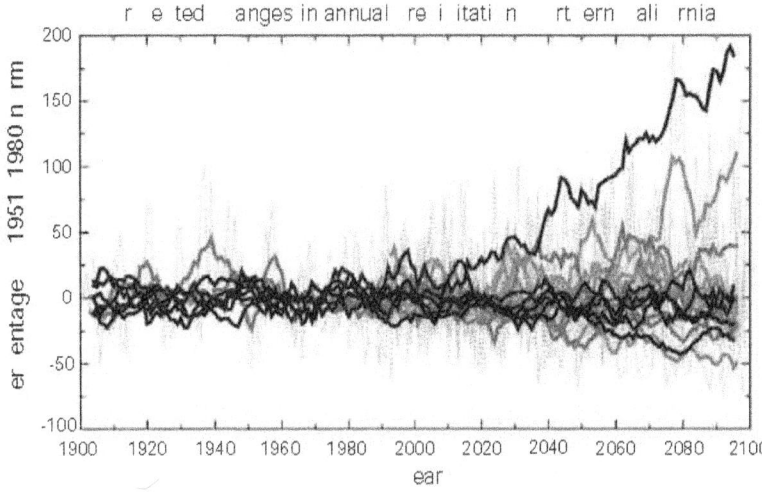

Figure 7—Simulated and projected precipitation changes, expressed as percentages, between Reno, Nevada and Susanville, California, 1900-2100, from six climate models using three emissions scenarios, compared with baseline case. From Dettinger (2004).

For purposes of forecast interpretation, the NOAA Climate Prediction Center has computed successive trends for each climate division in the United States from 1941-1998, and for all 3-month seasons, with a hinge point at 1966 (CPC 2005c). The trend after this hinge (1966-1998) shows similar patterns of warming to those in figure 8, much more accentuated in winter than in summer. Cayan et al. (2001) used phenological evidence from a network of lilacs and honeysuckles [shows] that bloom dates have been occurring earlier each year for the last several decades. In the same paper they also presented further evidence of an earlier onset to spring in the West in the timing of the snowmelt "pulse." Spring runoff in snow-fed basins typically begins in a sudden burst that can usually be identified to within a day or two. Over the past 3-5 decades dates of this spring pulse have been occurring earlier by 1-4 weeks in the Western contiguous United States, Canada, and Alaska (Stewart et al. 2005). Conversion of the bloom and spring pulse dates into temperature terms shows that they agree with thermometer records for the late winter and spring that precede these events (Cayan et al. 2001). This correspondence has given us more confidence in all of the separate time series, especially those for temperatures that are based strictly on thermometers.

Western snowpack is critical to summer streamflow, and normally peaks between March 1 in the southern West and May 1 in the northern West; April 1 is commonly used as a west-wide date of maximum snowpack. Mote (2003a, 2003b) used data from the Natural Resources Conservation Service (NRCS) Snotel network and its predecessor, the snow course network, to show that the snowpack on this date has shown a recent decline over most of the West. Later studies, Mote et al. (2005) and Mote (submitted), expanded to the remainder of the West and showed a similar result, except in the southern portions. Subsequent diagnosis (Hamlet et al. 2005) has shown that both temperature and precipitation trends in winter have contributed to the observed trends in April 1 snow water equivalent (SWE, the water residing in the snowpack if melted).

...phenological evidence from a network of lilacs and honeysuckles [shows] that bloom dates have been occurring earlier each year for the last several decades.

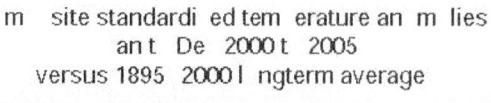

m site standardi ed tem erature an m lies
an t De 2000 t 2005
versus 1895 2000 l ngterm average

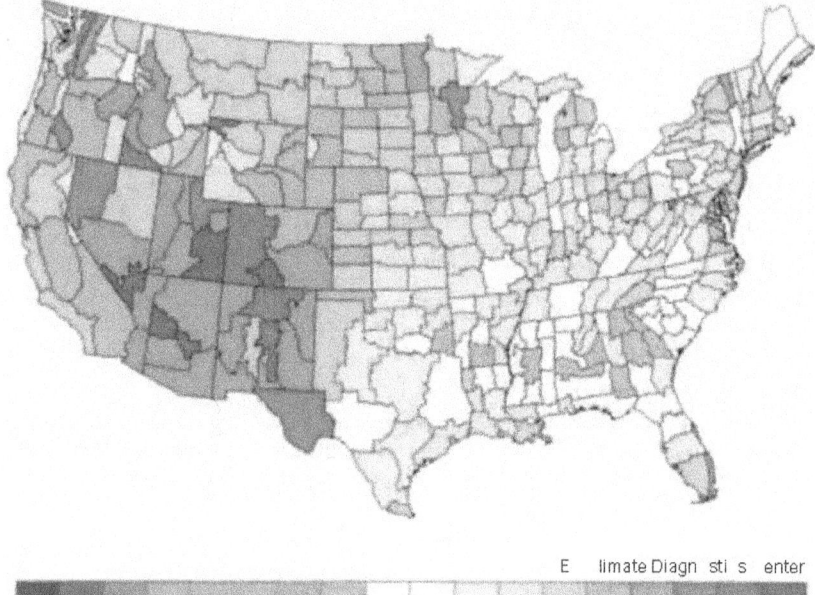

E   limate Diagn sti s enter

-2 00   -1 50   -1 00   -0 50   0 00   0 50   1 00   1 50   2 00

Figure 8—Departure from average temperature, 344 United States climate divisions, for the 72-month period from January 2000 through December 2005, expressed as departure in standard deviations from 1895-2000 mean. Analysis: NOAA Climate Diagnostics Center.

In the Western states late winter and early spring have shown the greatest rate of warming during the year...

In almost every location, temperature trends are acting to reduce late season snowpack, but in some locations, notably the southern Sierra Nevada, the effects from upward precipitation trends on snowpack (possibly from increased El Niño frequency) have overcome the effects of trends toward higher temperatures on snowpack.

The factors that control the properties of the spring snowmelt pulse can be deduced with the help of hourly streamflow data (Lundquist and Cayan 2002, Lundquist and Dettinger 2005). Lundquist and Dettinger (2004) examine the very interesting issue of the details of how the spring snowmelt pulse forms, and its synchroneity at different altitudes. Surprisingly, this does not always appear to steadily march up the elevation gradient as spring warms up, and varies considerably from one year to another. In the Western states late winter and early spring have shown the greatest rate of warming during the year (CPC 2005c). The ratio of early summer runoff to the annual total began to decrease in the latter quarter of the 20th Century (Aguado et al. 1992, Dettinger and Cayan 1995, Roos 1991). Subsequent studies (Dettinger 2005; Stewart et al. 2004, 2005) have shown that earlier spring pulses and runoff fractions are occurring from Mexico to Alaska. Regonda et al. (2005) show a variety of interlinked trends stemming from warming that are consistent with many of the foregoing results, and in aggregate constituting a significant change in western hydrology already under way.

Mountain glaciers in the western portions of the United States and Canada and in Alaska show widespread trends toward negative mass balances on an annual basis, cumulative mass loss, and retreat on a large scale (e.g., Burbank 1982, Hall and Fagre 2003, Hodge et al. 1998, Luckman 1998, Naftz et al. 2002, Rasmussen and Conway 2004, Reichert et al. 2002).

In recent years there have been large die-offs in western forests on spatial scales not hitherto witnessed directly. In some areas (the Southwest) these forest effects have been driven primarily by drought, but also by related causes such as warm temperatures and insect growth (Northern United States and southern Canadian Rockies, where temperature has been the issue more than drought). Weiss and Overpeck (2005) present phenological evidence from vegetation of recent warming, especially minimum temperature, in the Sonoran Desert. The Southwest has experienced two large and lengthy droughts in the last half century, one in the mid 1950s and one from 1999-2004 (maybe not over yet). The second drought was during the warmer regime shown in figures 1 and 2; the increased temperature appears to have exacerbated the effects of insects. In the Rockies of the Northern United States and Southern Canada, insect pests such as pine beetles are affecting elevations and tree species where they have not been previously seen. In some elevation bands, mild winters are permitting overwintering while longer summers are permitting a second generation in one year, speeding insect life cycles and overcoming the defense mechanisms of trees not accustomed to such assaults (Logan and Powell, submitted).

Long-term surface monitors at higher elevations are difficult to find, especially in North America and in the United States (see Diaz and Bradley 1997, and Diaz et al. 1997 and papers therein). Evidence of high elevation effects can be obtained from the National Center for Atmospheric Research/National Centers for Environmental Prediction (NCAR/NCEP) "Reanalysis" (Kalnay et al. 1996, Kistler et al. 2001). Operational weather models and data assimilation techniques are constantly being refined and changed. The concept of Reanalysis is to "freeze" the analysis and assimilation methods using a recent modern model, and re-process all the original input data from the last 3-5 decades (which has all been saved!) so that changes in processing are not the source of the subtle variations of interest for climate. Though laborious, this approach has proven to be well worth the trouble. Time series of temperature data at 700 mb (10,000 ft [3000 m]) taken from the Reanalysis shows winter and annual trends not too dissimilar from those of the cooperative network at the surface seen if figures 1, 2, and 4. These values, based largely on weather balloons, do not include precipitation. It is not known definitively whether high elevations have warmed or will warm differentially compared to low elevations, and it is very important to improve this understanding (Karl et al. 2006, Pepin and Seidel 2005).

In recent years there have been large die-offs in western forests on spatial scales not hitherto witnessed directly.

In the Rockies of the Northern United States and Southern Canada, insect pests such as pine beetles are affecting elevations and tree species where they have not been previously seen.

What is Expected with Climate Change, and with What Certainty

The climate elements of most interest to resource managers are precipitation and temperature. Fortunately, these are the most widely measured and reported and have the longest time series. Other common elements of interest to resource managers include snowfall, snow depth, absolute or relative humidity, wind speed and direction, solar radiation, clouds and sky conditions, and soil temperature and moisture. The relevant statistical climate descriptors of most interest are usually means or totals over days, months, or seasons. Others wish to know the likelihood of threshold exceedance, because natural resource systems are unduly affected by rare extreme events and disturbances, that result in, for example, mortality, lack of mortality (for pests), erosive events, fire, or other ecosystem disturbance. Redmond (1998) presented an overview of many of the principal climate change issues in the West.

Temperature is the element in which there is the most confidence in the ability to project future trends. Temperature is a continuous variable in the atmosphere (it is always present), we have ample experience with it, and many biological and chemical processes are highly correlated with temperature. In the West, with its many dependencies on snow, temperature is an important *hydrologic* element, even though it is not often thought of in those terms. As figure 4 shows, there is significant coherence among forecast models for the next several decades for a relatively steady rate of warming. This combination of expectations approximately matching ongoing observed trends seems sufficient to instill at least moderate confidence in further expectation of continued warming of the Western states. Furthermore, there is reason to believe that nighttime minimum temperatures are likely to warm more than daytime maximum temperatures. Humans may pay more attention to daylight conditions, but natural systems are exposed at all times. More generally, all natural systems take notice of all climatic factors in their immediate environment and respond to them, whether nearby humans in their buffered environments do or not.

It is interesting to note that in the nearly four decades since Manabe and Wetherald (1967) used a simple one-dimensional model to estimate that global climate would warm by about 2°C with doubled CO_2, a finding that has changed relatively little with far more sophisticated models. Nonetheless, until these models have attained a longer track record, and have proven themselves in more demanding contexts, there remains the possibility that they are missing or misrepresenting processes of importance, and results should not be accepted as gospel. They are tools for planning, diagnosing and understanding, and as long as this point is kept in mind, they can be extremely useful.

With respect to precipitation, as with daily weather this element is much harder than others (such as temperature) to forecast at longer time scales, weeks to decades. Precipitation is discontinuous in the atmosphere, not present everywhere and every moment, so one has to first forecast the development of a storm or cloud, and then secondly obtain the amounts.

Temperature is the element in which there is the most confidence in the ability to project future trends.

...there is reason to believe that nighttime minimum temperatures are likely to warm more than daytime maximum temperatures. Humans may pay more attention to daylight conditions, but natural systems are exposed at all times.

Cloud effects must be parameterized, since no present climate model can afford the resources to try to resolve the formation of individual clouds (and, there are many kinds of clouds). Winter systems are more likely to be simulated correctly, because of their large scale. Summer convection is much harder to simulate accurately. Likewise, monsoon systems present a real challenge to climate models. Manabe et al. (2004) note that on a global basis, current wet places are likely to become wetter, and other locations may experience more water stress.

For precipitation over regions the size of typical western river basins, there is much disagreement among models, there are many issues of scale (spatial and temporal), the track record does not seem impressive, and the best advice for managers is to be very circumspect, take care in trusting any of the model results too much, and to use model results for precipitation as scenarios and potential futures. Attempts are being made to address this uncertainty more directly by expressing results as probability distributions (e.g., Dettinger 2004). Trenberth et al. (2003) emphasized that too much focus may be placed on precipitation amount, rather than other important characteristics that may change (frequency, timing, intensity, statistical distributions, extremes, types of events, etc). Meehl et al. (2000) discuss the impacts of changes in extreme of climate. Groisman et al. (2001, 2004) report on changes in the frequency distribution of precipitation and streamflow in the United States, with upward trends especially in the heaviest end of the frequency distribution, and in recent decades. With such extreme differences in precipitation climatology over short horizontal distances, much care must be taken in the West when interpreting the correspondence between model projections and observations (examples in Groisman et al. 2005).

Snow and snowpack result from a combination of temperature and precipitation processes. To the extent that models can get the precipitation approximately correct, they have good prospects of utilizing their better temperature performance to provide diagnostic and prognostic inferences about snow depth and water content. Snow *depth* is important to plants (protection via coverage) and to animals (or their predators) that hibernate or that must forage or migrate through deep snow, and to snowplows, skiers and snowmobiles. Snow *water content* is important to water supplies, soil recharge, stream runoff, snow loading for design, rafters, early summer hikers, forest road design, and many others. Climate projections in nearly all cases are for snow levels to rise, and for end-of-winter snowpack and snow depth to decline, except at the highest elevations (less cold, but still below freezing) and in those locations where precipitation might increase (Christensen et al. 2004; Knowles and Cayan 2002, 2004; Van Rheenen et al. 2004). Barnett et al. (2005) estimate that about $1/_6$ of the world population receives its water supply from ice and snow, and is at risk of disruption from warming. Models, and empirical studies (see below), indicate that lower mountains, closer to the mean freezing level, are especially vulnerable to decreases in snowpack.

Along these lines, Mike Dettinger (reported in Bales et al., submitted) has performed a very informative vulnerability analysis, based largely on observed behavior, using the Variable Infiltration Capacity (VIC) model

For precipitation over regions the size of typical western river basins, there is much disagreement among models, there are many issues of scale (spatial and temporal), the track record does not seem impressive, and the best advice for managers is to be very circumspect…

Models, and empirical studies, indicate that lower mountains, closer to the mean freezing level, are especially vulnerable to decreases in snowpack.

(Liang et al. 1994, 1996) at the University of Washington. In important catchments much snow falls near the freezing point. For example, in the Sierra Nevada, Blue Canyon at elevation 5,280 ft (1609 m) averages about 248 in (630 cm) of snow with a mean winter temperature of 36°F (+2°C), whereas the Central Sierra Snow Lab 20 mi (35 km) east toward the Sierra crest on Interstate 80 at 6,883 ft (2098 m) receives 451 in (1145 cm) of snow with a mean winter temperature of 28°F (–2°C). Both locations have similar total winter precipitation. Assuming a modest change in temperature of about +3°C, daily time series are examined at each $^1/_8$ degree VIC grid point to estimate the change in likelihood of a former snow event changing to a rain event because of the temperature increase. These results are shown in figure 9.

> This analysis shows that the entire West Coast (Sierra/Cascades) is seen to be quite vulnerable to modest increases in temperature.

This analysis shows that the entire West Coast (Sierra/Cascades) is seen to be quite vulnerable to modest increases in temperature. Much precipitation that now falls as snow would fall in the future as rain, so that snowpack would decline if precipitation amounts stayed the same. The state of Idaho and parts of the Great Basin are next most vulnerable. The highest, and thus coldest, mountains in Colorado, and the southern High Sierra, with its limited spatial area, are less vulnerable. Heavy rain events in winter, and rain-on-snow events, would likely increase (even with no increase in precipitation). Knowles et al. (submitted) report that rain/snow ratios have already begun to change in the Western United States; Huntington et al. (2004) are reporting a similar result for the Northeast United States. These have significant consequences for reservoir management, in attaining a seasonally evolving balance between flood control (empty reservoirs are best) and preservation of water supplies (full reservoirs are best). In many of these model runs, higher precipitation variability leads to the seemingly paradoxical and perverse result that the likelihood of *both* floods *and* dry spells and droughts goes up. This odd result does indeed appear physically plausible, and perhaps we have been witnessing this in the past 30 years. The summer dry season would generally begin earlier and end later, so that the evaporative demand season would be longer, and likely exaggerate fire danger.

> …higher precipitation variability leads to the seemingly paradoxical and perverse result that the likelihood of *both* floods *and* dry spells and droughts goes up.

Additional studies (Dettinger et al. 2004, Hamlet and Lettenmeier 1999, Jeton et al. 1996, Kim 2005, Kim et al. 2002, Leung et al. 2004) anticipate changes in the timing of many snowmelt driven systems. Miller et al. (2003) examine the effects of climate change on California hydrology. Others have gone further and attempted to determine biological effects of warmer streams, such as on fish populations (e.g., Gooseff et al. 2005 and references therein). Hayhoe et al. (2004) discuss a variety of issues pertinent to climate change in California.

Models with subsurface structure indicate that warming seems more likely to reduce rather than to increase soil moisture. In part this stems from a longer and warmer vegetative water demand season, and from less efficient recharge in the mountains in winter. With respect to atmospheric moisture, we do not have high quality long-term observations of humidity trends, and are unlikely to obtain these soon from in situ ground-based sensors. Wind also affects soil moisture and evapotranspiration, but is one of the most difficult elements to measure accurately and consistently

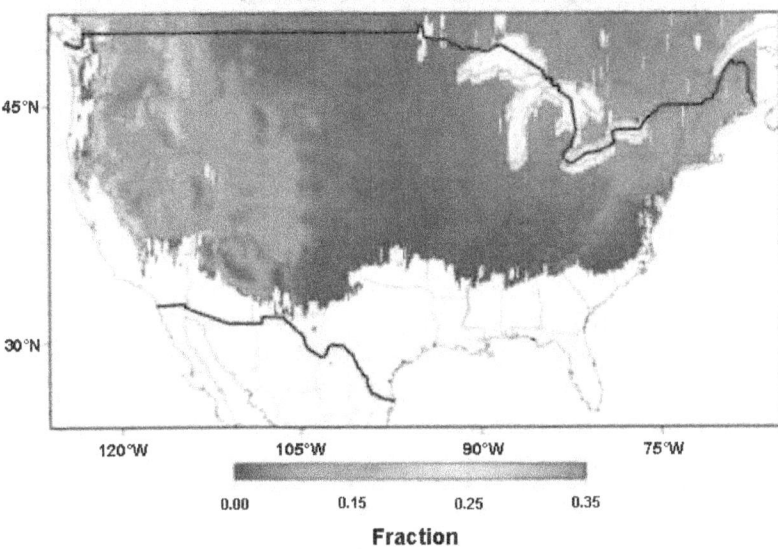

**Fraction of annual precipitation falling
in the daily tempture range: -3C < Tavg < 0C**
[from 1950-1999 VIC 1/8-degree INPUT DATA]

Figure 9—Fractional change of mean annual precipitation falling as snow to falling as rain, with a +3 C change in mean temperature. Redder areas are more vulnerable to small temperature rises. Courtesy Mike Dettinger, from Bales et al. (2005).

over many years, and we have very few first-class long-term wind records. Probably the best wind record in the West is the one starting 1944 at the Hanford Meteorology Station tower that continues to the present.

Unlike CO_2, aerosols vary greatly in their concentrations and properties from place to place (Kaufman et al. 2002), can travel long distances (Koch and Hansen 2005), and can affect climate in a variety of ways (Ramanathan et al. 2001). Increased numbers of small particulates can create too many small droplets, which make the mechanisms of precipitation formation less efficient. Small droplets do not coalesce well into drops large enough to fall to the surface. Evidence exists suggesting that particulate pollutants are changing the amount of precipitation in western mountains (Borys et al. 2000, 2003; Givati and Rosenfeld 2004; Rosenfeld 2000; Rosenfeld and Givati, in press). Clouds in general continue to provide one of the most vexing problems in climate simulation (Randall et al. 2003). Contrails have both cooling and warming effects and are becoming more common (Minnis et al. 2003, 2004). Together, clouds and aerosols pose some of the most daunting challenges to more accurate modeling of climate. Much of the basic problem has to do with how radiation flows through the atmosphere, a subject concisely described by NRC (2005). The global effect of human aerosol contributions is proving to be quite substantial (Bellouin et al. 2005). In general these aerosols act as a cooling influence on global climate by reflecting radiation from the system. Because they originate from processes similar to those that produce greenhouse gasses, there remains a possibility that removal of these aerosols from the air for health reasons may release what is in effect now a partial "brake" on climate warming.

Together, clouds and aerosols pose some of the most daunting challenges to more accurate modeling of climate.

19

Mountains enhance precipitation, often greatly. The mechanisms are complex and subtle, and evidence and theoretical considerations suggest that the amount of enhancement varies within storms, from storm to storm, from winter to winter, and on longer time scales. In some mountain ranges the phase of ENSO makes a difference (Dettinger et al. 2004). Numerical experiments (e.g., Grubisic et al., submitted) and experience (Leffler et al. 2001) strongly suggest that orographic effects operate at scales of hundreds of meters or less. A clear need exists for model studies at finer scales (Leung and Qian 2003; Leung et al. 2003a, 2003b). Changes in cloud microphysics, flow trajectories, and temperatures can cause changes in orographic enhancement (ratios of high elevation to low elevation precipitation). Orographic effects can be highly sensitive to slight changes in trajectory and enhanced or changed by barrier winds (Nieman et al. 2002, 2004; Ralph et al. 2003; White et al. 2003).

The reasons for summer to summer variations in regional precipitation systems like the Southwest monsoon (July, August and sometimes September) are only dimly understood. Monsoon precipitation is difficult to forecast more than a few days in advance. It is known that monsoon season precipitation totals in Arizona and New Mexico are not highly correlated (Gutzler 2000, Mitchell et al. 2002). Gutzler and Preston (1997), Gutzler (2000), and Lo and Clark (2002) report on a potential relation between prior winter snow cover and timing and amount of monsoon rains.

Our confidence in accuracy of attribution will improve when there is a better match between theory and observation, and when we can successfully trace changes in energy flow and storage in the climate system.

Our confidence in accuracy of attribution will improve when there is a better match between theory and observation, and when we can successfully trace changes in energy flow and storage in the climate system. The oceans represent a major sink for energy; Hansen et al. (2005) has recently reported progress on accounting for Earth's energy imbalance, which appears to be going into warming of the world's oceans (Levitus et al. 2000, 2001, 2005; Willis et al. 2004). Pielke (2003) has argued that ocean energy storage rates constitute an important climate metric and must be better known. At this point there is no single improvement that is widely foreseen that would provide a quantum leap in quality and accuracy of climate forecasts. Rather, any improvements are likely to be the result of numerous incremental advances, slowly chipping away at this difficult problem. New techniques to combine multiple runs of multiple models ("super-ensembles;" Kharin and Zwiers 2002, Krishnamurti et al. 2000) offer additional promise for improved bounds on uncertainty. It is certainly clear that this arid region cannot be understood or predicted well until we incorporate better its relations to the world ocean.

...any improvements are likely to be the result of numerous incremental advances, slowly chipping away at this difficult problem.

Large Scale Teleconnections

Spatial patterns of climate variability in the Western United States are correlated with patterns of climate variability in other parts of the world, the *teleconnections* referred to earlier. For example, it is known that winter precipitation in the West frequently exhibits a "dipole" pattern (wet in the Pacific Northwest and dry in the Desert Southwest, or vice versa), and that this pattern is strongly related to tropical Pacific ocean temperatures and to atmospheric pressure patterns in the Southern Hemisphere (Redmond and Koch 1991). The sense of the relation is such that El Niño is associated with wet winters in the Southwest and dry winters in the Northwest and northern Rockies; La Niña is associated with dry winters in the Southwest (very reliably: no exceptions in 75 years) and wet winters in the Northwest and northern Rockies.

There is much popular confusion between El Niño *itself* and the *effects* of El Niño. El Niño refers (only, and exclusively) to ocean warming in the top 100-200 meters in a narrow band between South America and the Date Line, typically within 5 degrees latitude of the equator. The effects of El Niño, by contrast, are global in reach. At time scales of a few years or less, outside of the seasons El Niño is the largest contributor to climate variability on earth. The warm area may look small on a map of the Pacific, but can easily be larger than the United States. The exact shape, magnitude, extent, duration, and longitudinal position of the warm water patch can vary from one episode to the next, factors that can significantly influence the impacts on the West (Hoerling and Kumar 2002). Typical events last 6-18 months, and recur irregularly at 2-7 year intervals. La Niña refers to unusually cool temperatures in this same area. El Niño exhibits characteristics of an oscillation in the sense that during one phase of the cycle forces are at work that lead to the demise of that phase and often even the eventual growth of the opposite phase, like a very complicated pendulum, albeit one subject to irregular forcing by short term weather events.

The atmospheric pressure difference Tahiti minus Darwin (Australia) is negatively correlated with ocean temperatures in the El Niño /La Niña area, a phenomenon known as the Southern Oscillation. For historical reasons these two descriptions have been lumped together as ENSO ("El Niño /Southern Oscillation"). The magnitude of this correlation, usually strong, has varied somewhat through time (McCabe and Dettinger 1999), so the atmosphere and the ocean each carry somewhat different information. Other descriptive measures have been developed more recently, such as the Multivariate ENSO Index (MEI) by Wolter and Timlin (1993). El Niño and La Niña are now simulated by many models that couple the atmosphere to the ocean, a necessity for El Niño to appear in them. They can thus be predicted with some success, as can their effects in North America and elsewhere. In the Western United States the effects of El Niño and La Niña are experienced in the cold half of the year, from approximately October through March; summer signals are very weak. The climatic effects of ENSO are also found in streamflow (Andrews et al. 2004, Barnett et al. 2004) where they are greatly accentuated with respect to precipitation (Cayan et al. 1999) in the Western states. Because annual tree growth in the Southwest is strongly dependent on prior winter precipitation, these ENSO effects are clearly seen in tree ring widths (Swetnam and Betancourt 1990). The West is "fortunate" in that temperature and precipitation over large areas can be predicted with some skill at 3-7 month lead times, and 6-9 month lead times for the summer streamflow runoff.

There is much popular confusion between El Niño *itself* and the *effects* of El Niño.

In the Western United States the effects of El Niño and La Niña are experienced in the cold half of the year, from approximately October through March…

The frequency of El Niño has varied through time. During the period 1947-1976 El Niño occurred relatively infrequently and La Niña was common. A sudden and still unexplained change (the "1976 shift") in the Pacific ushered in an era of much more common El Niño and a virtual dearth of La Niña. This appeared to many observers to have switched again in the late 1990s, though present evidence remains somewhat ambiguous. This long "cycle" of about 50 years duration is expressed in a pattern of ocean temperatures, atmospheric pressures, jet stream positions, and ocean currents seen from the tropics to the high latitudes in the Pacific, first described by Mantua et al. (1997) and Mantua and Hare (2002) as the Pacific Decadal Oscillation (PDO) and elaborated by others. They related the PDO to strong differences in salmon abundance between Alaska and the Pacific Northwest. There is much debate about the origin of the PDO, whether it truly is an oscillation, and even whether it really exists except as a (multi-year) filtered effect of El Niño (Newman et al. 2003) with strong elements of chaotic behavior (Overland et al. 2000). Thus far, models have been unable to faithfully simulate the behavior of the PDO, particularly transitions from one phase to the other, or its possible effects on temperature or precipitation in Western North America, despite tantalizing evidence that there are such effects. For now, ENSO has predictive value, but the PDO remains primarily diagnostic. Brown and Comrie (2004) saw the same western "dipole" at longer time frames in the PDO signal as seen on the shorter time scales of ENSO (e.g., Redmond and Koch 1991); McCabe and Dettinger (2002) see this dipole on both time scales in the historical Western United States snow course data.

Another kind of connection operates in the Pacific at intermediate time scales of approximately 40-70 days. Pairs of mostly cloudy and mostly clear regions slowly drift eastward from the Indian Ocean toward the Western Pacific, a phenomenon known as the Madden-Julian Oscillation (MJO), or sometimes, Intra-Seasonal Oscillation (ISO). Interactions with the eastward flowing jet stream coming off Asia can lead to multi-day precipitation episodes on the West Coast 5-10 days later (Mitchell and Blier 1997, Mo 1999, Mo and Higgins 1998). These are important because much of the annual precipitation occurs in the largest 3-5 storms of the 20-25 that typically strike the coast of California in winter.

Quite clearly, there are long term phenomena in the Pacific that require explanation and understanding (see Zhang et al. 1998, for an overview). Attempts to further extend these records must rely on proxy paleoclimatic data, such as tree rings (Biondi et al. 2001; D'Arrrigo et al. 2001, 2005; Gedalof and Smith 2001; MacDonald and Case 2005; Wiles et al. 1998), corals (Gedalof et al. 2002) and nitrogen isotopes in salmon (Finney et al. 2002). The relevance of variations on these scales is that slow natural changes appearing in the short sample afforded by historical records (50-150 years) can masquerade (perhaps) as "climate change" if our temporal perspective for interpretation is too short. The PDO shifted abruptly in 1976, at about the time when the temperatures shown in figure 1 began to warm. Our best global climate observations are unfortunately from this very same post-World War II period, and thus nearly coincide with this approximately 50-year long period of the PDO (1947 to latter 1990s). One might interpret this in two ways: (1) some of the recent warming in Western North America is a natural effect due to the mid-1970s phase change of the PDO, or (2) the climate system has "selected" this pattern to express the effects of climate warming (some climatic changes are likely to appear in the form of pattern changes). However, western warming has continued into 2005, seemingly independent of the phase of the PDO. From a management perspective, it is of interest to note that climate variations of 2-3 decade duration roughly correspond to the length of a typical career.

Emboldened by these findings of recurrent behavior, the research community has been examining connections between additional aspects of Western United States climate and hydrology and other oscillatory phenomena. Among the latter are the North Atlantic Oscillation (NAO) for both instrumental (Hurrell 1995, Marshall et al. 2001) and millennial time scales eras (Cook et al. 2002), the related Arctic Oscillation (AO) (Thompson and Wallace 1998, 2000, 2001; Wu and Straus 2004), and the Atlantic Multidecadal Oscillation (AMO) (Enfield et al. 2001, Gray et al. 2004b, McCabe et al. 2004). It is more difficult to understand the cause and effect chain with a "downwind" ocean like the Atlantic compared with an "upwind" ocean like the Pacific, but the statistical associations are suggestive and intriguing. Also, one would expect these Atlantic couplings to vary between winter and summer. The Atlantic would seemingly have more "opportunity" to affect Western North America when the Bermuda High shifts northward in early summer and a broad flow from east toward west develops at lower latitudes on its southern flank. In winter, the broad flow over Western North America nearly always has a component directed from west toward east.

Much of the (relatively modest) skill that now exists at lead times of 1-12 months arises from two sources, ENSO and (continuation of) recent trends (Quan et al., submitted). Until about 2004 statistical approaches and dynamical models showed rough parity in their respective abilities to forecast upcoming seasons. However, after about 50 years of long-lead forecasting in the United States, in an inevitable development dynamical models have begun to pull slightly ahead of statistical models, and in the long run they will have much more potential. To maintain this progress, a new framework, known as the Climate Test Bed, has emerged, currently centered around the Climate Forecast System (Saha et al. in press). The goal is to systematically add and improve the representation of climate factors in forecast models for the upcoming 1-12 months (CPC 2005a, 2005b).

The climate research community has recently begun to make a concerted effort to understand the cause of decadal-to-centennial scale climate variability. In the West, modern (e.g., Cayan et al. 1998) and paleoclimate (e.g., Cook et al. 2004; Fye et al. 2003; Gray et al. 2004a, 2004b; Hughes and Brown 1992; Stahle et al. 2000, 2001; Woodhouse 2003; Woodhouse and Overpeck 1998; Woodhouse et al. 2005) records have firmly established that long-term drought (5-20 years and more) is an inherent part of climate variability in this dry region. Recent model

From a management perspective, it is of interest to note that climate variations of 2-3 decade duration roughly correspond to the length of a typical career.

The climate research community has recently begun to make a concerted effort to understand the cause of decadal-to-centennial scale climate variability.

23

studies to understand the source of the 1930s Dust Bowl (Schubert et al. 2004a, 2004b; Seager et al. 2005), the 1950s Southwest drought, and the intense 2000-2004 drought (Hoerling and Kumar 2003) have shown that a major part of the answer lies in the world's oceans, in particular the Western Pacific and the Indian Oceans. These parts of the world ocean are also slowly warming (Levitus et al. 2000, 2005), with potential additional implications for the West. Hansen et al. (2005) have pointed to the energy imbalance at the top of the earth's atmosphere arising from increased greenhouse gasses. These imply another 0.6°C of ocean warming yet to be realized at the surface (excess energy already residing in the system), even if all present human greenhouse emissions were to cease. The direct and immediate effect of greenhouse gasses is to reduce the radiative energy loss to space, without appreciably affecting the solar supply. The climate must warm to increase this energy loss rate so that it approximately equals the solar supply rate, but this warming cannot occur instantly.

Major Sectors

The impacts of climate variability and climate change are experienced differently by every sector, and often differently within sectors, depending on the exact set of circumstances. The manner in which events are sequenced can be a significant determinant of whether their impact is serious or inconsequential. Considerations for a selected set of sectors are discussed next. This list is not exhaustive and there is a continuum of variations on the underlying themes.

Drought

The already arid West is the most drought prone part of the United States. At this writing the region has experienced its most significant drought in half a century, with no certainty that this episode is finished. Regardless, water supply systems for urban and rural populations, and for environmental needs, must be engineered to work with expected variability and long periods of shortage. Drought involves a mismatch between supply and demand, and consequent impacts, and thus is better defined in such terms (Redmond 2002). Burgeoning populations, and migrations to new locations, are placing new demands and increasing stress on western water supplies. New knowledge of past climates has led to the realization that very long droughts could occur and raise the question as to whether we are adequately buffered or otherwise prepared should they materialize. Swetnam and Betancourt (1998) discuss the major synergistic effects of drought, fire and insects that can be seen in the Southwest paleoclimate records, and how these can hinge on subtleties in their relationships.

Water Resources

The West is the most urban region (percentage of people living in cities) in the United States. A slow but inexorable shift is taking place as growing western cities and towns exert more influence on large scale water management decisions, and as agriculture steadily yields to development. Unlike agriculture, cities cannot lie fallow to during a poor water year, and

The already arid West is the most drought prone part of the United States. At this writing the region has experienced its most significant drought in half a century, with no certainty that this episode is finished. Regardless, water supply systems for urban and rural populations, and for environmental needs, must be engineered to work with expected variability and long periods of shortage.

thus reliability is paramount. The environmental footprints of the West's cities extend all the way to the headwaters of its major river systems, and increasingly to groundwater, both typically recharged by snow. Systems have been designed to accommodate the measured climates and flows. Lately, some water managers have taken an interest in utilizing longer estimates from paleo (pre-historical) records. However, the prospect of climate change leads to a major and unanswered question: What part of the climatic past is relevant to what part of the climatic future? Already, snowpack appears to be declining. Very few cities have factored in the prospect of climate change with respect to water planning, or even know how to do so. This is emerging as a significant issue, and is commingled with the ubiquitous growth issue affecting nearly every part of the West (Lund et al. 2003). Water decisions by the urban centers will have significant repercussions well upstream and often out of the basin. Few studies have comprehensively examined vegetative demand changes. Rind et al. (1990) did examine this issue from a drought perspective, but western droughts are typically more associated with snowfall deficit. Hidalgo et al. (2005) estimate that a +3 C temperature change in California would (all else unchanged) lead to about a 6 percent increase in evapotranspiration. Pan evaporation values have decreased (Roderick and Farquhar 2002) in the United States, but there are many possible reasons for this, climatic and observational. The geographic synchroneity of variations in streamflow greatly affects whether there is inter-regional "compensation" among anomalies, and thus is of much interest to water and power managers (Cayan et al. 2003, Hirschboeck and Meko 2005); evidence exists that such relations are not constant (Jain et al. 2005).

Very few cities have factored in the prospect of climate change with respect to water planning, or even know how to do so. This is emerging as a significant issue, and is commingled with the ubiquitous growth issue affecting nearly every part of the West...

Timber and Forestry

The eventual fate of a tree is to be blown down, burned down, or cut down. Two of these involve the atmosphere, and the susceptibility to those outcomes is increased by weather and climate behavior and often by insects. Much of the life of insects is in turn controlled by climate, particularly temperature. Changes in climate have potentially significant consequences for insects (Williams and Liebold, 2002). Trees can also be harmed by pollutants that are either advected from afar or created in place through photochemical reactions. Both sources are closely tied to weather and climate. As with other plants, trees also will exhibit differential physiological responses to increased CO_2 concentrations, a direct consequence of this greenhouse gas, and CO_2 may modulate the response to factors such as ozone. Climate affects the growth of seedlings, and changes in microclimate induced by clearcuts have been shown to affect regeneration (Childs and Flint 1987). Thus, even neglecting fire, there are many ways in which weather and climate phenomena can affect forest management.

Fire

Fire is an integral component of forest and range communities, and knowledge of its many roles is improving steadily (Baird et al. 1999, Brown and Smith 2000, Christensen et al. 1989, Foster et al. 1988, Grissino-Mayer and Swetnam 2000, Heyerdahl et al. 2001, Johnson and Miyanishi 2001, many others). Climate and weather events are major factors affecting fire vulnerability and potential, ignition, spread, suppression when needed, and regeneration. Climate information, expressed probabilistically, can be useful for planning of prescribed burns, with adjustments that take into account the presence or absence of drought, and forecasts at various lead times from two weeks to a day are available when active intervention is desired. Westerling et al. (2002, 2003) have developed techniques that show some skill at longer lead times in forecasting aspects of upcoming fire seasons. Precipitation can increase or decrease fire potential, depending on the time of year, the particular seasonal climatological background, the type of fuel, and the recent weather history. On longer time scales, the general effect of warming, with no change in precipitation patterns, would be for increased dryness of soils and vegetation, lengthened summer dry seasons, and lower relative humidity. Brown et al. (2004) discuss climate change effects on wildland fire. Some areas that presently do not burn often, such as coastal fog belts and higher elevations, might experience significant change toward greater susceptibility, especially in the zone below timberline. Some forests of significant aesthetic and economic value (e.g. the redwoods) are tied to small scale phenomena (coastal winds and upwelling, systems with dimensions of 5-50 km [3-31 miles]) that await high-resolution long-term climate simulations likely embedded in large scale global models. At present it is unknown whether the summer fog belt along the West Coast will change appreciably, though some models hint at modest warming and lower humidity. Few climate studies have addressed whether wind and cloudiness, both factors that affect plant and soil moisture budgets, will increase or decrease, or which general settings will experience which effects.

Recreation

Every corner of the diverse western landscape is host to some form of recreation, including tourism, camping, rafting, windsurfing, biking, hiking, snowmobiling, climbing, motorcycling, boating, four-wheeling, fishing, hunting, backpacking, skiing, boating, picnicking, photographing and just plain relaxing, to name but a few. The West has a long-standing outdoor orientation. All such activities are greatly affected by long and short term events in the atmosphere, exposure to ultraviolet radiation, and the condition of streams, lakes and reservoirs. Preparation for visitation to national parks and other public lands is often planned according to expected climate, and numerous last minute decisions are made on the basis of recent or upcoming weather. In some locations climate is a primary park attractant (the Olympic rain forest, the ice of Glacier and Rainier and North Cascades, the fog of Channel Islands, the snow of Crater Lake, even the heat of Death Valley). Festivals and gatherings are planned on the basis of climate expectations. A large number of local and regional economies are tied to seasonal recreation. Forest closures from drought or fires have significant financial impacts, and political dimensions. Summer homes extend the wildland-urban interface and habitat fragmentation ever farther out from cities. Warmer temperatures will drive people to cooler, higher, more comfortable climate zones.

> Climate and weather events are major factors affecting fire vulnerability and potential, ignition, spread, suppression when needed, and regeneration.

> A large number of local and regional economies are tied to seasonal recreation. Forest closures from drought or fires have significant financial impacts, and political dimensions.

Grazing

The rural and agrarian traditions in the West remain alive in the widespread presence of cattle and sheep on public lands. Managers of these range and forest lands would prefer that grazing intensity be optimized according to the present status and expected trends of forage and drought indicators. Personnel limitations do not allow on-site visits to evaluate conditions on every patch of ground. Automated climate monitoring sites feeding into spatial and temporal models, in concert with satellite information, is greatly desired. Such sites need long records for calibration, and for ground truth of remote sensing data. Techniques are needed to interpolate and map such information, in forms that assist with making decisions. Invasive plants and animals are a major issue in much of the interior West, and indeed in nearly ecotone. Climate is a major factor in the invasion process itself, as well as in establishment and consolidation of new species. Disturbances that facilitate invasions (such as fire or drought) often have a climatic origin or strong component.

Monitoring Needs

There are a number of motivations for monitoring of climate, from reasons related to forecasting and modeling (Goody et al. 2002) to those that support myriads of operational and practical decisions (NRC 1998, 1999, 2001). Although Lewis and Clark carried thermometers from 1804-1806 (Knapp 2004, Solomon and Daniel 2004), systematic weather and climate measurements did not begin until the settlement of the West commenced in earnest, particularly through the forts and the Signal Corps (recounted in, e.g., Moran and Hopkins 2002). A large increase in the number of stations occurred during 1890s, and these form the backbone of our current historical surface climate data set. Most historical networks are biased toward locations where humans live and work, and thus the higher and more remote locations of the West have generally been severely underrepresented. These regions are, however, the source of most of the natural resources that urban centers depend on. Because the underrepresented areas have very different climates (colder, wetter, snowier, windier) from those of population concentrations, spatial averages that do not account for these differences will be biased toward values representative of lower elevations. Figure 10 shows that in the Great Basin, the upper elevations supply a disproportionate share of annual precipitation.

The Nation has long relied on the NOAA (National Oceanic and Atmospheric Administration) cooperative network maintained by the National Weather Service (NWS) and on airports (NWS and Federal Aviation Administration, FAA) sites. However in the Western states the interagency RAWS (Remote Automatic Weather Station) and U.S. Department of Agriculture/Natural Resources Conservation Service (USDA/NRCS) Snotel system provide an invaluable and substantial augmentation, as both are designed for duty in the locations where crucial natural resources are located. Neither of these were designed or deployed specifically as "climate" networks, though they are increasingly used in that way and will continue to be. With improved technology,

Invasive plants and animals are a major issue in much of the interior West...Climate is a major factor in the invasion process itself, as well as in establishment and consolidation of new species. Disturbances that facilitate invasions (such as fire or drought) often have a climatic origin or strong component.

Although Lewis and Clark carried thermometers from 1804-1806...systematic weather and climate measurements did not begin until the settlement of the West commenced in earnest...

27

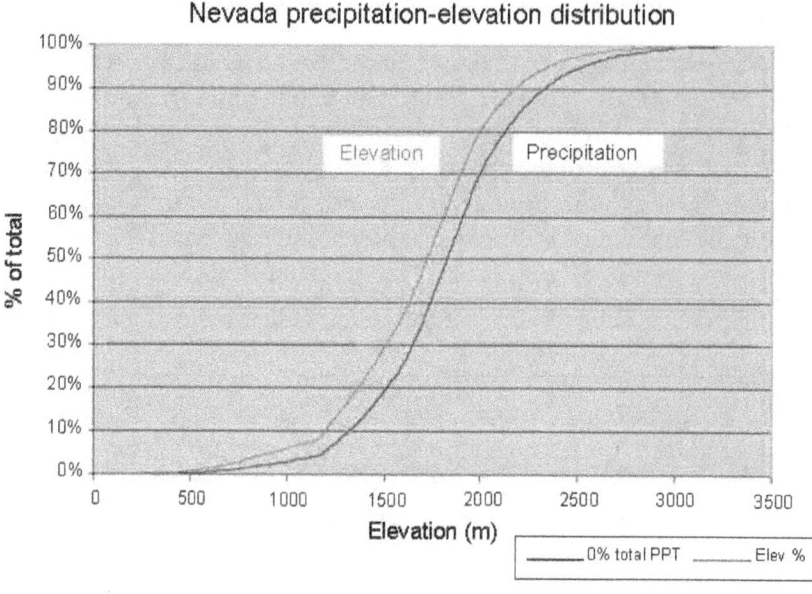

Figure 10—Cumulative distribution of elevation and of precipitation for the state of Nevada, based on 30-year means from PRISM. Figure courtesy Chris Daly, Oregon State University.

There is presently no coherent strategy among all public, or even federal, agencies to coordinate the location, sensors, communications, siting, and maintenance criteria, or expected minimum standards, needed to establish a West-wide climate observing network.

added stations and networks are appearing. Most networks were deployed to serve particular constituencies that must continue to be satisfied, whereas a few (e.g., NWS cooperative network) have served a general multipurpose role of benefit to every citizen. Lists of uses for climate information can be found in NRC (1998, 2001).

However, there still remains no comprehensive coordination to these observing efforts, and the special need of climate–long term consistency and careful attention to siting–is not a mandated priority. This, especially, remains a critical need for the region. Detailed discussions of these issues can be found in Redmond and McCurdy (2005) and Redmond et al. (2005). The West is unevenly sampled, mostly as a consequence of a large variety of individual decisions pertaining to expressed local needs. The high elevations are especially undersampled, with most of the West's approximately one thousand mountain ranges having no instrumentation at all. There is presently no coherent strategy among all public, or even federal, agencies to coordinate the location, sensors, communications, siting, and maintenance criteria, or expected minimum standards, needed to establish a West-wide climate observing network. Many bits and pieces do exist, however. Strategies have been developed for estimating desired station density (e.g., Janis et al. 2004, Vose and Menne 2004) but these often address a well-defined observing need. Observation needs vary widely, depending on intended use, and there are difficult issues of spatial scale, because climates in physically close locations can exhibit very different properties. This is especially true for ecological studies, where the climate at the scales of communities and organisms and their ranges is the most relevant. A major shortcoming with the present observing system is the shortage of soil moisture observations. Soil moisture status is affected by a variety of processes and parameters, and serves as an integrating property. Likewise, snow is a critical element for western hydrology, and stands to be greatly affected if climate changes. Snow is difficult to measure (Doesken and Judson 1996) and although some studies of valley snows have been conducted (Karl et al. 1993, Scott and Kaiser 2004) we still do not understand the strengths and limitations of the national snow data base (Knowles et al., submitted; Kunkel et al., submitted).

Greater coordination is being promoted, through such efforts as the Consortium for Integrated Climate Research in Western Mountains (CIRMOUNT 2005), which has sponsored several meetings since 2004, advocating improved high elevation observations and understanding of fundamental processes and vulnerability to climate change. The highest such station is White Mountain Summit, east of the Owens Valley in California at 1,4245 ft (4342 m) reporting every ten minutes on the Web. Another similar effort is the interagency Western Mountain Initiative (WMI 2005). Of note is NSF's effort to develop a series of "observatories" and associated communications and computer access infrastructure: NEON (National Ecological Observatory Network), Hydrologic Observatories through CUAHSI (Consortium of Universities for the Advancement of Hydrologic Science, Inc.), engineering and sensing with CLEANER (Collaborative Large-scale Engineering Analysis Network for Environmental Research), and ORION (Ocean Research Interactive Observatory Networks). NOAA has been attempting to upgrade its legacy cooperative network to 5-minute live reporting with NERON (National Environmental Realtime Observing Network), and USDA is similarly attempting to deploy a large number of Soil Climate Analysis Network (SCAN) sites to measure soil moisture (a major shortcoming identified by Western Governors Association 2004) and temperature (e.g., Hu 2004). Both NERON and SCAN have been adding stations at a relatively slow pace, however. Many other smaller or specialty networks could be mentioned. Practical considerations lead to the clear conclusion that there is an enormous need for improved coordination among a very diverse cast of characters.

Increasingly, resource management agencies are being urged to shore up the scientific underpinnings for their management decisions. It is also vital to know whether slow changes in abundance of individual species (e.g., Chavez 2003) is due to changes in climate or to changes in resource management; one phase of the PDO lasts about the length of a typical career. The requirement that baseline climate monitoring stations be sited in settings that will remain undisturbed (except for natural successional processes) leads to the need for land devoted primarily to research needs. Many of the West's federal agencies have something to offer in this regard. The NOAA Climate Reference Network, for example, has attempted to take advantage of the natural platforms, automatically protected from encroachment, offered by the lands of the National Park Service (NPS), with the further advantage of tying in to the NPS Inventory and Monitoring Program. Such efforts should be encouraged and expanded.

The NOAA Regional Climate Center (RCC) program has recently teamed with the National Weather Service and the National Climatic Data Center to develop a distributed infrastructure for ingesting and disseminating climate data from various networks. At this writing the system now ingests manually observed daily cooperative data supplied by

Practical considerations lead to the clear conclusion that there is an enormous need for improved coordination among a very diverse cast of characters.

NWS, and transforms this into temperature and precipitation anomaly maps for various periods extending back into the past from a week to 36 months, updated each day for the nation and for subregions. This infrastructure is known as the Applied Climate Information System (ACIS) (ACIS 2005, Hubbard et al. 2004, WRCC-CIP 2006 "related sites"). Such information is very useful for resource management.

The National Park Service (NPS) Inventory and Monitoring (I&M) Program is an ambitious and comprehensive effort to utilize about 285 park units as platforms to monitor ecological health in a wide variety of settings (NPS 2006, Oakley et al. 2003). NPS has organized 32 groups of geographically distributed park units (I&M Networks) to address regional aspects. Climate and weather are a major environmental driver and indicator in all park units with significant natural resources. Climate is being addressed at the network level; for representative examples see Oakley and Boudreau (2000), MacCluskie and Oakley (2002, 2003), MacCluskie et al. (2004), and Sousanes (2004). The NPS and Western Regional Climate Center (WRCC 2006) are collaborating on the development of inventories of weather and climate information for each of 32 NPS groups of park units (I&M Networks) to help guide future activities. This depends heavily on the ACIS structure (WRCC-CIP, 2006, "related sites"). Initial emphasis on central Alaska (Redmond and Simeral 2006) and the Greater Yellowstone ecosystem (Davey et al. 2006) build on earlier work for the Channel Islands (Redmond and McCurdy 2005) and southwest Alaska (Redmond et al. 2005). The methods, findings, data and metadata, web pages, and activities associated with this effort are directly relevant to those of many other resource management agencies.

> The highly convoluted topography of the West necessitates mapping and descriptive techniques that can resolve individual mountains ranges and mountains … for uses such as ongoing monitoring, quality control of data, understanding changing elevational relationships, and the elevational details of climate variability and change.

The highly convoluted topography of the West necessitates mapping and descriptive techniques that can resolve individual mountains ranges and mountains (e.g., to a mile or less), such as PRISM (Daly et al. 1994, 2002, 2004), for uses such as ongoing monitoring, quality control of data, understanding changing elevational relationships, and the elevational details of climate variability and change. Simpson et al. (2005) have evaluated different approaches to mapping of climate in regions of exceptional topographic relief.

In addition to tracking of the physical elements of climate, measures of the consequences and impacts of climate behavior are needed to identify and understand how these connect. Efforts to establish a National Integrated Drought Information System (NIDIS) must address this issue. Monitoring of the impacts of climate is haphazard and very uneven (Western Governors Association 2004), with very few systematic efforts. NIDIS represents the kind of broadly based activity able to provide a common framework and coordination for a wide variety of climate-related operational and research needs. Furthermore, the bulk of climate impacts are felt at the smaller scales of individuals and businesses, where such information is even harder to acquire, manipulate and distill. For such work a database of economic impacts is also much needed (Changnon 2005).

Concluding Remarks

The needs for climate information span a very broad range. The National Research Council (2001) laid out the ingredients and attributes of a comprehensive program of national *climate services*, defined after careful deliberation over each word as:

> The timely production and delivery of useful climate data, information, and knowledge to decision makers.

The key point is that the desired information is centered around assisting with some sort of decision, narrow or broad, trivial or momentous. Monitoring, data stewardship, active programs of research, and the engagement of diverse governmental, academic and private communities constitute other essential components, interacting in an iterative fashion.

There is an extraordinary amount of information currently "out there," much of it greatly underutilized, often not in a convenient, meaningful, or accessible form. The United States Climate Change Science Program, currently budgeted at around $2 billion annually, and allied efforts, continue to churn out new knowledge about global, regional and local climate behavior at a rapid pace. The pipeline between knowledge production and use needs to be shorter and wider, to reduce the time lag between discovery or observation and application. To provide this capacity, there is a great need for trusted and knowledgeable information brokers, acting as intermediaries to connect providers and users. These individuals must be comfortable and credible within each of the respective communities they are attempting to bridge.

State, regional, and national climate centers have operated in this milieu for a number of years. Over the last ten years additional institutional structures have arisen, with a special, but not exclusive, emphasis on better understanding of the decision environment of users, a necessity for effective use of knowledge (e.g., Rayner et al. 2005). A special NOAA activity, the Regional Integrated Sciences and Assessments (RISA) Program, has made significant headway in this direction. The process is long, iterative, nonlinear, organic, and features mutual learning. Four of these projects operate in the Western states (RISA 2006). Collectively, among all these varied players, there is a significant amount of capability waiting to be harnessed. New technologies for sensing, storing, retrieving, displaying, and disseminating information offer a great deal of promise.

With all the multiple complexities found in the West in observational systems, information repositories, economic sectors, user communities, climatic diversity, topographic juxtapositions, and a potential trajectory toward a different kind of future, apparently endlessly nested like Russian dolls, the whole situation may seem hopelessly complex. However, in spite of this appearance, there is also ample evidence to suggest that with care and diligence we can nonetheless harness what we know and what is being discovered to effectively navigate our way through this maze, and achieve satisfactory solutions. To do so simply requires an ability and willingness to stretch in new ways on the part of information providers and users alike.

There is an extraordinary amount of information currently "out there," much of it greatly underutilized, often not in a convenient, meaningful, or accessible form.

...there is also ample evidence to suggest that with care and diligence we can nonetheless harness what we know and what is being discovered to effectively navigate our way through this maze, and achieve satisfactory solutions.

References

Aguado, E.; Cayan, D.R.; Riddle, L.; Roos, M. 1992. Climatic fluctuations and the timing of west coast streamflow. Journal of Climate. 5: 1468-1483.

Andrews, E.D.; Antweiler, R.C.; Nieman, P.J.; Ralph, F.M. 2004. Influence of ENSO on flood frequency along the California coast. Journal of Climate. 17(2): 337-348.

Applied Climate Information System [ACIS]. 2005. Current anomaly maps. http://www.hprcc.unl.edu/products/current. html. (20 November).

Baird, M.; Zabowski, D.; Everett, R.L. 1999. Wildfire effects on carbon and nitrogen in inland coniferous forests. Plant and Soil. 209(2): 233-243.

Bales, R.; Dozier, J.; Molotch, N.; Painter, T.; Rice, R.; Dettinger, M. [Submitted]. Mountain hydrology of the semi-arid western United States. Water Resources Research.

Barnett, T.; Malone, R.; Pennell, W.; Sammer, D.; Semtner, B.; Washington, W. 2004. The effects of climate change on water resources in the West: introduction and overview. Climate Change. 62: 1-11.

Barnett, T.P.; Adam, J.C.; Lettenmaier, D.P. 2005. Potential impacts of a warming climate on water availability in snow-dominated region. Nature. 438(7066): 303-309. doi:10.1038/nature04141.

Bellouin, N.; Boucher, O.; Haywood, J.; Reddy, M.S. 2005. Global estimate of aerosol direct radiative forcing from satellite measurements. Nature. 438(22): 1138-1141.

Biondi, F.; Gershunov, A.; Cayan, D.R. 2001. North Pacific decadal climate variability since 1661. Journal of Climate Letters. 14: 5-10.

Borys, R.D.; Lowenthal, D.H.; Cohn, S.A.; Brown, W.O.J. 2003. Mountaintop and radar measurements of anthropogenic aerosol effects on snow growth and snowfall rate. Geophysical Research Letters. 30(10): 1538. doi:10.1029/2002GL016855, 45-1/45-4.

Borys, R.D.; Lowenthal, D.H.; Mitchell, D.L. 2000. The relationships among cloud microphysics, chemistry, and precipitation rate in cold mountain clouds. Atmospheric Environment. 34: 2593-2602.

Brown, D.P.; Comrie, A.C. 2004. A winter precipitation 'dipole' in the western United States associated with multidecadal ENSO variability. Geophysics Research Letters. 31: L09203. doi:10.1029/2003GL018726.

Brown, J.K.; Smith, J.K., eds. 2000. Wildland fire in ecosystems: effects of fire on flora. Gen Tech. Rep. RMRS-GTR-42. U.S. Department of Agriculture, Forest Service, Rocky Mountain Research Station. 257 p. Vol. 2.

Brown, T.J.; Hall, B.L.; Westerling, A.L. 2004. The impact of twenty-first century climate change on wildland fire danger in the western United States: an applications perspective. Climatic Change. 62(1): 365-388. doi:10.1023/B:CLIM.0000013680.07783.de.

Burbank, D.W. 1982. Correlations of climate, mass balances, and glacial fluctuations at Mount Rainier, Washington, USA, since 1850. Arctic and Alpine Research. 14: 137–148.

Cayan, D.R.; Dettinger, M.D.; Diaz, H.F.; Graham, N.E. 1998. Decadal variability of precipitation over western North America. Journal of Climate. 11: 3148-3166.

Cayan, D.R.; Dettinger, M.D.; Redmond, K.T.; McCabe, G.J.; Knowles, N.; Peterson, D.H. 2003. The transboundary setting of California's water and hydropower systems. In: Diaz, H.F.; Morehouse, B.J., eds. Climate and water: transboundary challenges in the Americas. Dordrecht, The Netherlands: Kluwer Academic Publishers: 237-262, Chapter 10.

Cayan, D.R.; Kammerdiener, S.A.; Dettinger, M.D.; Caprio, J.M.; Peterson, D.H. 2001. Changes in the onset of spring in the western United States. Bulletin of the American Meteorological Society. 82: 399-415.

Cayan, D.R.; Redmond, K.T.; Riddle, L.G. 1999. ENSO and hydrologic extremes in the western United States. Journal of Climate. 12: 2881-2893.

Changnon, S.A. 2005. Economic impacts of climate conditions in the United States: past, present, and future: an editorial essay. Climatic Change. 68: 1-9. doi:10.1007/s10584-005-1673-4.

Chavez, F.P.; Ryan, J.; Lluch-Cota, S.E.; Niquen, M. 2003. From anchovies to sardines and back: multidecadal change in the Pacific Ocean. Science. 299: 217-221.

Childs, S.W.; Flint, L.E. 1987. Effect of shadecards, shelterwoods, and clearcuts on temperature and moisture environments. Forest Ecology and Management. 18: 205-217.

Christensen, N.L.; Agee, J.K.; Brussard, P.F.; Hughes, J.; Knight, D.H.; Minshall, G.W.; Peek, J.M.; Pyne, S.; Swanson, F.J.; Thomas, J.W.; Wells, S.; Williams, S.E.; Wright, H.A. 1989. Interpreting the Yellowstone fires of 1988: ecosystem responses and management implications. BioScience. 39(10): 678-685.

Christensen, N.S.; Wood, A.W.; Voisin, N.; Lettenmeier, D.P.; Palmer, R.N. 2004. The effects of climate change on the hydrology and water resources of the Colorado River Basin. Climatic Change. 62(1): 337-363.

CIRMOUNT. 2005. Consortium for integrated climate research in Western Mountains. www.fs.fed.us/psw/cirmount/about.shtml. (3 December).

Climate Prediction Center [CPC]. 2005a. Climate forecast system forecast of seasonal anomalies. www.cpc.ncep.noaa.gov/products/analysis_monitoring/lanina/ensoforecast.html. (2 December).

Climate Prediction Center [CPC]. 2005b. Climate test bed. www.cpc.ncep.noaa.gov/products/ctb. (3 December).

Climate Prediction Center [CPC]. 2005c. U.S. temperature and precipitation trends. NOAA Climate Prediction Center. www.cpc.ncep.noaa.gov/trndtext.shtml. (1 December).

Cook, E.R.; D'Arrigo, R.D.; Mann, M.E. 2002. A well-verified, multiproxy reconstruction of the winter North Atlantic Oscillation Index since A.D. 1400. Journal of Climate. 15(13): 1754-1764.

Cook, E.R.; Woodhouse, C.A.; Eakin, M.; Meko, D.M.; Stahle, D.W. 2004. Longterm aridity changes in the western United States. Science. 306: 1015-1018.

Daly, C.; Gibson, W.; Doggett, M.; Smith, J.; Taylor, G. 2004. Up-to-date monthly climate maps for the conterminous United States. 14th AMS Conference on Applied Climatology. 8 p.

Daly, C.; Gibson, W.P.; Taylor, G.H.; Johnson, G.L.; Pasteris, P. 2002. A knowledgebased approach to the statistical mapping of climate. Climate Research. 22: 99-113.

Daly, C.; Neilson, R.P.; Phillips, D.L. 1994. A statistical-topographic model for mapping climatological precipitation over mountain terrain. Journal of Applied Meteorology. 33: 140-158.

D'Arrigo, R.; Villalba, R.; Wiles, G. 2001. Tree-ring estimates of Pacific decadal climate variability. Climate Dynamics. 18: 219-224.

D'Arrigo, R.; Wilson, R.; Deser, C.; Wiles, G.; Cook, E.; Villalba, R.; Tudhope, S.; Cole, J.; Linsley, B. 2005. Tropical-North Pacific climate linkages over the past four centuries. Journal of Climate. 18(24): 5253-5265.

Davey, C.A.; Redmond, K.T.; Simeral, D.B. 2006. Weather and climate inventory: Natioinal Park Service Greater Yellowstone inventory. Western Regional Climate Center. 96 p. www.wrcc.dri.edu/nps. (May 2006).

Dettinger, M.D. 2004. From climate-change spaghetti to climate-change distributions for 21st Century California. San Francisco Estuary Watershed Science. 3(1): 14 p. Article 4. http://repositories.cdlib.org/cgi/viewcontent.cgi?article=1025&context=jmie/sfews.

Dettinger, M.D. 2005. Changes in streamflow timing in the western United States in recent decades. Fact sheet 2005-3018. U.S. Geological Survey. 6 p. water.usgs.gov/pubs/fs/2005/3018/. (March 2005).

Dettinger, M.D.; Cayan, D.R. 1995. Large-scale atmospheric forcing of recent trends toward early snowmelt runoff in California. Journal of Climate. 8: 606-623.

Dettinger, M.D.; Cayan, D.R.; Meyer, M.K.; Jeton, A.E. 2004. Simulated hydrologic responses to climate variations and change in the Merced, Carson, and American River basins, Sierra Nevada, California, 1900-2099. Climatic Change. 62: 283-317.

Diaz, H.F.; Beniston, M.; Bradley, R.S., eds. 1997. Climatic change at high elevation sites. Dordrecht, The Netherlands: Kluwer Academic Publishers. 298 p. Reprinted from Climatic Change 1997(36): 3-4.

Diaz, H.F; Bradley, R.S. 1997. Temperature variations during the last century at high elevation sites. Climatic Change. 59: 33-52.

Doesken, N.J.; Judson, A. 1996. The snow booklet: a guide to the science, climatology, and measurement of snow in the United States. Fort Collins, CO: Colorado State University, Department of Atmospheric Science. 85 p.

Ebbesmeyer, C.C.; Cayan, D.R.; McClain, D.R.; Nichols, F.H.; Peterson, D.H.; Redmond, K.T. 1991. 1976 step in Pacific climate: forty environmental changes between 1968-1975 and 1977-1984. Tech Rep. 26. Sacramento, CA: California Department of Water Resources, Interagency Ecological Study Program. 235 p.

Enfield, D.B.; Mestas-Nuñez, A.M.; Trimble, P.J. 2001. The Atlantic Multidecadal Oscillation and its relation to rainfall and river flows in the continental U.S. Geophysical Research Letters. 28: 2077-2080.

Finney, B.P.; Gregory-Eaves, I.; Douglas, M.S.V.; Smol, J.P. 2002. Fisheries productivity in the northeastern Pacific Ocean over the past 2200 years. Nature. 416: 729-733.

Foster, D.R.; Knight, D.H.; Franklin, J.F. 1998. Landscape patterns and legacies resulting from large, infrequent forest disturbances. Ecosystems. 1(6): 497-510.

Fye, F.K.; Stahle, D.W.; Cook, E.R. 2003. Paleoclimatic analogs to twentieth-century moisture regimes across the United States. Bulletin of the American Meteorological Society. 84(7): 901–909.

Gedalof, Z.; Mantua, N.J.; Peterson, D.L. 2002. A multi-century perspective of variability in the Pacific decadal oscillation: new insights from tree rings and coral. Geophysical Research Letters. 29(24): 2204. doi:10.1029/2002GL015824.

Gedalof, Z.; Smith, D.J. 2001. Interdecadal climate variability and regime-scale shifts in Pacific North America. Geophysical Research Letters. 28: 1515-1518.

Givati, A.; Rosenfeld, D. 2004. Quantifying precipitation suppression due to air pollution. Journal of Applied Meteorology. 43(7): 1038–1056.

Goody, R.; Anderson, J.; Karl, T.; Miller, R.B.; North, G.; Simpson, J.; Stephens, G. Washington, W. 2002. Why monitor the climate? Bulletin of the American Meteorological Society. 83(6): 873–878.

Gooseff, M.N.; Strzepek, K.; Chapra, S.C. 2005. Modeling the potential effects of climate change onwater temperature downstream of a shallow reservoir, lower Madison River, Montana. Climatic Change. 68: 331-353. doi:10.1007/s10584-005-9076-0.

Gray, S.T.; Graumlich, J.L.; Betancourt, J.L.; Pederson, G.T. 2004a. A tree-ring based reconstruction of the Atlantic multidecadal oscillation since 1567 A.D. Geophysical Research Letters. 31: L12205. doi:10.1029/2004GL019932.

Gray, S.T.; Fastie, C.L.; Jackons, S.T.; Betancourt, J.L. 2004b. Tree-ring-based reconstruction of precipitation in the Bighorn Basin, Wyoming, since 1260 A.D. Journal of Climate. 17(19): 2855-3865.

Grissino-Mayer, H.D.; Swetnam, T.W. 2000. Century-scale climate forcing of fire regimes in the American Southwest. Holocene. 10(2): 213-220.

Groisman, P.Ya; Knight, R.W.; Easterling, D.R.; Karl, T.R.; Hegerl, G.C.; Razuvaev, V.N. 2005. Trends in intense precipitation in the climate record. Journal of Climate. 18(9): 1326–1350.

Groisman, P.Ya; Knight, R.W.; Karl, T.R. 2001. Heavy precipitation and high streamflow in the contiguous United States: trends in the twentieth century. Bulletin of the American Meteorological Society. 82(2): 219–246.

Groisman, P.Ya; Knight, R.W.; Karl, T.R.; Easterling, D.R.; Sun, B.; Lawrimore, J.H. 2004. Contemporary changes of the hydrological cycle over the contiguous United States: trends derived from in situ observations. Journal of Hydrometeorology. 5: 64-84.

Grubisic, V.; Vellore, R.K.; Huggins, A.W. [Submitted]. Quantitative precipitation forecasting of wintertime storms in the Sierra Nevada: sensitivity to the microphysical parameterization and horizontal resolution. Revised version March 2005 to Monthly Weather Review.

Gutzler, D.S. 2000. Covaribility of spring snowpack and summer rainfall across the southwest United States. Journal of Climate. 13: 4018-4027.

Gutzler, D.S.; Preston, J.W. 1997. Evidence for a relationship between spring snow cover in North American and summer rainfall in New Mexico. Geophysical Research Letters. 24: 2207-2210.

Hall, M.P.; Fagre, D.B. 2003. Modeled climate-induced glacier change in Glacier National Park, 1850-2100. Bioscience. 53(2): 131-140.

Hamlet, A.F.; Lettenmeier, D.P. 1999. Effects of climate change on hydrology and water resources in the Columbia River basin. Journal of American Water Resources Association. 35: 1597-1623.

Hamlet, A.F.; Mote, P.W.; Clark, M.P.; Lettenmeier, D.P. 2005. Effects of temperature and precipitation variability on snowpack trends in the western United States. Journal of Climate. 18(21): 4545–4561.

Hansen, J.; Nazarenko, L.; Ruedy, R.; Sato, M.; Willis, J.; Del Genio, A.; Koch, D.; Lacis, A.; Lo, K.; Menon, S.; Novakov, T.; Perlwitz, J.; Russell, G.; Schmidt, G.A.; Tausnev, N. 2005. Earth's energy imbalance: confirmation and implications. Published online 2005 May 2; 10.1126/science.1110252 (Science Express Research Articles).

Hayhoe, K.; Cayan, D.; Field, C.B.; Frumhoff, P.C.; Maurer, E.P.; Miller, N.L.; Moser, S.C.; Schneider, S.H.; Cahill, K.N.; Cleland, E.E.; Dale, L.; Drapek, R.; Hanemann, R.M.; Kalkstein, L.S.; Lenihan, J.; Lunch, C.K.; Neilson, R.P.; Sheridan, S.C.; Verville, J.H. 2004. Emissions pathways, climate change, and impacts on California. Proceedings of National Academy of Sciences. 101(34): 12422-12427. 10.1073/pnas.0404500101.

Heyerdahl, E.K.; Brubaker, L.B.; Agee, J.K. 2001. Spatial controls of historical fire regimes: a multiscale example from the interior West, USA. Ecology. 82(3): 660-678.

Hidalgo, H.G.; Cayan, D.R.; Dettinger, M.D. 2005. Sources of variability of evapotranspiration in California. Journal of Hydrometeorology. 6: 3-19.

Hirshboeck, K.K.; Meko, D.M. 2005. A tree-ring based assessment of synchronous extreme streamflow episodes in the Upper Colorado and Salt-Verde-Tonto River basins. Final report to Salt River Project. 31 p. fp.arizona.edu/khirschboeck/SRP%20WEB/Final.Report/Final.Final.Report.pdf.

Hodge, S.M.; Trabant, D.C.; Krimmel, R.M.; Heinrichs, T.A.; March, R.S.; Josberger, E.G. 1998. Climate variations and changes in mass of three glaciers in western North America. Journal of Climate. 11: 2161-2179.

Hoerling, M.; Kumar, A. 2003. The perfect ocean for drought. Science. 299: 691-694.

Hoerling, M.P.; Kumar, A. 2002. Atmospheric response patterns associated with tropical forcing. Journal of Climate. 15(16): 2184-2203.

Hu, Q.; Feng, S. 2004. U.S. soil temperature and its variation: a new dataset. Bulletin of the American Meteorological Society. 85(1): 29–31.

Hubbard, K.G.; DeGaetano, A.T.; Robbins, K.D. 2004. A modern applied climate information system. Bulletin of the American Meteorological Society. 85(6): 811–812.

Hughes, M.K.; Brown, P.M. 1992. Drought frequency in central California since 101 B.C. recorded in giant sequoia tree rings. Climate Dynamics. 6: 161-167.

Huntington, T.G.; Hodgkins, G.A.; Keim, B.D.; Dudley, R.W. 2004. Changes in the proportion of precipitation occurring as snow in New England (1949-2000). Journal of Climate. 17(13): 2626-2636.

Hurrell, J.W. 1995. Decadal trends in the North Atlantic Oscillation, 1995: regional temperatures and precipitation. Science. 269: 676-679.

Jain, S.; Hoerling, M.; Eischeid, J. 2005. Decreasing reliability and increasing synchroneity of western North American streamflow. Journal of Climate Letters. 18: 613-618.

Janis, M.J.; Hubbard, K.G.; Redmond, K.T. 2004. Station density strategy for monitoring long-term climatic change in the contiguous United States. Journal of Climate. 17(1): 151-162.

Jeton, A.E.; Dettinger, M.D.; Smith, J.L. 1996. Potential effects of climate change on streamflow, eastern and western slopes of the Sierra Nevada, California and Nevada. Rep. 95-4260. Sacramento, CA: U.S. Geological Survey Water Resources Investigations. 44 p.

Johnson, E.A.; Miyanishi, K. 2001. Forest fires: behavior and ecological effects. Academic Press. 549 p.

Kalnay, E.; Kanamitsu, M.; Kistler, R.; Collins, W.; Deaven, D.; Gandin, L.; Iredell, M.; Saha, S.; White, G.; Woolen, J.; Zhu, Y.; Chelliah, M.; Ebisuzaki, W.; Higgins, W.; Janowiak, J.; Mo, K.C.; Ropelewski, C.; Wang, J.; Leetma, A.; Reynolds, R.; Jenne, R.; Joseph, D. 1996. The NCEP/NCAR 40-year reanalysis project. Bulletin of the American Meteorolgocial Society. 77: 437-471.

Karl, T.R.; Groisman, P.Ya; Knight, R.W.; Heim, R.R. 1993. Recent variations of snow cover and snowfall in North America and their relation to precipitation and temperature variations. Journal of Climate. 6: 1327-1344.

Karl, T.R.; Hassol, S.J.; Miller, C.D.; Murray, W.L., eds. 2006. Temperature trends in the lower atmosphere: steps for understanding and reconciling differences. U.S. Climate Change Assessment Program, Synthesis and Assessment Product 1.1. 164 p. www.climatescience.gov/Library/sap/sap1-1/finalreport/default.htm.

Kaufman, Y.J.; Tanre, D.; Boucher, O. 2002. A satellite view of aerosols in the climate system. Nature. 419: 215-223.

Kharin, V.V.; Zwiers, F.W. 2002. Climate predications with multimodel ensembles. Journal of Climate. 15: 793-799.

Kistler, R.; Kalnay, E.; Collins, W.; Saha, S.; White, G.; Woollen, J.; Chelliah, M.; Ebisuzaki, W.; Kanamitsu, M.; Kousky, V.; VanDenDool, H.; Jenne, R.; Fiorino, M. 2001. The NCEP-NCAR 50-year reanalysis: monthly means. [CD-ROM and documentation]. Bulletin of the American Meteorological Society. 82: 247-268.

Kim, J. 2005. A projection of the effects of the climate change induced by increased CO_2 on extreme hydrologic events in the western U.S. Climatic Change. 68: 153-168. doi:10.1007/s10584-005-4787-9.

Kim, J.; Kim, T.K.; Arritt, R.W.; Miller, N.L. 2002. Impacts of increased atmospheric CO_2 on the hydroclimate of the western United States. Journal of Climate. 15(14): 1926-1942.

Knapp, P.A. 2004. Window of opportunity: the climatic conditions of the Lewis and Clark Expedition of 1804–1806. Bulletin of the American Meteorological Society. 85(9): 1289–1303.

Knowles, N.; Cayan, D. 2002. Potential impacts of climate change on the Sacramento/San Joaquin watershed and the San Francisco estuary. Geophysical Research Letters. 29(18): 1891. doi:10.1029/2001GL014339.

Knowles, N.; Cayan, D. 2004. Elevational dependence of projected hydrologic changes in the San Francisco estuary and watershed. Climatic Change. 62: 319-336.

Knowles, N.; Dettinger, M.D.; Cayan, D.R. [Submitted]. Trends in snowfall versus rainfall for the western United States, 1949-2004. Journal of Climate.

Koch, D.; Hansen, J. 2005. Distant origins of Arctic black carbon: a Goddard Institute for Space Studies ModelE experiment. Journal of Geophysical Research. 110: D04204. doi:10.1029/2004JD005296.

Krishnamurti, T.N.; Kishtawal, C.M.; LaRow, T.E.; Bachiochi, D.R.; Zhang, Z.; Willifor, C.E.; Gadgil, S.; Surendran, S. 2000. Multimodel ensemble forecasts for weather and seasonal climate. Journal of Climate. 13: 4196-4216.

Kunkel, K.E.; Easterling, D.; Robinson, D.; Hubbard, K.G.; Redmond, K.T. [Submitted]. Issues with identification of trends in 20th Century U.S. snowfall. Geophysical Research Letters.

Leffler, R.J.; Horvitz, A.; Downs, R.; Changery, M.; Redmond, K.T.; Taylor, G. 2001. Evaluation of a national seasonal snowfall record at the Mount Baker, Washington, Ski Area. National Weather Digest. 25(1,2): 15-20.

Leung, L.R.; Qian, Y. 2003. The sensitivity of precipitation and snowpack simulations to model resolution via nesting in regions of complex terrain. Journal of Hydrometeorology. 4: 1025-1043.

Leung, L.R.; Qian, Y.; Bian, X. 2003a. Hydroclimate of the Western United States based on observations and regional climate simulation of 1981-2000. Part I: seasonal statistics. Journal of Climate. 16: 1892-1911.

Leung, L.R.; Qian, Y.; Bian, X.; Hunt, A. 2003b. Hydroclimate of the Western United States based on observations and regional climate simulation of 1981-2000. Part II: Mesoscale ENSO anomalies. Journal of Climate. 16(12): 1912-1928.

Leung, L.R.; Qian, Y.; Bian, X.; Washington, W.M.; Han, J.; Roads, J.O. 2004. Mid-century ensemble regional climate change scenarios for the western United States. Climatic Change. 62 (1): 75-113. doi:10.1023/B:CLIM.000001369 2.50640.55

Levitus, S.; Antonov, J.L.; Boyer, T.P. 2005. Warming of the world ocean, 1955-2003. Geophysical Research Letters. 32: L02604. doi:10.1029GL021592.

Levitus, S.; Antonov, J.L.; Boyer, T.P.; Stephens, C. 2000. Warming of the world ocean. Science. 287(5461): 2225-2229.

Levitus, S.; Antonov, J.L.; Wang, J.; Delworth, T.L.; Dixon, K.W.; Broccoli, A.J. 2001. Anthropogenic warming of Earth's climate system. Science. 292: 267-270.

Liang, X.; Lettenmaier, D.P.; Wood, E.F.; Burges, S.J. 1994. A simple hydrologically based model of land surface water and energy fluxes for GSMs. Journal of Geophysical Research. 99(D7): 14,415-14,428.

Liang, X.; Wood, E.F.; Lettenmaier, D.P. 1996. Surface soil moisture parameterization of the VIC-2L model: evaluation and modifications. Global and Planetary Change. 13: 195-206.

Lo, F.; Clark, M.P. 2002. Relationships between spring snow mass and summer precipitation in the southwestern United States associated with the North American Monsoon System. Journal of Climate. 15(11): 1378-1385.

Logan, J.A.; Powell, J.A. [Submitted]. Ecological consequences of climate change altered forest insect disturbance regimes. In: Wagner, F.H., ed. Climate change in western North America: evidence and environmental effects. Allen Press.

Luckman, B.H. 1998. Landscape and climate change in the central Canadian Rockies during the 20th Century. Canadian Geographer. 42: 319-336.

Lund, J.R.; Howitt, R.E.; Jenkins, M.W.; Zhu, T.; Tanaka, S.K.; Pulido, M.; Tauber, M.; Ritzema, R.; Ferriera, I. 2003. Climate warming and California's water future. Rep. 03-01. Davis, CA: University of California Davis Center for Environmental and Water Resource Engineering. http://ee.engr.ucdavis.edu/faculty/lund/CALVIN/ReportCEC/CECReport2003.pdf. (23 May 2006)

Lundquist, J.D.; Cayan, D. 2002. Seasonal and spatial patterns in diurnal cycles in streamflow in the western United States. Journal of Hydrometeorology. 3: 591-603.

Lundquist, J.D.; Dettinger, M. 2004. Spring onset in the Sierra Nevada: When is snowmelt independent of elevation? Journal of Hydrometeorology. 5: 325-340.

Lundquist, J.D.; Dettinger, M.D. 2005. How snowpack heterogeneity affects diurnal streamflow timing. Water Resources Research. 41: W05007. doi:10.1029/2004/WR003649, 2005.

MacCluskie, M.; Oakley, K. 2002. Central Alaska network vital signs monitoring plan, phase 1 report. 126 p. http://www.nature.nps.gov/im/units/cakn/reportpubs.cfm.

MacCluskie, M.; Oakley, K. 2003. Central Alaska network vital signs monitoring plan, phase 2 report. 114 p. http://www.nature.nps.gov/im/units/cakn/reportpubs.cfm.

MacCluskie, M.; Oakley, K.; McDonald, T.; Wilder, D. 2004. Vital signs monitoring plan, phase 3 report. 303 p.

MacDonald, G.M.; Case, R.A. 2005. Variations in the Pacific Decadal Oscillation over the past millenium. Geophysical Research Letters. 32: L08703.doi:10.1029/2005GK022478.

Manabe, S.; Wetherald, R.T. 1967. Thermal equilibrium of the atmosphere with a given distribution of relative humidity. Journal of Atmospheric Science. 24 (3): 241-259.

Manabe, S.; Wetherald, R.T.; Milly, T.C.D.; Delworth, T.L.; Stouffer, R.G. 2004. Century-scalechange in water availability--CO_2-quadrupling experiment. Climatic Change. 64(1,2): 59-76.

Mantua, N.J.; Hare, S.R. 2002. The Pacific Decadal Oscillation. Journal of Oceanography. 58: 35-44.

Mantua, N.J.; Hare, S.R.; Zhang, Y.; Wallace, J.M.; Francis, R.C. 1997. A Pacific interdecadal climate oscillation with impacts on salmon production. Bulletin of the American Meteorological Society. 78: 1069-1079.

Marshall, J.; Kushnir, Y.; Battisti, D.; Chang, P.; Czaja, A.; Dickson, R.; Hurrell, R.; McCartney, M.; Saravanan, R.; Visbeck, M. 2001. North Atlantic climate variability: phenomena, impacts and mechanisms. International Journal of Climate. 21: 1863–1898.

McCabe, G.J.; Dettinger, M.D. 1999. Decadal variations in the strength of ENSO teleconnections with precipitation in the Western United States. International Journal of Climatology. 19(13): 1399-1410.

McCabe, G.J.; Dettinger, M.D. 2002. Primary modes and predictability of year-to-year snowpack variations in the western United States from teleconnections with Pacific Ocean climate. Journal of Hydrometeorology. 3: 13-25.

McCabe, G.J.; Palecki, M.A.; Betancourt, J.L. 2004. Pacific and Atlantic Ocean influences on multidecadal drought frequency in the United States. Proceedings of the National Academy of Sciences. 101: 4136-4141.

Meehl, G.A.; Karl, T.; Easterling, D.R.; Changnon, S.; Pielke, R., Jr.; Changnon, D.; Evans, J.; Groisman, P.Ya; Knutson, T.R.; Kunkel, K.E.; Mearns, L.O.; Parmesan, C.; Pulwarty, R.; Root, T.; Sylves, R.T.; Whetton, P.; Zwiers, F. 2000. An introduction to trends in extreme weather and climate events: observations, socioeconomic impacts, terrestrial ecological impacts, and model projections. Bulletin of the American Meteorological Society. 81(3): 413–416.

Miller, N.L.; Bashford, K.E.; Strem, E. 2003. Potential impacts of climate change on California hydrology. Journal of the American Water Resources Association. 39: 771-784.

Minnis, P.; Ayers, J.K.; Nordeen, M.L.; Weaver, S.P. 2003. Contrail frequency over the United States from surface observations. Journal of Climate. 16(21): 3447–3462.

Minnis, P.; Ayers, J.K.; Palikonda, R.; Phan, D. 2004. Contrails, cirrus trends, and climate. Journal of Climate. 17(8): 1671-1685.

Mitchell, D.L.; Ivanova, D.; Rabin, R.; Brown, T.J.; Redmond, K. 2002. Gulf of California sea surface temperatures and the North American Monsoon: mechanistic implications from observations. Journal of Climate. 15(17): 2261–2281.

Mitchell, T.P.; Blier, W. 1997. The variability of wintertime precipitation in the region of California. Journal of Climate. 10: 2261-2276.

Mo, K.C. 1999. Alternating wet and dry eipsodes over California and intraseasonal oscillations. Monthly Weather Review. 127: 2759-2776.

Mo, K.C.; Higgins, R.W. 1998. Tropical influences on California precipitation. Journal of Climate. 11: 412-430.

Moran, J.M.; Hopkins, E.J. 2002. Wisconsin's weather and climate. Madison, WI: University of Wisconsin Press. 321 p.

Mote, P.W. 2003a. Trends in snow water equivalent in the Pacific Northwest and their climatic causes. Geophysical Research Letters. 30: 1601. doi:10.1029/2003GL017258.

Mote, P.W. 2003b. Trends in temperature and precipitation in the Pacific Northwest during the twentieth century. Northwest Science. 77(4): 271-282.

Mote, P.W. [submitted]. Climate-driven variability and trends in mountain snowpack. Journal of Climate.

Mote, P.W.; Hamlet, A.F.; Clark, M.P.; Lettenmeier, D.P. 2005. Declining mountain snowpack in western North America. Bulletin of the American Meteorological Society. 86: 39-49. doi:10.1175/BAMS-86-1-39.

Naftz, D.L.; Susong, D.D.; Schuster, P.F.; Cecil, L.D.; Dettinger, M.D.; Michel, R.L.; Kendall, C. 2002. Ice core evidence of rapid air temperature increases since 1960 in alpine areas of the Wind River Range, Wyoming, United States. Journal of Geophysical Research. 107(D13): 4171. 10.1029/2001JD000621.

National Park Service [NPS]. 2006. National Park Service inventory and monitoring web pages. http:science.nature.nps.gov/im/inventory/index.cfm. (20 May).

National Research Council [NRC]. 1998. Future of the national weather service cooperative observer network. Washington, DC: National Academy Press. 78 p.

National Research Council [NRC]. 1999. Adequacy of climate observing systems. Washington, DC: National Academy Press. 66 p.

National Research Council [NRC]. 2001. A climate services vision: first steps toward the future. Washington, DC: National Academy Press. 84 p.

National Research Council [NRC]. 2005. Radiative forcing of climate change. Washington, DC: National Academy Press. 207 p.

Newman, M.; Compo, G.P.; Alexander, M.A. 2003. ENSO-forced variability of the Pacific decadal oscillation. Journal of Climate. 16: 3853-3857.

Nieman, P.J.; Ralph, F.M.; Horgensen, D.P.; White, A.B.; Kingsmill, D.E. 2004. Modification of fronts and precipitation by coastal blocking during an intense landfalling winter storm in Southern California: observations during CALJET. Monthly Weather Review. 132: 242-273.

Nieman, P.J.; Ralph, F.M.; White, A.B.; Kingsmill, D.E.; Persson, P.O.G. 2002. The statistical relationship between upslope flow and rainfall in California's coastal mountains: observations during CALJET. Monthly Weather Review. 130: 1468-1492.

Oakley, K.L.; Boudreau, S.L. 2000. Conceptual design of the long-term ecological monitoring program for Denali National Park and Preserve. Anchorage, AK: U.S. Geological Society and National Park Service. 116 p. www.absc.usgs.gov/research/Denali_USGS/downloads/Denali_LTEM_Report_without_cover.pdf.

Oakley, K.L.; Thomas, L.P.; Fancy, S.G. 2003. Guidelines for long-term monitoring protocols. Wildlife Society Bulletin. 31: 1000-1003.

Overland, J.E.; Adams, J.M.; Mofjeld, H.O. 2000. Chaos in the North Pacific: spatial modes and temporal irregularity. Progress in Oceanography. 47: 337-354.

Pepin, N.C.; Seidel, D.J. 2005. A global comparison of surface and free-air temperatures at high elevations. Geophysical Research. 110: DO3104. doi:10.1029/2004JD005047.

Pielke, R.A., Sr. 2003. Heat storage within the Earth system. Bulletin of the American Meteorological Society. 84: 331-335.

Quan, X.; Hoerling, M.; Whitaker, J.; Bates, G.; Xu, T. [Submitted]. Diagnosing sources of U.S. seasonal forecast skill. Journal of Climate.

Ralph F.M.; Neiman, P.J.; Kingsmill, D.E.; Persson, P.O.G.; White, A.B.; Strem, E.T.; Andrews, E.D.; Antweiler, R.C. 2003. The impact of a prominent rain shadow on flooding in California's Santa Cruz Mountains: a CALJET case study and sensitivity to the ENSO cycle. Journal of Hydrometeorology. 4(6): 1243–1264.

Ramanathan, V.; Crutzen, P.J.; Kiehl, J.T.; Rosenfeld, D. 2001. Aerosols, climate and the hydrological cycle. Science. 294: 2119-2124.

Randall D.; Khairoutdinov, M.; Arakawa, A.; Grabowski, W. 2003. Breaking the cloud parameterization deadlock. Bulletin of the American Meteorological Society. 84(11): 1547–1564.

Rasmussen, L.A.; Conway, H. 2004. Climate and glacier variability in western North America. Journal of Climate. 17(9): 1804-1815.

Rayner, S.; Lach, D.; Ingram, H. 2005. Weather forecasts are for wimps: why water resource managers do not use climate forecasts. Climatic Change. 69: 197-227. doi:10.1007/s10584-005-3148-z.

Redmond, K.T. 1998. Climate-change issues in the mountainous and intermontane West. In: Wagner, F.H.; Baron, J., eds. Proceedings, Rocky Mountain/Great Basin regional climate-change workshop. Logan, UT: Utah State University: 34-40.

Redmond, K.T. 2002. The depiction of drought: a commentary. Bulletin of the American Meteorological Society. 83(8): 1143-1147.

Redmond, K.T. 2003. Climate variability in the intermontane West: complex spatial structure associated with topography, and observational issues. In: Lewis, W.M., Jr., ed. Water and Climate in the Western United States, Boulder, CO: University Press of Colorado: 29-48, Chapter 2.

Redmond, K.T.; Koch, R.W. 1991. Surface climate and streamflow variability in the western United States and their relationship to large-scale circulation indexes. Water Resources Research. 27: 2381-2399.

Redmond, K.T.; McCurdy, G.D. 2005. Channel Islands National Park: design considerations for weather and climate monitoring. Rep. WRCC-02. Reno, NV: Western Regional Climate Center. 118 p. ftp.wrcc.dri.edu/nps/chis/chisdesignfinal.pdf. (23 May).

Redmond, K.T.; Simeral, D.B. 2006. Weather and climate inventory: National Park Service central Alaska network. Western Regional Climate Center. 122 p. www.wrcc.dri.edu/nps. (May 2006).

Redmond, K.T.; Simeral, D.B.; McCurdy, G.D. 2005. Climate monitoring for southwest Alaska national parks: network design and site selection. Rep. WRCC-01. Reno, NV: Western Regional Climate Center. 92 p. ftp.wrcc.dri.edu/nps/alaska/swanreportfinal.pdf. (23 May)

Regonda, S.K.; Rajagapolan, B.; Clark, M.; Pitlick, J. 2005. Seasonal cycle shifts in hydroclimatology over the western United States. Journal of Climate. 18: 372-384.

Reichert, B.K.; Bengsson, L.; Oerlemans, J. 2002. Recent glacier retreat exceeds internal variability. Journal of Climate. 15(21): 3069-3081.

Rial, J.A.; Pielke, R.A., Sr.; Beniston, M.; Claussen, M.; Canadell, J.; Cox, P.; Held, H.; De Noblet-Ducoudre, N.; Prinn, R.; Reynolds, J.F.; Salas, J.D. 2004. Nonlinearities, feedbacks and critical thresholds within the earth's climate system. Climatic Change. 65: 11-38.

Rind, D.; Goldberg, R.; Hansen, H.; Rozenzweig, C.; Ruedy, P. 1990. Potential evapotranspiration and the likelihood of future drought. Journal of Geophysical Research. 95: 9983-10004.

RISA. 2006. NOAA Regional Integrated Sciences and Assessments Program. www.climate.noaa.gov/cpo_pa/risa/. Brochure: www.climate.noaa.gov/cpo_pa/risa/brochure.pdf. (21 May).

Roderick, M.L.; Farquhar, G.D. 2002. The cause of decreased pan evpaoration over the past 50 years. Science. 298: 1410-1411.

Roos, M. 1991. A trend of decreasing snowmelt runoff in northern California. In: Proceedings 59th Western Snow Conference: 29-36.

Rosenfeld, D. 2000. Suppression of rain and snow by urban and industrial air pollution. Science. 287: 1793-1796.

Rosenfeld, D.; Givati, A. [In press]. Evidence of orographic precipitation suppression by air pollution induced aerosols in the western U.S. Journal of Applied Meteorology.

Saha, S.; Nadiga, S.; Thiaw, C.; Wang, J.; Wang, W.; Zhang, Q.; van den Dool, H.M.; Pan, H.L.; Moorthi, S.; Behringer, D.; Stokes, D.; White, G.; Lord, S.; Ebisuzaki, W.; Peng, P.; Xie, P. [In press]. The NCEP climate forecast system. Journal of Climate.

Schubert, S.D.; Suarez, M.J.; Pegion, P.J.; Koster, R.D.; Bacmeister, J.T. 2004a. Causes of long-term drought in the U.S. Great Plains. Journal of Climate. 17(3): 485-503.

Schubert, S.D.; Suarez, M.J.; Pegion, P.J.; Koster, R.D.; Bacmeister, J.T. 2004b. On the cause of the 1930s Dust Bowl. Science. 303: 1855-1859.

Scott, D.; Kaiser, D. 2004. Variability and trends in United States snowfall over the last half century. Preprint, 15th Symposium on global climate variations and change. [CD-ROM]. Pap. 5.2. American Meteorological Society.

Seager, R.; Kushnir, Y.; Herweijer, C.; Naik, N.; Velez, J. 2005. Modeling of tropical forcing of persistent droughts and pluvials over western North America: 1856-2000. Journal of Climate. 18(19): 4068-4091.

Simpson, J.J.; Hufford, G.L.; Daly, C.; Berg, J.S.; Fleming, M.D. 2005. Comparing maps of mean monthly surface temperature and precipitation for Alaska and adjacent areas of Canada produced by two different methods. Arctic. 58(2): 137-161.

Solomon, S.; Daniel, J.S. 2004. Lewis and Clark: pioneering meteorological observers in the American West. Bulletin of the American Meteorological Society. 85(9): 1273–1288.

Sousanes, P.J. 2004. Climate monitoring protocol for the Central Alaska network: Denali National Park and Preserve, Yukon-Charley Rivers National Preserve, and Wrangell-St. Elias National Park and Preserve. Draft version 1.0.

Stahle, D.W.; Cook, E.R.; Cleaveland, M.K.; Therrell, M.D.; Meko, D.M.; Grisino-Mayer, H.D.; Watson, E.; Luckman, B.H. 2000. Tree-ring data document 16th century megadrought. Eos. 81(12): 121, 125.

Stahle, D.W.; Therrell, M.D.; Cleaveland, M.K.; Cayan, D.R.; Dettinger, M.D.; Knowles, N. 2001. Ancient blue oak reveal human impact on San Francisco Bay salinity. Eos. 82(12): 141, 144-145.

Stewart, I.T.; Cayan, D.R.; Dettinger, M.D. 2004. Changes in snowmelt runoff timing in western North America under a "business as usual" climate change scenario. Climatic Change. 62: 217-232.

Stewart, I.T.; Cayan, D.R.; Dettinger, M.D. 2005. Changes toward earlier streamflow timing across western North America. Journal of Climate. 18: 1136-1155.

Swetnam, T.W.; Betancourt, J.L. 1990. Fire-Southern oscillation relations in the southwestern United States. Science. 249: 1017-1020.

Swetnam, T.W.; Betancourt, J.L. 1998. Mesoscale disturbance and ecological response to decadal climatic variability in the American Southwest. Journal of Climate. 11: 3128-3147.

Thompson, D.W.; Wallace, J.M. 1998. The Arctic oscillation signature in the wintertime geopotential height and temperature fields. Geophysical Research Letters. 25: 1297–1300.

Thompson, D.W.; Wallace, J.M. 2000. Annular modes in the extratropical circulation. Part I: Month to month variability. Journal of Climate. 13: 1000-1016.

Thompson, D.W.; Wallace, J.M. 2001. Regional climate impacts of the Northern Hemisphere annual mode. Nature. 293: 85-89.

Trenberth, K.E.; Dai, A.; Rasmussen, R.M.; Parsons, D.B. 2003. The changing character of precipitation. Bulletin of the American Meteorological Society. 84(9): 1205–1217.

Trenberth, K.E.; Hurrell, J. 1994. Decadal atmosphere–ocean variations in the Pacific. Climate Dynamics. 9: 303–319.

Van Rheenen, N.T.; Wood, A.W.; Palmer, R.N.; Lettenmeier, D.P. 2004. Potential implications of PCM climate change scenarios for Sacramento-San Joaquin River basin hydrology and water resources. Climate Change. 62: 257-281.

Vose, R.S.; Menne, M.J. 2004. A method to determine station density requirements for climate observing networks. Journal of Climate. 17(15): 2961-2971.

Weiss, J.L.; Overpeck, J.T. 2005. Is the Sonoran Desert losing its cool? Global Change Biology. 11: 2065-2077. soi:10.1111/j.1365-2486.2005.01020.x.

Westerling, A.L.; Gershunov, A.; Brown, T.J.; Cayan, D.R.; Dettinger, M.D. 2003. Climate and wildfire in the Western United States. Bulletin of the American Meteorological Society. 84(5): 595–604.

Westerling, A.L.; Gershunov, A.; Cayan, D.R.; Barnett, T.P. 2002. Long lead statistical forecasts of area burned in western U.S. wildfires by ecosystem province. International Journal of Wildland Fire. 11: 257–266.

Western Governors Association [WGA]. 2004. Creating a drought early warning system for the 21st Century: the National Integrated Drought Information System. Adopted June 2004. Santa Fe, NM: Western Governors Association. 16 p.

Western Mountain Initiative [WMI]. 2005. Western Mountain Initiative. www.cfr.washington.edu/research. FME/wmi. (3 December).

Western Regional Climate Center [WRCC-CIP]. 2006. Climate inventory project. www.wrcc.dri.edu/nps. (20 May).

Western Regional Climate Center [WRCC]. 2006. Western Regional Climate Center web pages. www.wrcc.dri.edu. (20 May).

White, A.B.; Neiman, P.J.; Ralph, F.M.; Kingsmill, D.E.; Persson, P.O.G. 2003. Coastal orographic rainfall processes observed by radar during the California Land-Falling Jets Experiment. Journal of Hydrometeorology. 4(2): 264–282.

Wiles, G.C.; D'Arrigo, R.D.; Jacoby, G.C. 1998. Gulf of Alaska atmosphere-ocean variability over recent centuries inferred from coastal tree-ring records. Climatic Change. 38: 289-306.

Williams, D.W.; Liebold, A.M. 2002. Climate change and the outbreak ranges of two North American bark beetles. Agricultural and Forest Entomology. 4(2): 87-99. doi:10.1046/j.1461-9563.2002.00124.x.

Willis, J.K.; Roemmich, D.; Cornuelle, B. 2004. Interannual variability in upper ocean heat content, temperature, and thermosteric expansion on global scales. Journal of Geophysical Research. 109: C12036. doi:10.1029/2003JC002260.

Wolter, K.; Timlin, M.S. 1993. Monitoring ENSO in COADS with a seasonally adjusted principal component index. In: Proceedings of the 17th climate diagnostics workshop, Norman, OK, NOAA/N MC/CAC, NSSL, Oklahoma Climate Survey, CIMMS and the School of Meteorology. Norman, OK: University of Oklahoma: 52-57.

Woodhouse, C.A. 2003. A 431-yr reconstruction of western Colorado snowpack from tree rings. Journal of Climate. 16(10): 1551-1561.

Woodhouse, C.A.; Kunkel, K.E.; Easterling, D.R.; Cook, E.R. 2005. The 20th Century pluvial in the western United States. Geophysical Research Letters. 32: L07701. doi:10.1029/2005GL022413, 2005.

Woodhouse, C.A.; Overpeck, J.T. 1998. 2000 years of drought variability in the central United States. Bulletin of the American Meteorological Society. 79(12): 2693-2714.

Wu, Q.; Straus, D.M. 2004. AO, COWL, and observed climate trends. Journal of Climate. 17(11): 2139-2156.

Zhang, X.; Sheng, J.; Shabbar, A. 1998. Modes of interannual and interdecadal variability of Pacific SST. Journal of Climate. 11: 2556-2569.

Terrestrial and Aquatic Natural Ecosystems: Potential Responses to Global Climate Change

Hermann Gucinski[1]

Olympic National Park

foreground Gary M. Stolz
U.S. Fish and Wildlife Service
background Erik Ackerson

Erik Ackerson, EarthDesign, Ink

[1]Was an assistant director (retired), USDA Forest Service, Southern Research Station, Asheville, NC 28802.

Abstract

Evidence that climate is warming is increasingly obvious. Responses include the earlier onset of green-up, the displacement of high-latitude species by low-latitude ones in both terrestrial and coastal regions, and the infilling of alpine tundra by sub-alpine. For the American West models and projections of current climate trends show reductions of desert and increase in shrubland, except for the great basin, and reduction or disappearance of alpine biomes for the 21st century. Already multiple stresses influence western ecosystems; climate change is an added stressor. Fire frequencies and intensities may hasten ecosystem degradation from other causes; vegetation shifts can be accelerated or slowed by fire. Invasive species will affect fire regimes and induce positive or negative feedback mechanisms. Insects and pathogens, as well as their natural predators will change in numbers, population dynamics and areal extent. Resource systems are not static, with climate change their dynamism may be accelerated. This changes how we approach conservation reserves, view development at the wildland-urban interface, think about habitat and future migration corridors. Seed dispersal, the role of pollinators, influence of topographic and human constraints to migration, and conflicting demands between community, agricultural and aquatic system water needs will require new thinking over multiple organizational levels.

Keywords: Climate changes, ecosystems responses.

Introduction

Natural resource managers of today face an uncertain world that poses many challenges, among them the threat of invasive species, fuel accumulations and risk of catastrophic fire, alteration and loss of habitat, encroachment from human development such as urban expansion, and the interaction of processes that produce difficult to predict synergistic effects. Managers have further come to realize that to that plethora must be added the risk of potential climate change and altered climate variability. How ecosystems will respond to these added stressors, and how these might play out with the other impacts is of concern when it has become apparent that attaining sustainability in the delivery of goods and services from natural systems can at times appear a losing proposition.

In this paper we will attempt to describe the current knowledge of ecosystem responses to climate change and variability in the American West and explore the implications managers may wish to be aware of both from the short-term tactical perspective and from the long-range, policy position. It is a foregone conclusion that uncertainty and the framework within which to manage in an uncertain world will be a significant part of the problem, and it is hoped some helpful hints will be found here.

The scope of this paper, in addition to limiting itself to the American West, is to touch on topics that were insufficiently advanced for consideration 4 years ago when the National Assessment was completed.

…will attempt to describe the current knowledge of ecosystem responses to climate change and variability in the American West and explore the implications managers may wish to be aware of…

We will analyze several broad areas from the perspective of the added risk of climate change and variability in relation to ecosystem response:

a. Vegetation re-distribution ranging from the biome to the species level

b. Fire-affected processes

c. Aquatic ecosystems

d. Biodiversity impacts, disturbance and invasive species

e. Multiple interactions and feedbacks

Finally, we will make some recommendations that reflect the implications of the advances in recent learning.

Background

The concept that man-made releases of CO_2 could alter climate goes back to some very early thinking by Arrhenius (1896, cited in the National Assessment 2001) and was given more substantive thought in the late 1950s by Roger Revelle (Revelle and Waggoner 1984). Revelle's hypothesis led to experimental verification that CO_2 was rising in the earth's atmosphere by Keeling and Whorf (1999), whose measurement record at the Mauna Loa dates back to 1958. The interpretation of choice by atmospheric scientists is that radiative forcing produced by additions of "greenhouse" gases to the atmosphere is the driver for climate change. Greenhouse gases (water vapor is the most potent among them) absorb energy within the solar spectrum, and that energy "capture" leads to a rise in temperature, ultimately balanced by emission of radiation at much lower wavelengths.

The interpretation of choice by atmospheric scientists is that radiative forcing produced by additions of "greenhouse" gases to the atmosphere is the driver for climate change.

However, changes in radiative forcing alone do not tell the whole story of climate change. We must also take into account the processes that take up and redistribute energy (such as changes in the atmospheric moisture and the storage capacity of oceans), and interchanges between these reservoirs and the biosphere. Coupled ocean-atmosphere physics models have grown in sophistication and account for most of the known processes. However, the complexity a multitude of variables, and a certain degree of stochasticity, permits the models to provide predictions at continental scales, but not regional ones. This is shown by the divergence in results of different GCMs (Global Circulation Models). Nevertheless, the confidence level for global interpretation has continued to rise; in fact, a group of National Science Academies, representing 16 countries, say: "We support the IPCC's—Intergovernmental Panel on Climate Change—conclusion that it is at least 90 percent certain that temperatures will continue to rise, with average global surface temperature projected to increase by between 1.4 and 5.8°C above 1990 levels by 2100" (Gucinski et al. 2004, excerpted therein from HYPERLINK "http://www.royalsoc.ac.uk/files/statfiles/document-138.pdf").

For insights regarding the ecosystem responses to climate change, the inadequacy of regional-scale predictability has lead scientists to consider a second approach. Here, trends within the period of record for meteorological observations (a little over a century) are extrapolated over the next few decades; in many cases this is generally consistent with GCM model runs for the same period, but perhaps allows greater insight into events at the regional scale.

The dichotomy can be usefully employed in examining ecological responses. One may build ecological models driven by the climate scenarios—using several GCM outputs, a "fix" is derived for the range of possible responses—and analyze the most likely trends in ecosystem behavior. Alternatively, one can use empirical extrapolation from observed ecosystem function. Given the current level of understanding, the safest approach is to employ both methods and use the contradictions, real or apparent, to refine and improve the science, as was done in the National Assessment (2001).

State-of-Science by 2000

The state of science up to the year 2000 can be found in the "Climate Change Impacts on the United States" effort (NAST or National Assessment Synthesis Team 2001) and a series of papers that are derived from it, such as Aber et al. (2001), Dale et al. (2001), Hansen et al. (2001); we will recap its major conclusions for the American West.

The assessment team used the two broad approaches mentioned above, extrapolating the historical records and using general circulation model simulations to assess the climate change effects. In the former approach, direct observations of temperature and precipitation for the past 100 years were supplemented by space-based observations, along with paleoclimate surrogate data inferred from tree ring, sediment, ice core and related proxies. In the National Assessment sensitivity studies that examine ecosystem impacts were taken from VEMAP (Vegetation-Ecosystem Modeling and Analysis Project, Kittel et al. 1997) used to supplement the historical data.

The 20th century climate simulations show general agreement for the U.S. data as a whole, are a bit warmer than observations along mountain ridges such as the Sierra Nevada and Cascade Mountains, colder over mountain basins, and diverge even more over the southern Rocky Mountains and Great Basin. Direct model outputs must be modified, or modeled further to arrive at secondary information such as soil moisture and snow pack extent and depth, or extrapolated to provide a measure of changes such as the nature of precipitation events, or the likelihood of temperature extremes or other extreme events.

With these inputs, the National Assessment Synthesis Team and Wagner (2003) concluded the following regarding global climate change and variability and potential ecosystems responses for the West:

- Where wetter conditions are likely, we can expect an increase in vegetative biomass and a reduction in desert area. In the Pacific Northwest, average increases in precipitation were 11 percent for the 20th century, with the far northwestern region experiencing as much as a 50 percent increase. The northwest is additionally subject to cyclical changes strongly correlated to El Niño/La Niña and the

Direct model outputs must be modified, or modeled further to arrive at secondary information such as soil moisture and snow pack extent and depth...

Pacific Decadal Oscillation (PDO). These cycles tend to correlate warm temperatures with summer drought, and cool temperatures with wetter winters. At the time of publication of the assessment, little was known about how such pattern will be affected by altered climate. Using GCM scenarios for the relative small size of the Pacific Northwest region is made problematic by the coarse grid cells of the GCMs, few grid cells cover the northwest, and the montane topography add further complications due to elevation difference effects.

- Where reduced precipitation is expected, as in areas of southwestern Arizona, the opposite is likely, i.e., forest productivity may decline and desertification increase. In either case, increases in forest fire frequency are possible.

- Biodiversity is already impacted by habitat fragmentation, increases in migration barriers and invasive species. It will likely decline further with climate change as an added stressor. While some species may be able to migrate to higher elevations, habitats specific to high elevations now may disappear. Adaptive strategies having the most promise for implementation include lessening the impact of rural development and consciously removing existing migration barriers and preventing new ones from arising.

- Aquatic systems are likely to be impacted by the reduction of snowpack extent due to warming, which may offset scenarios of increased precipitation. Earlier melting and changed run-off intensities could alter hydrographs significantly, affecting spawning and altering stream habitat. For example, in the northwest, clear correlation between salmon abundance and climate exists for the freshwater portion of their life cycle, which includes spawning, of course, and here, potential summer warming and reduced summer stream flow will be negatives. In regions of lessened precipitation increased competition for water resources could impact stream productivity and reduce available habitat for aquatic organisms. Means for using technological approaches to mitigate these impacts are available and could be applied if policy for such steps is promulgated and accepted.

Examples from the NAST (2001) Selected to Conveythe Scope of the Impacts:

In a quantitative estimate of climate change impacts on runoff for selected western basins (taken NAST 2001), the authors note that where runoff remains the same or is reduced, added stresses to stream habitat can be inferred from increased temperatures, with attendant reductions in dissolved oxygen levels, particularly in slow-flowing systems (table 1).

They note further that in montane areas, significant temperature rise may put alpine, coldwater species at risk of extinction. Increases in runoff will have varying effects, depending on the extent of accompanying changes in the hydrograph; flashier flow regimes are likely to produce negative changes while well-distributed ones could be beneficial.

egi n	ist ri al run	ange in annual run			
	1961-1990	2025-2034 (mm/y)		2090-2099 (mm/y)	
Upper Colorado	43	-15	3	2	28
Lower Colorado	2	-1	6	0	33
Great Basin	21	-1	4	16	29
California	232	60	63	320	273

Table 1—Current and estimated changes in runoff from CGCM1 and HadCM2

Large regions of the American West are covered by fire-prone vegetation; these ecosystems have evolved adaptations to survive these conditions. The appearance of humans has at times upset that balance, such as when reforestation has lead to denser tree growth...

The direct effect of atmospheric carbon increases, sometimes seen as "fertilization" that enhances forest productivity, has remained elusive...

Alteration in habitat characteristic can drive competition among species, change dominance patterns, and drive some toward extinction (this applies to more than aquatic systems). A confounding factor here is the competitive advantage that permits introduced species to thrive, exacerbating biodiversity issues.

Large regions of the American West are covered by fire-prone vegetation; these ecosystems have evolved adaptations to survive these conditions. The appearance of humans has at times upset that balance, such as when reforestation has lead to denser tree growth, inviting more crown- and stand-replacement fires, or where human development in wildland areas took no heed or precautions to fire risk. The introduction of xenobiotics (foreign invasives) has further exacerbated the problem. Where climate warming leads to increased evapotranspiration, increased fire frequency may result, and increased precipitation may not routinely reduce fire risk. The latter is likely where the increases in precipitation occur in winter months, but leave summer drought unchanged, which is typical for much of the Far West. For example, the dynamic ecosystem model MC1, using both Hadley (HadCM2) and a Canadian GCM (CGCM1), shows a gradual trend of increasing forest biomass consumption by fire and greater consumption for single year events (catastrophic fires), with the Hadley scenario appearing somewhat more benign (Bachelet et al. 2001). There have been several new studies to provide further insights into these dynamics, along with increased emphasis on understanding the interaction between multiple ecosystem changes, and these will be considered in the next section.

The direct effect of atmospheric carbon increases, sometimes seen as "fertilization" that enhances forest productivity, has remained elusive for the writers of the National Assessment. The initial responses of increased CO_2 seen in chamber and other exposure studies were only maintained under conditions of adequate water and nutrient availability. Otherwise a down-regulation by trees resulted, leading to only small and variable increases in forest productivity (Orem et al. 2001). But the data were not yet conclusive at the time of writing.

In the next section we will attempt two things: one, to bring the insights of new studies, experiments and modeling efforts to bear; and two, to attempt to synthesize the state-of-science findings based on the interaction of multiple variables, of which climate change and climate variability are but two elements. Throughout, we will hark to "the big picture" that we believe is of greater relevance to the resource manager than a host of details, many of which may be contradictory.

New Insights into Climate Change and the Potential Range of Ecological Responses

Climate Change

Examining specific developments in climate science itself goes beyond the scope of this paper, and will be addressed in a parallel effort. Our interest here is in understanding how progress in the climate science arena has benefited analyses of ecosystem, hydrologic/aquatic and related responses.

We will digress briefly, however, to broach a topic that received only the merest mention in the National Assessment, and one that may be relegated to the topic of "climate surprises." That is the possibility of global cooling triggered by the temperature rise at high latitude. A recent Pentagon study (Schwartz and Randall 2003) forcefully calls attention to the need to plan for such a scenario. A subsequent comprehensive review done by Clark et al. (2002) re-states the importance of the ocean's thermohaline circulation (THC) in redistributing the globally uneven input of solar atmosphere. The thermohaline circulation is the density driven movement of ocean water, fresh or warm water will tend to stay on top, salty or cold below. However, very cold water such as formed in some polar regions, will sink and displace water below, this leads to exchange of deep waters and helps balance energy input differences between the northern and southern hemisphere. This interaction is complex and has added uncertainly in general circulation models. Recently obtained proxy records (radionuclide ratios in ice cores) show that the thermohaline circulation has collapsed several times over millennial time scales. The THC is driven in part by the formation of Atlantic deep water by sinking of surface water near Greenland (the Irminger Sea and Davis Strait areas). In past ice-ages, the THC has been interrupted because a fresh water lens is formed by increased melting of the Greenland ice cap (for a discussion of the value and need to use multiple proxy records, see Mann 2002 and for a discussion for statistical approaches to quantify climate model uncertainties, see Katz 2002). Coupled atmosphere-ocean GCMs are known to have several equilibria that reflect the altered thermohaline flow. This, and the relationship between the circulation status and cold periods like the Younger Dryas, as well as additional recent modeling, appear to point to the potential for a modest increase in freshwater runoff leading to a significant decrease in North Atlantic density driven flow. That could produce the cooling that has occurred historically (on geologic time scales) and has come about abruptly. Hansen (2005) points out in a recent editorial that glacial retreat and melting proceeds at a far more accelerated rate than does accretion, in large part because of positive feedback loops that come into play, and examines critical points in the melting regime that could lead to abrupt change—he warns that a "business as usual" scenario for man-made climate change could quickly take us to such a point.

...glacial retreat and melting proceeds at a far more accelerated rate than does accretion, in large part because of positive feedback loops that come into play... critical points in the melting regime that could lead to abrupt change...

The above serves as an added dimension to examine the spectrum of possible ecological responses. While we cannot as yet translate this emerging thinking into recommendations for resource managers, we shall return to this when discussing management in a climate of open-ended uncertainties.

There is a rapid and increasing accumulation of observations of consequences of the current warming trend. We will not attempt to cover the climatological data records, instead focusing on observed ecosystem and related responses, but wish to cite one review paper in order to address briefly the continued controversy regarding extreme climate events. Easterling et al. (2000) state that recent model studies further strengthen earlier outputs, that we can expect more intense precipitation events and increased summer drought, and that the future climate could resemble El Niño years more often. While there is poor agreement between GCMs on large storm intensity and frequency, work with nested models suggest that there will be increases in surface wind speeds and a 28 percent increase in near-storm precipitation. Unfortunately, the current level of scientific analysis has not yet allowed breaking out particulars for the Western United States.

Ecosystem Responses

Vegetation Redistribution at the Biome and Species Level

We now return to the more commonly accepted climate change scenarios of global warming. We begin with a discussion of vegetation change in response to climate forcing. The observational evidence since the National Assessment continues to give instances that match the trend previously reported (Iverson and Prasad 2001, Julius et al. 2003). In their report on a longitudinal transect (CLIMET) from the Olympic Peninsula in Washington State to Montana, Fagre et al. (2003) note the continued reduction of alpine tundra due to the replacement by sub-alpine forest. They caution that the process is not linear and not simply elevational, but appears to favor areas such as avalanche paths and infilling, and has aspect-dependent differences. However, upward migration has been observed to reach as much as 250 m in elevation. By contrast, elevational changes during the Holocene appear to have been generally less than 100 m. Accompanying the sub-alpine forest expansion is the glacial retreat. Glacier National Park had 150 glaciers in 1850; today 37 remain. Glacial ice thickness has decreased along with the retreat, as determined by use of ground penetrating radar. Simple extrapolation of this pattern could lead to the disappearance of the park's glaciers as early as 2030 (see references within Fagre et al. 2003). Lastly, the authors note that high elevation forest productivity has risen when compared to that of lower elevation forest. In Mexico, the drought of the 1950s led to changes in the pine to pinion-juniper forest up to 5 km, and these shifts have not reversed to the present time, though the drought abated (Easterling et al. 2000).

A full understanding of the relationship of climate to ecosystem productivity and processes will not come from observational evidence alone. To test one's understanding, models can provide considerable opportunity, and, once sufficiently robust and grounded in dominant physiological and biochemical mechanisms, can have predictive value. Lacking that, the models can deliver insight for potential scenarios that may delineate the range of potential ecosystem responses.

The National Assessment delineated ecosystem responses by considering both a biome-level, biogeographic—essentially, a life zone approach—to vegetation distribution. This approach has been developed further to incorporate hydrology, such as the equilibrium model MAPSS (Neilson 1995) and the MC1 model [the latter is dynamic and incorporates biogeography, biogeochemistry and fire dynamics (Bachelet et al. 2001, Daly et al. 2000, Lenihan et al. 2003)]. These models have continued to be used and refined, as has species-specific work relying on the development of response surfaces from empirical consideration of species requirements, as will be explained below.

Bachelet et al. (2001) used both MAPSS and MC1 to simulate vegetation distribution for historical climate and future scenarios, and to determine changes in leaf-area index (LAI) and changes in areas of stress as reflected by reduction in vegetation density for the conterminous United States. Their approach compares the two models, which can inspire confidence where good agreement is observed, or invite improvement where differences remain. In more recent work, the Canadian GCM (CGCM1) and the British Hadley Centre model (HadCM2) have principally been used; these agree in positing a slight conifer forest expansion. Figure 1 is a coarse scale representation of that expansion, done for both GCMs.

Model outputs further show shrubland losses in the Great Basin; farther west, they show reductions in desert area, i.e., increased shrubland biomass, due to the increased precipitation. Under increased warming the cold tolerant, high elevation alpine tundra, and even some sub-alpine trees may have nowhere to climb and disappear. The fate of western coniferous forests is of great interest, and here the models leave room for speculation. One model, MC1, posits an increase in forest area, but accompanied by decreased biomass (as reflected in carbon stores) in their present range, while the other, MAPSS, posits little areal change, but yields a decrease in LAI (i.e., a loss of productivity). In other words, the expanding forest may have a savannah-like structure.

Another interesting concept included in the simulations by Bachelet et al. (2001) is that of the stressed area as the fraction of the total land surface under consideration where a decline in vegetation density occurs. The simulation of historical climate shows the 1930s drought, which affected 49 percent of U.S. forested area and 60 percent of the land area, and also shows the 1972 climate shift toward wetter conditions. The sharp difference between the models' stress index for future climates reflects differences in the GCMs, when comparing the Hadley with the Canadian model. Such divergence reflects interpretation of large-scale atmospheric behavior in the GCMs, which are influenced by such factors as the positioning or shift in summer high-pressure fields such as the Bermuda High, or differences in the location of the jet stream.

Under increased warming the cold tolerant, high elevation alpine tundra, and even some sub-alpine trees may have nowhere to climb and disappear.

49

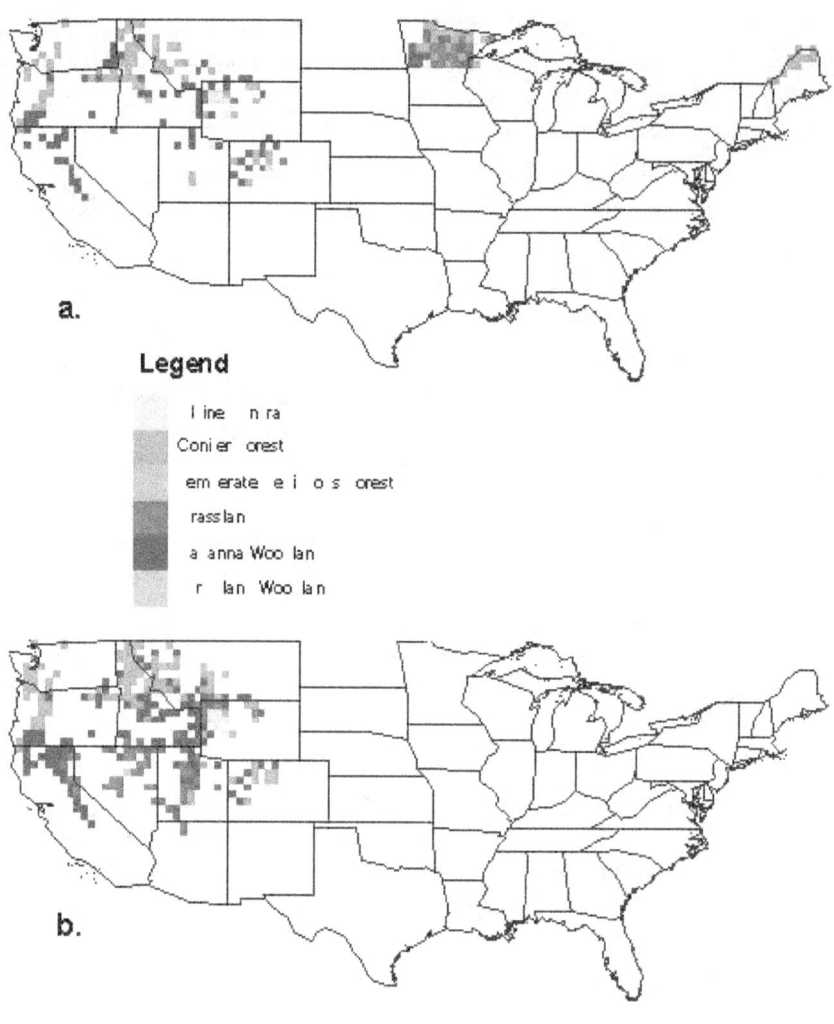

Legend

- line n ra
- Conifer orest
- emperate e i o s orest
- rassland
- a anna Woo lan
- r lan Woo lan

Figure 1—Conifer expansion in the American West under future climate shown as a DIFFERENCE map from current climate for a) the HadCM2 GCM and b) the Canadian GCM (CGCM1) scenario (courtesy of D. Bachelet, Oregon State University).

There are, as yet, no *a priori* considerations that allow either an atmospheric physicist or a layperson to accept or reject one scenario over another. Hence, the resource manager will face a wider spectrum of uncertainty. The implications of these findings will be taken up subsequently.

The conclusions of the above work are amplified by a more refined analysis applied by Lenihan et al. (2003) to California. Based on the use of the same two GCM (Canadian and Hadley) above, their results show similar vegetation dynamics, such as the shift in dominance of needle-leaved to broadleaved forests, accompanied by increases in productivity. Additionally, their work serves to highlight the role of fire in these ecosystems. Fire dynamics are not only altered by annual as well as seasonal trends in precipitation, but may initiate feedback loops to strengthen emerging trends. For example, the Modoc Plateau in northern California, now dominated by shrubland-conifer vegetation, will experience reduced precipitation that allows ingress of grass species. The fine fuel flammability will lead to higher fire frequencies, which serves to discourage tree/shrub recovery, solidifying the competitive advantage of the grasses. One somewhat ironic effect is that the wetter climate under the Hadley scenario can increase fire frequency or severity. California is influenced by the cyclical nature of both short-term events such as El Niño/La Niña cycles and the longer term PDO. Wet years will permit greater productivity and hence greater fuel accumulation. The following dry cycle will not only lead to higher ignition rates, but to more intense, and possibly more extensive fires because of fuel availability.

Although the simulations of MAPSS and MC1 yield potential redistribution of major biome components such as forest, savannas, shrublands or deserts, they say nothing of species. Yet the response of vegetation will be borne at the species level, under a multiplicity of reactions that include species-specific responses in productivity, root-shoot carbon allocation, competitive interactions, seed dispersal mechanisms, influence of soils, herbivory, pollination, and so on. This will affect plant behavior *in situ* as well as the plants' ability to new habitats.

Current efforts at predicting species-based vegetation response rely on empirical bioclimatic correlations. For example, Shafer et al. (2001) use the mean temperature of the coldest month of the year, growing degree days, and a moisture index to derive "response surfaces" that reflect the "exploitable" habitat for a given species. However, the treatment of these response surfaces allows imposition of future climate scenarios and can be used to infer new zones of species "habitability." The results are instructive. Selected species relevant to the West include Douglas-fir (*Pseudotsuga menziesii* (Mirbel) Franco), Ponderosa (*Pinus ponderosa* P.& C. Lawson), Pacific yew *(Taxus brevifolia* Nutt.), big sagebrush (*Artemisia tridentate* Nutt.), Saguaro (*Carmegiea gigantean* (Engelm.) Britt. & Rose), and creosote bush *(Larrea tridentate* (Sessé & Moc. ex DC.) Coville).

Response surfaces can be generated for future climate using GCM scenarios. In general, the authors report that resulting species shifts are potentially large—hundreds of miles—in all three GCM scenarios used (CGCM1, HadCM2, and CSIRO [Commonwealth Scientific and Industrial Research Organization, Australia]). The actual patterns of the shifts are affected by topography, and are not simply a northward or upward expansion as warming only would suggest.

In the northwest, higher coldest month temperature may lead to a contraction of Pacific silver fir (*Abies ambilis* (Dougl. ex Loud.) Dougl. ex Forbes) habitat. Interestingly, the authors report a shift eastward of species typical of the west-side mountains of Oregon and Washington; these species include Douglas fir, Pacific yew, as well as red alder (*Alnus rubra* Bong.) and Oregon white oak (*Quercus gerryana* Dougl. ex Hook.). Conversely, drought tolerant species such as Ponderosa will shift westward across the crest of the Cascades. Big sagebrush, a cold steppe component, will shift northward, but also contract from its current range, presumably driven by summer moisture stress, which in part limits its southern range. At the same time, both saguaro and creosote bush will expand into some of the present range of big sagebrush, and saguaro could expand both east and westward from its current distribution.

Wet years will permit greater productivity and hence greater fuel accumulation. The following dry cycle will not only lead to higher ignition rates, but to more intense, and possibly more extensive fires because of fuel availability.

...drought tolerant species such as Ponderosa will shift westward across the crest of the Cascades.

These simulations do not take into account limiting factors such as barriers to migration, seed dispersal issues, absence or lessening fire frequency effects on species requiring fire-hardening (e.g., having serotinous cones), and isolation of habitats or their fragmentation. The final distribution of species from such changes may be quite different than their potential range would indicate. One may surmise that periods of instability will create opportunities for invasive species where none exist now, further complicating predictions. Lastly, the simulations will be reliable to the extent that average temperature of coldest month, growing-degree days and moisture stress can be used to explain the principal response of the species examined; there may be cases where adaptation or other variables modify responses.

Fire

We have already mentioned the role of fire in western ecosystems, the conclusions regarding fire in the National Assessment, and the fire-vegetation interaction reported by Lenihan et al. (2003) for California. Figure 2 shows the simulation for both current and future climate. Fire alters the landscape, changes the vegetation patterns, affects succession, alters, and is altered by, invasive species. Understanding the effects of potential climate change includes understanding direct changes on present vegetation, vegetation-fire feedbacks, and fire regimes under vegetation shifts. Between 1989 and 1998, an average 100,000 fires consumed forests on 3.3 million acres per year in the United States. There is, of course, great variability (Flannigan et al. 2000); Whitlock at al. (2003) state that the paleo-record shows the fire-climate relationship quite clearly, they suggest that 20th century fire histories in the West portray a situation of "fire scarcity" when compared to the paleo-ecological record; it could be that the present-day fire regimes may be more ephemeral than previously thought.

Resource managers would like to know how fire regimes will change in both the near term, e.g., the next decade or two, and over the longer stretch, when the doubling of CO_2 might be expected. Fire danger is measured in several ways; indices have been developed to express differing aspects. Flanagan et al. (2000) used seasonal severity ratings (SSR), an index commonly used by fire managers that describes the seasonal average of the daily estimate of fire control difficulty. This measure can be projected using GCM outputs, and the authors state that both models (CGMC1 and HadCM2) show a 10 percent or less increase in SSR in the west.

More detailed is the work of Brown et al. (2004), who have used the Energy Release Component (ERC) to investigate climate change responses. The ERC (measured as heat energy per unit area) relates to fire severity, the higher the ERC, the more likely that a hot fire will grow and be hard to contain. The ERC is strongly influenced by relative humidity, which in turn affects fuel moisture. This relationship is quantified using a fuel model; climate model outputs, including humidity and temperature are inputs to the fuel model, which, combined with fuel abundance data, can be used to calculate ERC numbers. The model is calibrated

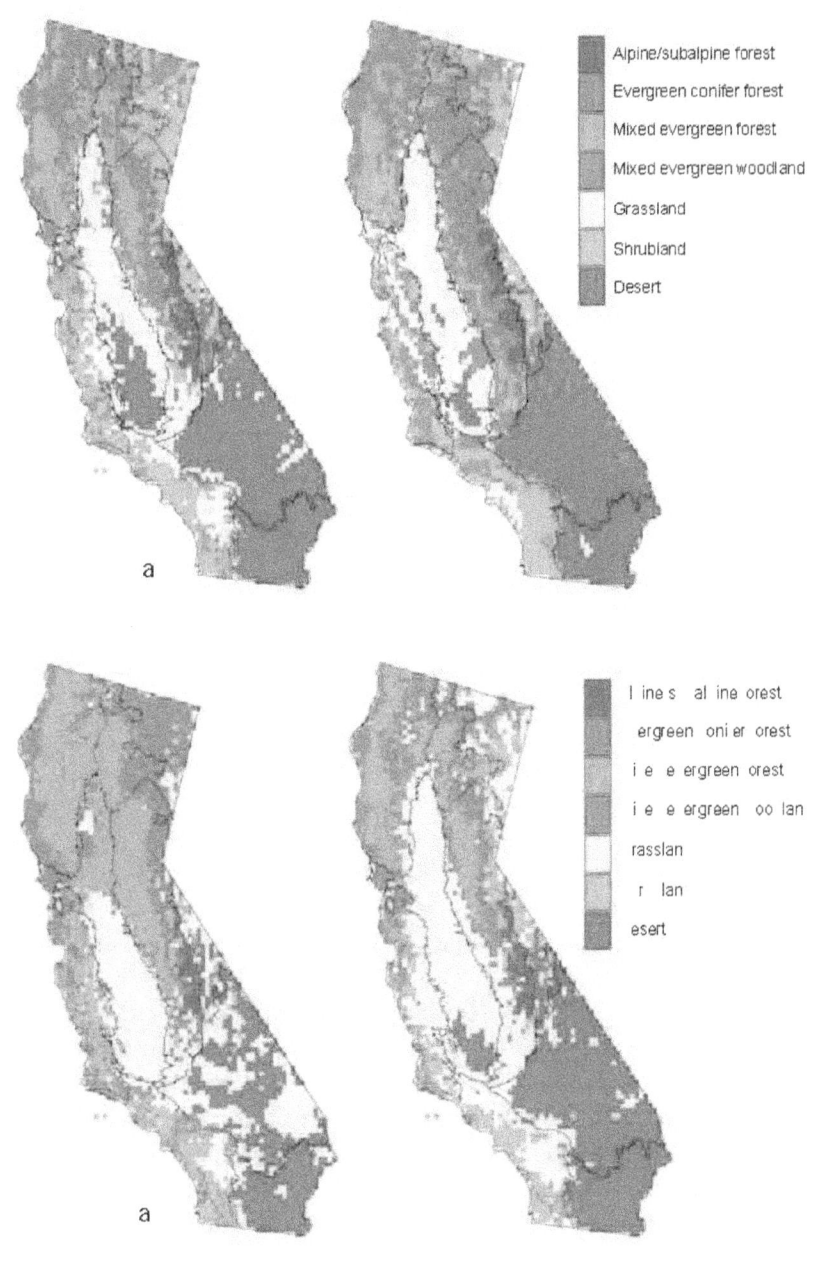

■	Alpine/subalpine forest
■	Evergreen conifer forest
■	Mixed evergreen forest
■	Mixed evergreen woodland
□	Grassland
■	Shrubland
■	Desert

Figure 2—California vegetation change for 2 global circulation model (GCC) scenarios, a) current and simulated distribution, and b) future distribution using the Parallel Climate model (PCN), top, and Hadley (HadCM2), bottom, models (Lenihan 2003, by permission).

by running it for historical periods for which ERC values have been determined independently, and then future scenarios are derived.

Brown et al. (2004) report on the Parallel Climate Model developed at NCAR (National Center for Atmospheric Research, Boulder, Colorado), which differs from those mentioned earlier. Using this model, they predict a drying trend, with more days of lower humidity compared to the present, for the Great Basin and the desert southwest. They arrive at an ERC threshold value of 60, a value presently reached at certain points in the fire season; Figure 3, taken from their work, shows the change in mean

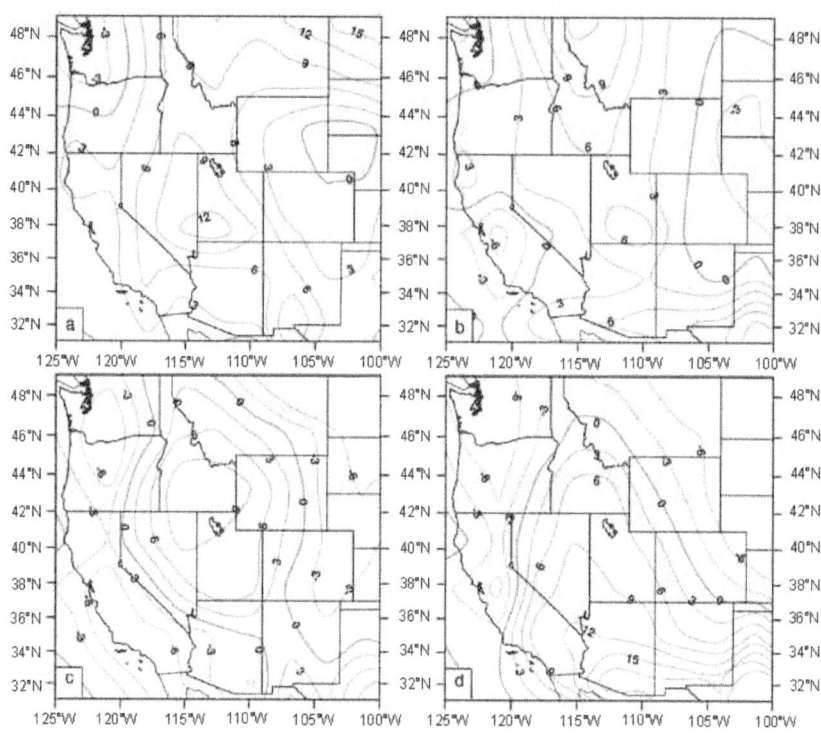

Figure 3—The change in mean number of days when the energy release component (ERC, see text for explanation) exceeds 60 for four future decades, based on PCM (parallel climate model) runs (Brown et al. 2004, by permission).

number of days when the energy release component exceeds 60 for four future decades, based on parallel climate model runs. At that threshold, fires have historically reached large proportions (> 40 ha), been difficult to control, and required a large containment effort, i.e., been expensive to fight. The Western United States is strongly affected by bidecadal climate patterns and the influence of these patterns can be seen in the predictions. The predicted threshold ERCs are reached 2 weeks earlier in the fire season in the Southwest, and earlier than at present nearly everywhere in the West, especially in the Great Basin and the northern Rockies, excepting the Front Range and High Plains. Neither group was able to include the effects of potential vegetation shifts, as theirs was a first-cut approach.

Added to potential vegetation shifts is the appearance of exotic species. These may not only alter the success rate of such shifts, outcompete native species, but influence fire with feedback mechanisms. Brooks at al. (2004) cite examples of both positive feedback—for example, the alien grass *Bromus tectorum* invades shrub steppe areas; by its creation of fine fuels it increases not only fire frequency, but the length of the fire season because fine fuels can dry out quickly—and negative feedback. The latter has been observed in maritime southwestern chaparral invaded by a South African succulent, *Carpobrotus edulis*, which, having a higher moisture content, reduces fire intensity. In both cases, the change enhances the competitive status of the invader, altering ecosystem properties, including herbivore status and their dependent predator-prey relationships. Brooks at al. (2004) develop a schema (fig. 4, taken

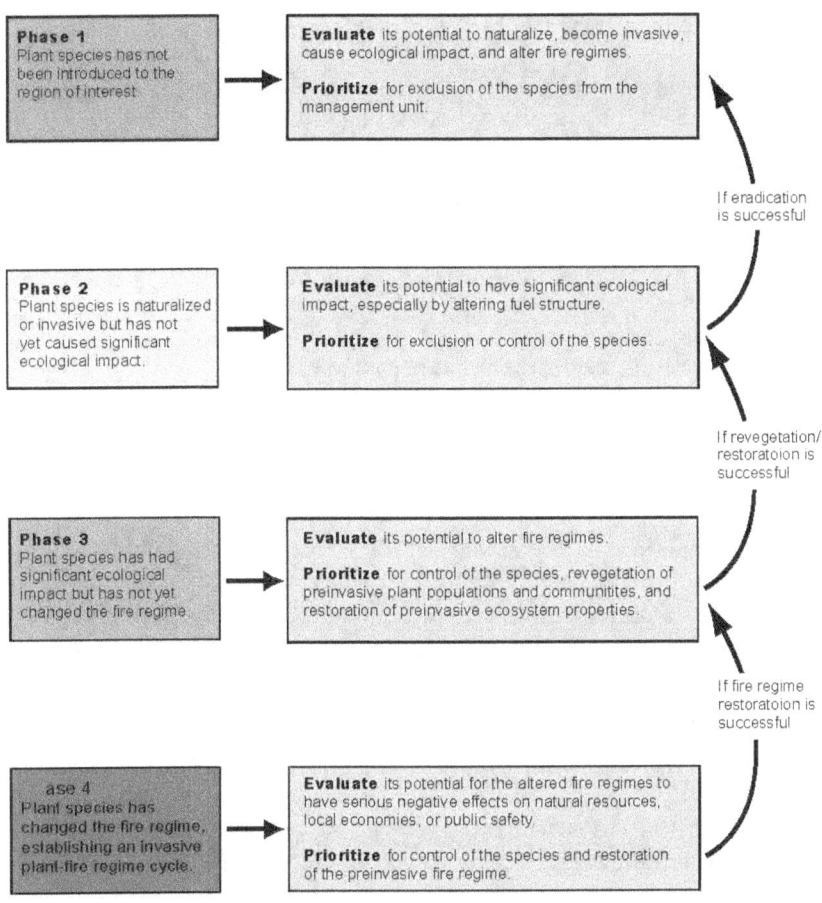

Phase 1
Plant species has not been introduced to the region of interest.

Evaluate its potential to naturalize, become invasive, cause ecological impact, and alter fire regimes.

Prioritize for exclusion of the species from the management unit.

If eradication is successful

Phase 2
Plant species is naturalized or invasive but has not yet caused significant ecological impact.

Evaluate its potential to have significant ecological impact, especially by altering fuel structure.

Prioritize for exclusion or control of the species.

If revegetation/ restoratoion is successful

Phase 3
Plant species has had significant ecological impact but has not yet changed the fire regime.

Evaluate its potential to alter fire regimes.

Prioritize for control of the species, revegetation of preinvasive plant populations and communitites, and restoration of preinvasive ecosystem properties.

If fire regime restoratoion is successful

ase 4
Plant species has changed the fire regime, establishing an invasive plant-fire regime cycle.

Evaluate its potential for the altered fire regimes to have serious negative effects on natural resources, local economies, or public safety.

Prioritize for control of the species and restoration of the preinvasive fire regime.

Figure 4—A system to evaluate the effects of invasive species and prioritize them for several stages of the fire regime cycle. (Brooks et al. 2004, by permission).

from their paper) for understanding the invasive plant fire-regime cycle with a four-phase conceptual model. Phase one, invasive plant potential depends on the life history and preadaptive status of the invasive in relation to the existing fire regime. Phase two, the establishment phase, addresses propagule characteristic, dispersal opportunities and barriers and related factors required for self-perpetuating populations. Phase three occurs when invasive populations reach a size sufficient to alter native community composition and functioning. The final phase is the one where the presence of the invader alters the fire regime, providing the feedback mechanism that effectively ends or greatly reduces the re-establishment potential of the native dominants. We cite this conceptual scheme, because it enables the resource manager to conceptualize more easily how and when to combat the invaders, and conveys a sense of how effective, or expensive, such measures might be. One compelling thought—one that comes as no surprise—is that prevention of initial introduction is probably the most cost-effective step that can be taken. However, managing fuel loads and ignitions are other actions that may hold promise once a manager is confronted with the growing presence of the invader. Of course, success is not easy to guarantee and may require manual native plant re-establishment efforts as well—hard to contemplate when resource budgets are scarce and manpower is limited.

…this conceptual scheme… enables the resource manager to conceptualize more easily how and when to combat the invaders, and conveys a sense of how effective, or expensive, such measures might be.

River Flow and Some Implications for Aquatics Systems

In order to understand the responses of aquatic ecosystems to climate change, one needs to understand how climate affects the hydrology of streams, rivers, and lakes. It appears there has been more progress in hydrology research than in the biological components. This may be a reflection of the state-of-science in both fields. We begin a brief review of the former.

An interesting development has been "downscaling," an attempt to take outputs of GCMs, which operate at a coarse scale (grid cells measure about 90 miles on edge), and use them as inputs to mesoscale models; the much higher resolution of the latter then provide input for yet finer scale hydrologic models (Barnett et al. 2004). Leung et al. (2004) used the NCAR Parallel Climate Model (PCN) to drive the accepted mesoscale MM5 model (40 km spatial resolution), which in turn provides the input for the hydrologic simulations. Using the Columbia River and the Sacramento-San Joaquin River basins, the author's simulations suggest that the 1 to 2.5°C warming from projected climate change will be greater on warm days, and less so on cold days (Payne et al. 2004, Van Rheenen et al. 2004). There will also be a strong effect on winter snowpacks, leading to a 60 to 70 percent reduction in the coastal mountains of these basins, and a 15 to 20 percent cold season increase in daily precipitation. This will be accompanied by an increase in rain-on-snow events—these are the events that frequently give rise to flooding episodes—and a shift of the snowmelt peak from May to April for many portions of the basins. The simulations show that during winter months in the Cascades and Sierras, daily precipitation will increase 15 to 20 percent, and 15 to 30 percent in the northern Rockies. Conversely, extremes in precipitation will be reduced in the southern portions of the Sierras and Oregon's coastal reaches, consequently snowpack reductions reach as much as 60-70 percent, which appears to be the effect of temperature varying about the freeing point. In areas now normally colder, the increase in temperature does not reach the freezing point; impacts on snowpack are much less. The predicted snowpack reductions and earlier melt, also reported by Stewart et al. (2004) for the Western United States in the same issue, will lead to diminished soil moisture in summer. Runoff increases by 40 percent for the December through February winter months, and is reduced by 28 percent for the March through April period. The reduced summer moisture appears to contradict the greater precipitation reported for northern California by the Hadley GCM (HadGCM2), which shows that the simulations have not yet converged to give the resource manager a simple picture of what the future holds. Finally, the authors assert that the climate-change-induced temperature rise in these regions points to a positive snow-albedo feedback enhancing the rise. Their claim makes sense from a physics standpoint, but was not well supported in their paper.

Christensen et al. (2004), also starting with the PCM, report a much similar result for the Colorado River Basin. They evaluate their simulations by giving results for the historical period and the future

> The simulations show that during winter months in the Cascades and Sierras, daily precipitation will increase 15 to 20 percent, and 15 to 30 percent in the northern Rockies.

scenario, thus they report a 10 percent reduction in basin-wide runoff for the historical period, and a 14, 18 and 17 percent reduction for 20-year periods beginning in 2010. Water storage is simulated at 7 percent less than the historic record, and 36, 32 and 40 percent less for the same future decadal intervals.

These simulations set the stage for examining aquatic ecosystem responses. The literature for these responses is not as systematic as one might wish; some speculative papers appeared a decade or more ago (e.g., Gucinski et al. 1990). The aquatic habitats and the fauna adapted to present ecosystems will be much influenced by the periodicity of runoff, such as the timing of annual peak runoff from snowmelt, summer low-flow stages, the flashiness of runoff events large enough to rework streams and alter spawning beds, and change in riffle and pool distributions.

Reductions in snowpack will alter the hydrograph of rivers in basins such as the Columbia, the Sacramento-San Joaquin and, perhaps to a lesser degree, the Colorado Rivers. For anadromous fishes, reductions in summer low flows may be of greater consequence than earlier peak runoff; in portions of western basins, this is already a problem because of water withdrawals for irrigation. We make no attempt in this paper to examine water resource issues for human uses, but must point to the fact that some climate change effects may exacerbate existing stresses from just such conflicts.

The flashiness of runoff, and the potential for greater flooding due to rain-on-snow events can have mixed consequences: aquatic fauna has co-evolved with disturbance. On short time-scales, flood disturbance generally brings population decreases for stream reaches. We also know that perpetually uniform stream flow does not lead to the highest stream productivity. The problem most likely lies with the degree of departure from historic extremes, and there may well be thresholds, that when exceeded with greater frequencies or exceeded beyond a certain point in single events, will have catastrophic impacts on aquatic ecosystem productivity. It is not clear if the events depicted in the simulations of basin hydrology are well within "normal" ranges or "push the envelope" beyond present tolerance limits. The stresses from human development, habitat degradation, water withdrawals, and dams are known to have pushed many populations toward tolerance limits, and disrupted the base on which aquatic productivity rests. Added negative changes from whatever source, climate included, could hasten deleterious degradation.

Biodiversity, Disturbance and Invasives

Observations, thinking, analysis, and modeling all show that potential climate change and variability can significantly influence species populations, community composition, reproductive success, competitive status, and resilience to disturbance patterns. Only fairly recently, it was believed that ecosystem processes were too subtle to allow the simple determination that observed changes could be attributed to climate change. Especially vexing is the added complexity when an ecosystem or an entire biome is subjected to the invasion and establishment of a foreign

The aquatic habitats and the fauna adapted to present ecosystems will be much influenced by the periodicity of runoff, such as the timing of annual peak runoff from snowmelt...

For anadromous fishes, reductions in summer low flows may be of greater consequence than earlier peak runoff; in portions of western basins, this is already a problem because of water withdrawals for irrigation.

(xenobiotic) species; Simberloff (2000) states, "how global climate change
will affect these impacts has scarcely been addressed." Fortunately, far-
reaching implications can be found in the painstaking search of long-term
records, comparison of old plots, the reexamination of data sets, and the
modeling efforts now mature enough to convey meaningful results.

The most trenchant summary is the report of the Pew Center
(Parmesan and Galbraith 2004, but also see Parmesan and Yohe 2003,
Root et al. 2003). Observations relevant to the American West include
disruptions to community structure because of earlier spring events
and the decline of cold-adapted species; the breeding season advance of
Mexican jays (*Aphelocoma ultramarina*), which requires parallel advance
of their food sources to permit continued survival; the earlier emergence
from denning of marmots (*Marmota flaviventris*); and a nearly 80 percent
decline of Edith's checkerspot butterfly *(Euphydryas editha)* in their
southern range (though populations at the northern range limit appear to
be doing well). On the aquatic side, long-term records in Monterey Bay
and kelp forest fish communities off southern California show the decline
of northern species and establishment and dominance of southern species.

The Pew Center report is not alone in delineating the significant
impact of potential climate change in the faunal community. Thomas et
al. (2004), writing in *Nature*, report an analysis of bird extinction risk
based on an empirical, but well-accepted relationship between the number
of species and the area occupied by them. The relationship is reported as
a reasonable predictor of the number of species that become threatened
or go extinct as the areas available to them is reduced from all possible
causes, including climate change. Their analysis compares habitat loss
from reasons other than climate to loss as a result of climate. Using results
from GCMs with moderate warming scenarios, they conclude that for the
taxa they examined in their sampling regions, from 15 to 37 percent of
species will be "committed to extinction," that to the degree the species/
area relationship applies, extinction is highly likely. The regions examined
(Mexico, South Africa, Queensland [Australia], Amazonia, and Europe)
do not include the American West, but can be deemed equally applicable.
It is important to note that the estimates from Thomas et al. (2004)
apply to the proportions of species committed to future extinction, not
the number of species. This observation parallels the work of Sekercioglu
et al. (2004), whose results are somewhat more ominous, stating that
by 2100, 6 to 14 percent of bird species will be extinct, and 7 to 25
percent of bird species will be extinction prone from the sum total of all
foreseeable causes, including climate change. The significance of birds to
ecosystem processes such as pollination, insectivory, seed dispersal, and
decomposition is hard to overstate, as the authors recognize.

Logan et al. (2003) assess the impact of global warming on forest pest
dynamics and begin with the premise that insects, diseases, and other
forest pathogens—anthropocentrically called pests—in general have been
an ever-present threat to "health" when a system is managed or exploited
for human use. With an affected area that is approximately 45 times
that of fire (although the per cent mortality may not be comparable) the
economic impact is 5 times that of fire (Dale et al. 2001, cited by Logan

et al. 2003), investigating the potential for exacerbation due to climate is not trivial. As with changes in phenology reported above, seasonally earlier insect activity compared to prior histories have been observed (Ayres and Lombardero 2000). Thus, one would expect changes in herbivory, altered predator-prey relations for insects, and regional as well as elevational effects (Bale et al. 2002). Logan et al. (2003) posit that the area occupied by an invader grows in proportion to the mean dispersal distance per reproductive cycle. Such relationships may be tied to climate model outputs to assess how insects will respond for future scenarios.

Multiple Interactions and Feedbacks

There is now considerable evidence that multiple interactions are occurring on the land; these will complicate the picture for the future. Fire will accompany vegetation shifts and exacerbate the decline where dense forests will give way to savannas due to water limitations on productivity. Moreover, as we observed, the change in fine fuel abundance will not only slow or stop forest reestablishment, but also speed the forest decline in those areas. This is exacerbated when the establishment of a grass-like invasive species is added to the mix. Stressed forests become much more susceptible to insect attack; the abundant opportunity for insects will lead to population surges. The eventual checks from insect predator populations may be at risk from unfavorable habitat conditions. The analysis of bird extinctions does not inspire confidence that such predators will be available. Lastly, we have mentioned that the promise of carbon fertilization that might offset some of the negative factors that lead to decline in vegetative productivity is not likely to be large and may be restricted by highly specific constraints.

The foregoing does not consider that expected dominant vegetation that characterizes the particular bird habitat may have changed as well. In turn, the analyses of such shifts are usually done without regard to human impediments to dispersal, re-establishment barriers, and habitat losses. Interdisciplinary work has made great strides in recent times (see for example references below that have climatologists, biologists, paleo-scientists, hydrologists and modelers in their list of authors). However, the science of modeling combined effects of entire suites of processes to obtain results that are meaningful, and not merely speculative, is in its infancy.

Implications for Management

At first blush the resource manager is faced with what seems an intractable problem. She or he is told that problems of potentially serious consequences are posing a threat, but that there is considerable uncertainty associated with the problems. Moreover, the consequences are reported as an initially disparate set, sometimes at odds with one another. Hints are given about their inter-connectedness, yet no self-consistent set of recommendations exists by which to approach the management needs.

We regret to say that we cannot provide any simple answers, but we do think we can identify some starting points. If everything is thrown at

There is now considerable evidence that multiple interactions are occurring on the land; these will complicate the picture for the future.

At first blush the resource manager is faced with what seems an intractable problem. She or he is told that problems of potentially serious consequences are posing a threat, but that there is considerable uncertainty associated with the problems.

us at once, it will be hard to respond in a logical and decisive manner that can yield improvement instead of adding to the chaos. We are told we are facing a global rise in temperatures, but one with wide regional differences accompanied by precipitation changes that could either increase or decrease. A potential increase in climatic variability is forecast, but as yet we see no identifiable change in hurricane frequency. We are told that these changes will come in concert with other stresses such as human encroachment at the urban-wildland interface, increasing pressure on conservation areas and perhaps on needed migration routes for both flora and fauna, changed timing and extent of run-off and changes in reservoir capacity and water demand for human consumption and agricultural priorities, and a growing threat from invasive species. Lastly, we are told that as yet unknown human responses to these stresses will affect which avenues for resource management will be closed or remain open

We can begin to face this challenge by a first-order approach and develop secondary options that can be prioritized and brought forward for implementation. Five to 10 years ago, the debate took the form of a dichotomy of mitigation versus adaptation. Then, mitigation referred to action needed to avert climate change, primarily by reductions in emissions of greenhouse gases and increases in the sequestration of some of them—principally CO_2—in the biosphere, and perhaps, the oceans. Adaptation strategies were based on the concept that climate change effects had a low probability of occurrence, had the potential of even being beneficial (who would argue that a warmer, wetter world would not be better than a colder, drier one?) and that resulting costs for adaptive strategies would be less than costs of mitigation, the latter was believed to have an economic slow-down as a by-product.

The discussion has changed since that time.

As stated earlier, the IPCC concluded that the certainty of warming from increasing man-made releases of greenhouse gases has a 90 percent probability. Then there is the concept of climate momentum. Increases in atmospheric CO_2 since the industrial revolution will result in climate change even if we are to stabilize emissions to earlier levels. Mitigation as initially envisioned is no longer an option—we are seeing the effects of climate change, as Parmesan and Galbraith (2004) and others report. Mitigation has taken on the new meaning of reducing the negative aspects of climate change by prudent action, and has become a part of adaptation. We hasten to add that this does not imply that action to reduce emissions or enhance sequestration would be useless. Even prolonging the time it takes CO_2 emissions to double may have significant benefits, but we want to alert the reader to a change in the operating framework we find ourselves.

We begin with recommendation at the local scale, and end with implications for managers at the broadest scale.

Recommendations of authors cited above reflect the perspective developed in their area of expertise after thorough study of climate change effects in their field. We cite those relevant to managers:

...the IPCC concluded that the certainty of warming from increasing man-made releases of greenhouse gases has a 90 percent probability.

Mitigation has taken on the new meaning of reducing the negative aspects of climate change by prudent action...

When considering vegetation change responses, Bachelet et al. (2003) suggest:

> ... managers would be well advised to develop contingency plans for alternative futures, increased vegetation growth, or increased vegetation stress, with specific regional patterns and timing to both. Monitoring could be configured to identify these alternative conditions as they occur.

Fagre et al. (2003) stress:

> It is critical that we understand the effects of climatic variability on mountains, because mountains support a high diversity of ecosystems and provide a wide range of ecological services to human populations. Mountains serve as the world's water towers by providing 50 percent of freshwater consumed by humans.

For range management Shafer et al. (2001) observe:

> ... range fragmentation may be a significant problem for some species. [In the West] areas of future bioclimatic habitat... are often small and disjunct, reflecting the heterogeneity of the landscape. Land-use activities will both severely restrict the amount of suitable habitat available... and impede [the species'] ability to successfully disperse...

Regarding fire and vegetation responses in California, Lenihan et al. (2003) state:

> ... results will indicate fire will play a critical role in the adjustment of vegetation to any of the later precipitation regimes for California, be it slowing the encroachment of woody vegetation in grasslands or hastening the transition from woody communities to grassland under drier conditions.

Sticking to the practical on the same subject, Flannigan et al. (2000) recommend:

> Possible manipulations of fuel type, load and arrangement could be used to help protect local areas of high value. A fine balancing act is required by managers to protect values (people and resources) from fire, while... allowing fire to resume... its role in ecosystem functioning and maintenance. Manage ignitions sources: create and adopt local ordinances to reduce human-caused ignitions.

By contrast, Brown et al. (2004) make sweeping recommendations on a broad scale, given with a pessimistic flavor—we will return to them at the end of this section:

> Policy makers face formidable challenges in ecosystem management and stewardship given socioeconomic desires and the physical outcomes from both climate change and human decisions. Our results suggest new fire management strategies and policies may be needed to address the added climatic risks.

...managers would be well advised to develop contingency plans for alternative futures

A fine balancing act is required by managers...

For dealing with the considerable problem of invasive species, large enough without the confounding factor of climate change and variability and interaction with fire regimes, Brooks et al. (2004) stick to the practical, proceeding from the tried and true to the more thorny areas by summarizing thus (paraphrased):

> **If invaders promote fire**: manage fuels: eradicate or reduce dominance; establish fire-resistant vegetation that competes; create firebreaks; manipulate to restore pre-invasion vegetation and fire regimes; limit land-use conditions that increase invader dominance.

> **If invaders reduce fire**: manage fuels: eradicate or reduce dominance; restore pre-invasion fuel structure; mechanically or chemically treat to increase flammability; restore pre-invasion fire regime; limit contrary land-use. Manage ignitions sources: use prescribed fire after fuel bed alteration for flammability; use prescribed fire often when possible.

The manager needs no primer to tell him or her the costs of undertaking such steps.

What are the manager's responsibilities in the broader arena, where policies must be developed or advocated, which may clash with political realities? What is or should be the role of the manager in situations where current knowledge is inadequate to allow future directions to be identified, and recommendations for new research direction may have to be stressed?

These are question we cannot answer as members of the research community. We would respectfully suggest, however, that managers, as do scientists and others possessing special expertise, bring their understanding of the implications of current practices to top level administrators, policy groups, and the general public. This is not done in an advocacy role, but in the neutral, objective role reflected in the "if, then…" approach. *If* you continue a particular policy, *then* it is our job to tell you the consequences you will find yourself faced with. These may be undesirable, or desirable, but may have side effects that cannot be minimized beyond a certain point; policy makers or policy advocates must take all of them into account when mapping the future.

If resource managers are faced with uncertain, but highly likely knowledge that effects such as the probable extinction of bird species that provide ecosystem services such as pollination, predator control, and decomposition is already occurring or becomes a near-term risk, *then* they must call attention to the fact that their assigned responsibility cannot be met given their existing resources and policy direction.

Hence the observation by Brown et al. that "… managers face formidable challenges…" and further emphasized by Thomas et al. (2004):

> … anthropogenic climate warming at least ranks alongside other recognized threats to global biodiversity… many of the most severe impacts of climate are likely to stem from interactions between

threats in many if not most regions. Returning to near pre-industrial global temperatures as quickly as possible could prevent much of the projected, but slower acting, climate related extinction from being realized.

The most comprehensive approach is that of Parmesan and Galbraith (2004), who restate "the big picture" interpretation of where we find ourselves today, and where this must take us. They give particular recognition to the problem of interaction among many stressors acting on natural resources:

> "*There is growing consensus within the scientific community that climate change will compound existing threats and lead to an acceleration of the rate at which biodiversity is lost* (emphasis added). Reducing the adverse effects of climate change on U.S. ecosystems can be facilitated through a broad range of strategies, including adaptive management, promotion of transitional habitat in non-preserved areas and the alleviation of non-climate stressors. [This includes] … promoting dynamic designs and management plans for nature reserves [which] may enable managers to facilitate adjustment of wild species to changing climate conditions.

They continue with a call that is both a plea for managers to continue to develop their expertise and for some research initiatives by stating:

> A major future challenge is to achieve a better understanding of which systems or species are most or least susceptible to projected climate change. [We need the] … development of … vulnerability assessment tools and methods … begun only recently, [and need to] reassess species and habitat classification to evaluate their relative vulnerabilities to GCC [as well as] design new reserves to allow for shift in distribution of target species, promote native habitat corridors between reserves, practice dynamic rather than static habitat conservation planning [and] alleviate effects of other stressors.

Conclusion

Observational evidence that climate is warming is increasingly obvious. The link of climate change to man-made inputs of greenhouse gases to the atmosphere is only slightly less clear. More importantly, responses to the climate change are manifest in both the physical and in the biological realm. The breakup of large parts of the Antarctic ice shelf, the receding of glaciers worldwide, the reduction in polar sea ice, the loss of arctic permafrost, and warming trends in high latitudes are strong indications of the former, while the earlier onset of green-up, the displacement or loss of high-latitude species in many regions both terrestrial and coastal, and the infilling of alpine tundra by sub-alpine forest are but a few examples of the latter.

Resource managers are only too aware that multiple stresses affect the systems they are charged to protect or from which they are expected to permit a sustainable flow of ecosystem services; to these stresses climate change is now added. In some cases, climate responses will exacerbate the

"There is growing consensus within the scientific community that climate change will compound existing threats and lead to an acceleration of the rate at which biodiversity is lost…"

A major future challenge is to achieve a better understanding of which systems or species are most or least susceptible to projected climate change.

existing stresses—fire frequencies and intensities may hasten ecosystem degradation from other causes; vegetation shifts can be accelerated or slowed by fire. Invasive species affect fire regimes and induce positive or negative feedbacks. Insects and pathogens, and their natural predators will change in numbers, population dynamics and areal extent. Some indications of how such processes play out has been suggested. However, comprehensive modeling of all of the above into forecasting a single outcome is in its infancy, and needs to be nurtured.

One emerging outcome is that the resources to be managed are not static systems, and that their dynamism is accelerated by climate change. This has profound implications for management. It changes how we approach conservation reserves, view development at the wildland-urban interface, think about habitat, and envision future migration corridors. It opens up the need for new thinking over that of the day-to-day priorities of a resource manager. Seed dispersal, the role of pollinators, influence of topographic, man-made constraints to migration, and potential conflicts between community, agricultural and aquatic-system water needs will require new thinking and demand responses at multiple organizational levels.

Knowing how to develop a "no-regrets" strategy, how to think about present and future costs of protecting ecosystem services, how to integrate such costs into economic analysis is needed. Classical analysis has historically viewed the environment as an inexhaustible reservoir. This is no longer tenable. On the issue of mitigating climate change versus adapting to its consequences, the manager may well want to think through the implications and costs of either strategy and voice his or her expert knowledge of which road to travel.

> Classical analysis has historically viewed the environment as an inexhaustible reservoir. This is no longer tenable.

n wledgments

The scientific, technical and editorial help of Linda Joyce, the expert editing assistance of Zoe Hoyle, the generous contributions of the figures by Dominique Bachelet and Jim Lenihan, as well as the library research by Michele Laskowski and others is hereby gratefully acknowledged.

e eren es

Aber, J.; Neilson, R.P.; McNulty, S.; Lenihan, J.M.; Bachelet, D.; Drapek, R.J. 2001. Forest processes and global environmental change: predicting the effects of individual and multiple stressors. BioScience. 51: 735-751.

Ayres, M.P.; Lombardero, M.J. 2000. Assessing the consequences of global change for forest disturbance from herbivores and pathogens. The Science of the Total Environment. 262: 263-286.

Bachelet, D.; Neilson, R.P.; Hickler, T.; Drapek, R.J.; Lenihan, J.M.; Sykes, M.T.; Smith, B.; Sitch, S.; Thonicke, K. 2003. Simulating past and future dynamics of natural ecosystems in the United States. Global Biogeochemical Cycles. 17(2): 1045.

Bachelet, D.; Neilson, R.P.; Lenihan, J.M.; Drapek, R.J. 2001. Climate change effects on vegetation distribution and carbon budget in the United States. Ecosystems. 4: 164-185.

Bale, J.S.; Masters, G.J.; Hodkinson, I.D.; Awmack, C.; Bezemer, M.; Brown, J.B.; Buse, A.; Coulson, J.C.; Farrar, J.; Good, J.E.G.; Harrington, R.; Hartley, S.; Jones, T.H.; Lindroth, R.L.; Press, M.C.; Symmioudis, I.; Watt, A.D.; Whittaker, J.B. 2002. Herbivory in global climate change research: direct effects of rising temperature on insect herbivores. Global Change Biology. 8: 1-16.

Barnett, T.; Malone, R.; Pennell, W.; Stammer, D.; Semtner, B.; Washington, W. 2004. The effects of climate change on water resources in the West: introduction and overview. Climatic Change. 62: 1-11.

Brooks, M.L.; D'Antonia, C.M.; Richardon, D.M.; Grace. J.B.; Keeley, J.E.; Ditomaso, J.M.; Hobbs, R.J.; Pellant, M.; Pyke, D. 2004. Effects of invasive alien plants on fire regimes. BioScience. 54(7): 677-688.

Brown, T.J.; Hall, B.L.; Westerling, A.L. 2004. The impact of twenty-first century climate change on wildland fire danger in the western United States: an applications perspective. Climatic Change. 62: 365–388.

Christensen, N.; Wood, A.; Voisin, N.; Lettenmaier, D.; Palmer, R. 2004. Effects of climate change on the hydrology and water resources of the Colorado River Basin. Climatic Change. 62: 337-363.

Clark, P.U.; Pisias, N.G.; Stolcker, T.F.; Weaver, A.J. 2002. The role of the thermohaline circulations in abrupt climate change. Nature. 415: 863-869.

Dale, V.H.; Joyce, L.A.; McNulty, S.; Neilson, R.P.; Ayres, M.P.; Flannigan, M.D.; Hanson, P.J.; Irland, L.C.; Lugo, A.E.; Peterson, C.J.; Simberloff, D.; Swanson, F.J.; Stocks, B.J.; Wotton, B.M. 2001. Climate change and forest disturbances. Bioscience. 51(9): 723-734.

Daly, C.; Bachelet, D.; Lenihan, J.M.; Neilson, R.P.; Parton, W.; Ojima, D. 2000. Dynamic interaction of tree-grass interactions for global change studies. Ecological Applications. 10(2): 449-469.

Easterling, D.R.; Meehl, G.A.; Parmesan, C.; Changnon, S.A.; Karl, T.R.; Mearns, L.O. 2000. Climate extremes: observations, modeling, and impacts. Science. 289(5487): 2068-2074.

Fagre, D.B.; Peterson, D.L.; Hessl, A.E. 2003. Taking the pulse of mountains: ecosystem responses and climatic variability. Climatic Change. 59: 263-282.

Flannigan, M.D.; Stocks, B.J.; Wotton, B.M. 2000. Science of the total environment. 262: 221-229.

Gucinski, H.; Lackey, R.T.; Spence, B. 1990. Implications of global climate change effects on fisheries. Fisheries. 5(6): 33-38.

Gucinski, H.; Neilson, R.P.; McNulty, S. 2004. Implications of global climate change for Southern forests: Can we separate fact from fiction? In: Rauscher, M.; Johnsen, K., eds. Southern forest science: past, present and future. Gen. Tech. Rep. GTR-SRS-75. Asheville, NC: U.S. Department of Agriculture, Forest Service, Southern Research Station: 365-371, Chapter 31.

Hansen, A.J.; Neilson, R.P.; Dale, V.H.; Flather, C.H.; Iverson, L.R.; Currie, D.J.; Shaffer, S.; Cook, R.; Bartlein, P.J. 2001. Global change in forests: response of species, communities, and biomes. Bioscience. 51(9): 765-779.

Hansen, J.E. 2005. A slippery slope: How much warming constitutes "dangerous anthropogenic interference? Climatic Change. 68: 269-279.

Iverson, L.R.; Prasad, A.M. 2001. Potential changes in tree species richness and forest community types following climate change. Ecosystems. 4: 186-199.

Julius, S.H.; Shafer, S.; Amthor, J.; Bontempi, P.; Buford, M.; Calder, J.; Coloff, S.; Conrad, S.; Mirabilio, S.; Nadelhoffer, K.; Peterson, B.; Scavia, D.; Stokes, B.; Turner, W. 2003. Ecosystems. In: Strategic plan for the U.S. climate change science program. Washington, DC: Climate Change Science Program and the Subcommittee on Global Change Research: 83-92, Chapter 8.

Katz, R.W. 2002. Techniques for estimating uncertainty in climate change scenarios and impact studies. Climate Research. 20: 167-185.

Keeling, C.D.; Whorf, T.P. 1999. Atmospheric CO_2 records from sites of the SIO air sampling network. In: Trends: a compendium of data on global change. Oak Ridge, TN: Carbon Dioxide Information Analysis Center: [Number of pages unknown].

Kittel, T.G.F.; Royle, J.A.; Daly, C.; Rosenbloom, N.A.; Gibson, W.P.; Fisher, H.H.; Schimel, D.S.; Berliner, L.M.; and VEMAP2 Participants. 1997. A gridded historical (1895– 1993) bioclimatic dataset for the conterminous United States. In: Proceedings of the 10th conference on applied climatology. Boston: American Meteorological Society: 219–222.

Lenihan, J.M.; Drapek, R.J.; Bachelet, D.; Neilson, R.P. 2003. Climate change effects on vegetation distribution, carbon, and fire in California. Ecological Applications. 13(6): 1667–1681.

Leung, L.R.; Qian, Y.; Bian, X.; Washington, W.M.; Han, J.G.; Roads, J.O. 2004. Mid-century ensemble regional climate change scenarios for the western United States. Climatic Change. 62: 75-113.

Logan, J.A.; Regniere, J.; Powell, J.A. 2003. Assessing the impact of global warming on forest pest dynamics. Frontiers in Ecology and the Environment. 1(3): 130-137.

Mann, M.R. 2002. The value of multiple proxies. Science. 297: 1481-1482.

National Assessment Synthesis Team. 2001. Climate change in the United States: the potential consequences of climatic variability and change. Report of U.S. Global Climate Change Research Program. Cambridge, UK: Cambridge University Press. 620 p.

Neilson, R.P. 1995. A model for predicting continental scale vegetation distribution and water balance. Ecological Applications. 5(2): 362–85.

Orem, R.; Ellsworth, D.S.; Johnsen, K.H.; Ewers, B.E.; Maier, C.; Schäfer, K.U.R.; McCarthy, H.; Hendrey, G.; McNulty, S.G.; Katul, G.G. 2001. Soil fertility limits carbon sequestration by forest ecosystems in a CO_2-enriched atmosphere. Nature. 411: 469-472.

Parmesan, C.; Galbraith, H. 2004. Observed impacts of global climate change in the U.S. Arlington, VA: Pew Center on Global Climate Change. 55 p.

Parmesan, C., Yohe, G. 2003. A globally coherent fingerprint of climate change impacts on natural systems. Nature. 421: 37-42.

Payne, J.; Wood, A.; Palmer, R.; Lettenmaier, D. 2004. Mitigating the effects of climate change on the water resources of the Columbia River Basin. Climatic Change. 62: 233-256.

Revelle, R.R.; Waggoner, P.E. 1984. Effects of a carbon dioxide-induced climatic change on water supplies in the Western United States. Washington, DC: National Academy Press.

Root, T.L.; Price, J.T.; Hall, K.R.; Schneider, S.H.; Rosenzweig, C.; Pounds, J.A. 2003. Fingerprints of global warming on wild animals and plants, Nature. 421: 57-69.

Schwartz, P.; Randall, D. 2003. An abrupt climate change scenario and its implications for United States national security. Pentagon paper. 22 p.

Sekercioglu, C.H.; Dailey, G.C.; Ehrlich, P.R. 2004. Ecosystem consequences of bird declines. PNAS. 101(52): 18042-18047.

Shafer, S.L.; Bartlein, P.J.; Thompson, R.S. 2001. Potential changes in the distribution of western North America tree and shrub taxa under future climate scenarios. Ecosystem. 4: 200-215.

Simberloff, D. 2000. Global climate change and introduced species in United States forests. The Science of the Total Environment. 262: 253-261.

Stewart, I.; Cayan, D.; Dettenger, M. 2004. Changes in snowmelt runoff timing in Western North America under a 'business as usual' climate change scenario. Climatic Change. 62: 217-232.

Thomas, C.D.; Cameron, A.; Green, R.E., Bakkenes, M.; Beaumont, L.J.; Collingham, Y.C.; Erasmus, B.F.N.; Ferreira De Siqueira, M.; Grainger, A.; Hannah, L.; Hughes, L.; Huntley, B.; Van Jaarsveld, A.S.; Midgley, G.F.; Miles, L.;Ortega-Huerta, M.A.; Peterson, A.T.; Phillips, O.L.; Williams, S.E. 2004. Extinction risk from climate change. Nature. 427: 145-148.

Van Rheenen, N.; Wood, A.; Palmer, R. 2004. Potential implications of PCM climate change scenarios for Sacramento-San Joaquin River Basin hydrology and water resources. Climatic Change. 62: 257-281.

Wagner, F.H., ed. 2003. Rocky Mountain/Great Basin regional climate-change assessment. Report for the U.S. Global Change Program. Logan, UT: Utah State University. 240 p.

Whitlock, C.; Shafer, S.L.; Marlon, J. 2003. The role of climate and vegetation change in shaping past and future fire regimes in northwestern US and the implications of ecosystem management. Forest Ecology and Management. 178: 5-21.

Social and Economic Issues of Global Climate Change in the Western United States

Randall S. Rosenberger[1]

Tom Iraci, USDA Forest Service

Erik Ackerson, EarthDesign, Ink

Mark Reid, USDA Forest Service

Erik Ackerson, EarthDesign, Ink

---

[1]Environmental economist, Department of Forest Resources, College of Forestry, Oregon State University, Corvallis, OR 97331.

Abstract

Global climate change and its attendant environmental changes will affect the functioning of our social and economic systems. This paper provides an overview of social and economic issues pertaining to global climate change impacts in the Western United States. A values typology that links human values with ecological functioning is introduced. This typology provides a motivation for developing strategies to minimize the impacts of climate change through mitigation and adaptation. Four research themes are introduced, including policy-relevant science, micro-scale analyses, non-market valuation, and local adaptation.

Keywords: Climate change, social, economic, mitigation, adaptation.

Introduction

The question is not whether climate is changing, but by how much, when, and what impacts it is likely to have on ecological, social and economic systems.

The Intergovernmental Panel on Climate Change (IPCC) projects mean global temperatures will increase by 2.5-10.4°F (1.4-5.8°C) this century, with continued increases in mean temperature thereafter (Houghton et al. 2001). In the United States, mean temperatures are expected to increase by about one-third greater than the global mean; i.e., 4-14°F (2-8°C) (Wigley 1999). In the United States, mean temperatures have already increased by 1°F (0.6°C) and precipitation has increased by 5-10 percent over the past century (Parmesan and Galbraith 2004). Generally there is scientific consensus that humans are contributing to climate change through increased atmospheric concentrations of greenhouse gases and land use changes (Oreskes 2004). The question is not whether climate is changing, but by how much, when, and what impacts it is likely to have on ecological, social and economic systems.

The IPCC (2001) and Smith (2004) identify several likely consequences of climate change on ecological, social and economic systems:

- **Agriculture**–changes in growing season; available soil moisture and nutrient balances; depleted water supplies;

- **Water**–variability in precipitation patterns resulting in droughts, floods and water shortages in certain areas, especially the arid southwest; reduced snowfall;

- **Coastal communities**–sea level rise from melting glaciers and ocean warming;

- **Human health**–more frequent and severe heat waves and increased air pollution; migration northward of tropical diseases;

- **Terrestrial ecosystems**–migration of colder regions northward and in elevation; reduced snowfall; changes in stream ecology through variable runoff and warmer water temperatures;

- **Forestry**–changes in growing conditions; increases in extreme events such as droughts, pest outbreaks, and wildfire frequency and intensity; expansion of timber production to agricultural lands;

- **Biodiversity**–changes in species composition from habitat losses, reduced in-stream flows, warmer water temperatures, and loss of wetlands; most at risk include coldwater species of fish, endangered species, and migratory waterfowl;

- **Energy**–increased energy demands for summer cooling, especially in the southwest but also expanding into regions with historically cool summer temperatures; and

- **Recreation**–changes in fishing opportunities; lengthening of summer season activities; reduction in skiing opportunities.

In a Pew Center report, Smith (2004: 19) summarized the likely impacts of temperature changes on different sectors in the United States based on evidence from the scientific literature. With a few degrees of warming (up to 7°F [4°C]) over the next century, national impacts are expected to be:

- **Agriculture**–a medium confidence in net benefits,

- **Water**–uncertain direction of impact,

- **Coastal communities**–high confidence in net damages,

- **Human health**–a medium confidence in some net benefits, some net damages,

- **Terrestrial ecosystem productivity**–a low to medium confidence in net benefits,

- **Terrestrial biodiversity**–a medium confidence in net damages,

- **Forestry**–a low to medium confidence in net benefits, and

- **Aquatic biodiversity**–a low confidence in net damages.

These likely impacts of climate change are a function of our expectations regarding the degree of warming, their effects on human and ecological systems, and the ability of these systems to respond to climate change signals. Economic and social systems (such as agriculture, forestry, and coastal developments) in the United States are less vulnerable (i.e., resilient) to climate changes than are natural ecosystems (Smith 2004). E.g., agriculture and forestry may benefit from lengthened growing seasons and increased carbon dioxide concentrations. The most recent analyses of climate change impacts on social and economic systems show that the U.S. economy is not greatly threatened by climate change over the 21st century (Mendelsohn 2001). In fact, these studies suggest national net benefits could range up to one percent of GDP. Smith (2004: iv) summarizes that while several sectors within the United States are sensitive to climate change, they are not vulnerable due to a significant capacity to adapt:

> The country's high per capita income, relatively low population density, stable institutions, research base, and health care system give the United States a strong capacity to adapt to climate change. … The country's large size and the population's mobility give it advantages in adapting to climate change. The lower 48 states span more than 20 degrees of latitude in the temperate zone, so while some southern parts of the country are at relatively higher risk from climate change, more northern areas are at less risk or may have many benefits.

The country's high per capita income, relatively low population density, stable institutions, research base, and health care system give the United States a strong capacity to adapt to climate change.

With greater than 7°F (4°C) of warming over the next century, national impacts are expected to be negative (net damages) with the exception of uncertainty regarding impacts on human health (Smith 2004). The expected impacts of climate change are prefaced on a gradual warming along with changes in regional precipitation patterns. If climate changes suddenly and catastrophically, all bets are off. The magnitude of likely impacts due to increasing temperatures varies across different regions of the United States.

Climate Change Impacts in the West

The Western United States is quite diverse not only in its topography and climate, but also in its distribution of people on the landscape. The West contains many states that have been the fastest growing in the nation over the last two centuries, compounding other issues such as resource allocation and land-use changes. While most of the population in the West resides in urban areas, communities are dispersed across the region with varying degrees of dependence on availability and access to natural resources. In addition, most rural areas in the West are dominated by public landownership (Travis 2003). Rural areas may be most at risk from changes in climate due to their relatively higher degrees of vulnerability to climate change (increased exposure, sensitivity, and lack of adaptive capacity). Miller and Gloss (2003: 251) note that the "west shows great heterogeneity in (1) the problems caused by climate variability, (2) current flexibility, (3) institutional constraints, (4) interests and perceptions of participants, (5) resources available to them, and (6) policy options." Therefore, the impacts of climate change cannot be evaluated out of context of existing stresses on natural, social and economic systems, including aridity, water shortage, burgeoning populations, and land use changes (Wagner 2003).

Climate change is a global phenomenon that will have some effect on all scales nested within the global framework. We can generally expect climate change to effect local economies, public health, water supplies, electric power production, and key industries such as tourism, agriculture and forestry in the long-term. In addition, we can expect an increase in the frequency and severity of weather events, and coastal areas could see an increased risk from sea level rise and storm surges. We can expect southern regions to be more vulnerable to climate change than northern regions (IPCC 2001, Shugart et al. 2003, Smith 2004).

A synthesis of evidence for the southwest (Smith 2004: 23) concludes:

> The Southwest has quite different vulnerabilities to climate change than the rest of the country. It is the most vulnerable region in terms of water supplies (Hurd et al. 1999) because of the combination of a semi-arid to arid climate and relatively high withdrawals of water resources. Earlier snowmelt could increase the risk of winter flooding and summer shortage of water supplies, thereby exacerbating current water scarcities. Should there be increased average annual runoff, some supply concerns may be alleviated, but flooding should increase. Agriculture in the region is projected by

The expected impacts of climate change are prefaced on a gradual warming along with changes in regional precipitation patterns. If climate changes suddenly and catastrophically, all bets are off.

We can generally expect climate change to effect local economies, public health, water supplies, electric power production, and key industries such as tourism, agriculture and forestry in the long-term.

economic models to fare relatively well. However, with about 90 percent of the region's water consumption going to agriculture, a reduction in water supplies could have a substantial negative effect on that sector. Biodiversity in the region is likely to be reduced because of the complex topography and human development (e.g., dams blocking migration of fish). Yet mountains such as the Rocky Mountains and Sierras also provide north-south and altitudinal migration corridors for some species. Interestingly, species in the Southwest (and Northwest) may not always migrate toward the north because of complex terrain and substantial variances in climate across these regions. Vegetation biomass could increase or decrease, depending on whether the Southwest becomes wetter or drier. There is generally less risk to coastal areas in California than in the Northeast, Southeast, or Southern Great Plains. Nonetheless, San Francisco Bay, the Sacramento-San Joaquin Delta, and many parts of southern California are at risk from sea-level rise. Risks to human health are relatively low because heat stress is not a significant risk in urban areas and there is limited risk of infectious disease outbreaks (although infectious diseases such as hantavirus are a problem in the region). The region's ski industry is likely to be harmed, although warm weather recreation activities could expand.

A synthesis of evidence for the Northwest (Smith 2004: 24) concludes:

> It can be argued that the Northwest's relatively cool climate and wet conditions (at least in the western portions of Oregon and Washington) make the region less vulnerable to climate change than warmer or drier regions, yet the region has some distinct vulnerabilities. Changes in the seasonality of runoff could be problematic for management of the region's water resources infrastructure (Hamlet and Lettenmaier 1999). Much of the coast is not vulnerable to sea-level rise, with the notable exception of the highly developed Puget Sound area. Agricultural production is estimated to increase in the region (Adams et al. 1999), and ranching could benefit if grassland productivity increases. The effects of climate on forests in the region are uncertain. Under some scenarios, productivity increases, while under others it decreases. Higher temperatures may benefit forests in the region only up to a point, and then they may become a detriment (Neilson and Drapek 1998). As in the other regions, biodiversity is expected to be harmed, although vegetation productivity could increase. The valuable salmon fishery may be at particular risk from rising temperatures and changes in runoff patterns.

The biggest winners from climate change are probably agriculture and summer recreation (high capacities to adapt), while the biggest losers are likely to be water resources and energy sectors (long-lived infrastructure with limited adaptive capacity) (Mendelsohn and Neumann 1999, Smith 2004). A shift of land from agricultural production to timber production is expected to be mainly an issue for the West (Sohngen and Mendelsohn 1999). However, the overall impact climate change will have on individual

The biggest winners from climate change are probably agriculture and summer recreation (high capacities to adapt), while the biggest losers are likely to be water resources and energy sectors (long-lived infrastructure with limited adaptive capacity)...

economic sectors, social systems, communities, and individuals depends on how well and when we decide to mitigate the causes of climate change, and to reduce or adapt to changes in ecological systems brought on by a changing climate.

Scientific Consensus and Social Values: A Prescription for Action

Given the level of scientific consensus and concern about climate change, why is the world barely beginning to take action? Part of the problem seems to lie in the void between scientific opinion and lay opinion (Robert Socolow as quoted in Kolbert 2005). Social, political and economic responses to climate change will require a shift in preferences for public and private managers, politicians, and consumers. These necessary shifts in preferences will take place when managers, politicians, and consumers accept the signals that climate is changing, that we need to do something about it, and we are willing to incur the (possibly substantial) costs of avoidance. Unfortunately, the lay public does not seem to see the signals or heed the warnings; scientific consensus is tenuously held by citizens and not supported by citizen's perceptions of climate patterns in the short term (e.g., marginal changes in climate patterns from year to year are not easily perceived by people). It may take a catastrophic, climate-related episode to finally get people's attentions to the likely future state of the world. A case in point is the recent tsunami in the Indian Ocean that affected Southeast Asia. It took this type of catastrophic event before politicians, managers and citizens would pay significant attention to warnings by scientific experts about tsunami preparedness in the Pacific Northwest.

Ecological and Socio-Economic Linkages

What is sustainability? In the context of their sustainable forest management initiative, the USDA FS (2005) defines sustainability as "the human desire for an environment that can provide for our needs now and for future generations." Sustainability is a human value that requires human judgment regarding the current and desired future condition of the world. Scientists, managers, politicians and citizens recognize the interconnectedness, complexity and dynamism of social, economic and ecological systems (USDA FS 2005). This recognition is based on decades of scientific and political debate, the evolution of people's preferences, and the development of our economic and social systems. The desire to improve human well-being is broadly recognized to be based on economic prosperity, social equity and environmental quality. However, the multitude of often competing human values and different desired future conditions not only necessitates continuing the debate about sustainable management, but expanding it to include all concerned parties (scientists, managers, politicians and citizens) in public discourse (USDA FS 2005). Climate change must be part of this discourse.

Humans, including their economic and social systems, are supported by ecological systems. Ecological systems affect and are affected by a wider network of systems, including social and economic ones. Sustainable

Unfortunately, the lay public does not seem to see the signals or heed the warnings; scientific consensus is tenuously held by citizens and not supported by citizen's perceptions of climate patterns in the short term...

Ecological systems affect and are affected by a wider network of systems, including social and economic ones.

management integrates these systems in an attempt to promote their sustainability across space and over time (fig. 1). Climate change and climate variability affect these systems directly and indirectly, as noted above. De Groot et al. (2002) identify four functions of ecosystems and the goods and services derived from them:

- **Regulation functions**–The maintenance of essential ecological processes and life support systems, including gas regulation, climate regulation, disturbance prevention, water regulation, water supply, soil retention, soil formation, nutrient regulation, waste treatment, pollination, and biological control;

- **Habitat functions**–The provision of habitat for wild plant and animal species, including refugium (adequate living space) and nursery (adequate reproduction habitat) services;

- **Production function**–The provision of natural resources, including food, raw materials, genetic resources, medicinal resources, and ornamental resources; and

- **Information functions**–The provision of opportunities for cognitive development, including aesthetic information, recreation, cultural and artistic information, spiritual and historic information, and science and education.

Through policy and regulations, management, and voluntary actions we may be able to curtail or at least slow down trends in human-caused climate change, or adapt to changes in ecosystem functioning that directly or indirectly affect social and economic systems. A better understanding of the link between those things we value and climate change seems a logical step in raising public awareness of the likely consequences if we continue to ignore the signals.

Economic value is generally defined as the amount of one good or service that must be given up to obtain an increase in another good or service. Therefore, economic values are relative in the sense that they are measured in terms of something else (opportunity cost). To measure these relative values, we must define the source of people's values for goods and services supported or provided by ecosystems. The following section on economic values is not to be confused with 'total valuation.' Total valuation would include the value of ecological functions themselves, of which people may not always be aware (NRC 2005). In addition, 'total economic value' as the aggregation of individual values may not be the same as the social value of an ecosystem. Social value would include broader considerations of the value of ecosystem functions beyond the values individuals gain from them. E.g., equity or fairness in the sharing of harms and benefits may be a social value that transcends individual values and interests. It is likely that the total value of ecosystems is more than the sum of their individual parts.

To measure value in economic terms, a link between ecological functioning and economic valuation must exist. Figure 2 labels this link as the ecological-economic interaction. Economic values of ecosystems depend on the functioning of these ecosystems. However, these functions are not necessarily directly valued by people. Economic values are derived

Through policy and regulations, management, and voluntary actions we may be able to curtail or at least slow down trends in human-caused climate change…

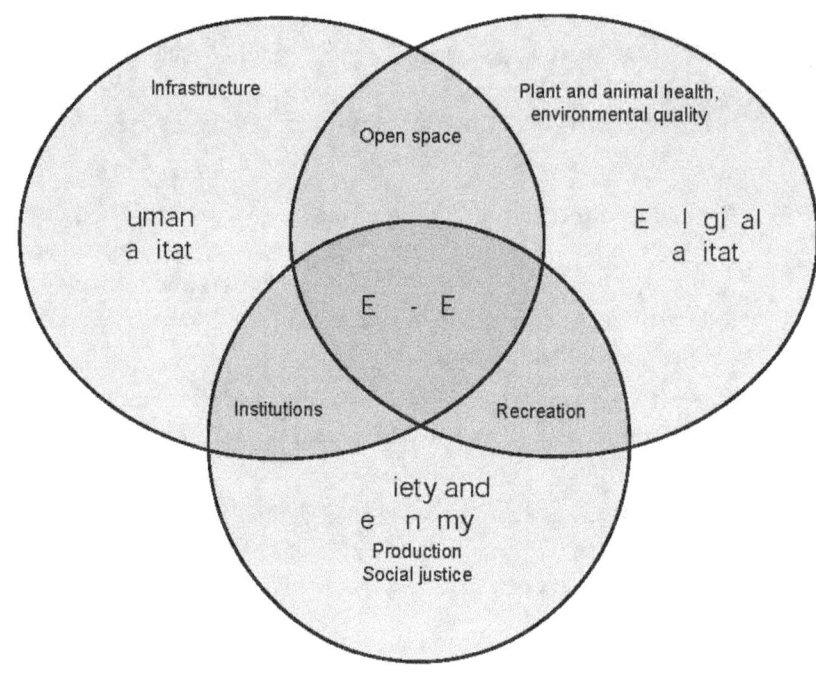

Figure 1—Integration of ecological, economic and social systems within an adaptive, sustainable management framework.

People's dispositions toward their natural environments motivate their behavior and decisions as they allocate scarce resources in pursuit of happiness or well-being.

from the goods and services supported by these functions. E.g., certain biotic characteristics are necessary to support viable fish populations, but it is fishing quality that is valued by the angler.

Why Should We Care About Climate Change? A Values Typology

The natural environment is important to people in a variety of ways. People value natural environments as part of what constitutes their quality of life. People's dispositions toward their natural environments motivate their behavior and decisions as they allocate scarce resources in pursuit of happiness or well-being. The quantity and quality of natural environments, along with climate and management-induced changes in natural environments, also affect individuals' abilities to produce value.

An environmental good or service has economic value if it increases human well-being. At the root of economic value is the individual human and it is based on this individual's preferences for one thing over another that constitutes economic value; i.e., we do not prefer a good or service because it is valuable, it is valuable because we prefer it. The economic value of a good or service is derived when an individual uses a resource to produce satisfaction (or value or benefit), where this use is an allocation of scarce resources (time and money) in the production of preferred outcomes, experiences, or knowledge. The appropriate context for economic valuation is estimation of the relative value of a good in relation to what a person is willing to give up ('willing to pay') or willing to accept compensation for a good or service.

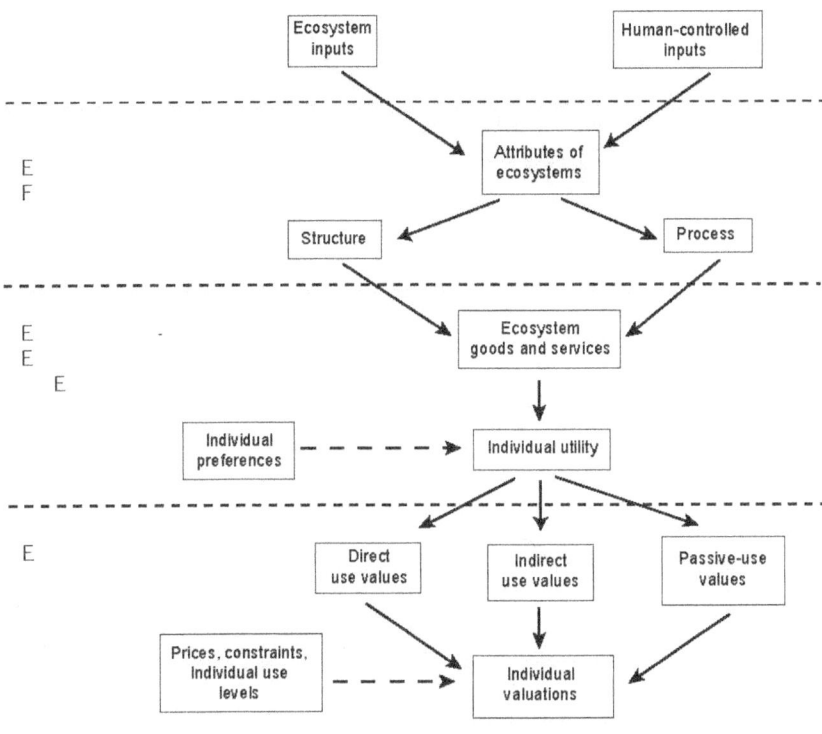

Figure 2—Schematic of valuing ecosystems (adapted from Randall 1984 and Turner et al. 2000).

An efficient outcome occurs when the benefits of an action (e.g., allocation of resources) outweigh the costs of that action. In a democratic society, values permeate resource allocation decisions related to land and resource management. An administrator's or manager's decisions should reflect the values held by their constituents, including the general public, in the formulation, selection and implementation of management alternatives (Lewis 1995). Therefore, understanding how the general public values natural systems and future conditions is critical to identifying efficient and effective responses to climate change. Thus, we complete the circle and return to the issue of public discourse regarding sustainable management and climate change.

Pete Morton (1999) merged an economic value classification schematic with an environmental philosopher's schematic of human-derived values from natural areas (Rolston 1985). Figure 3 reproduces Morton's value classification schematic.

- People may derive **direct use benefits** from natural areas, both managed and protected. Direct use benefits may include on-site recreation; mental, physical and/or spiritual regeneration; cultural heritage (both as natural history such as unique rock formations, cultural history such as archeological sites, or natural/cultural heritage and symbolization such as forestry's role in the history of the Pacific Northwest or the beaver as Oregon's state animal); and commercial uses (such as agriculture, timber harvesting, mineral extraction, and collection of non-timber resources).

...understanding how the general public values natural systems and future conditions is critical to identifying efficient and effective responses to climate change.

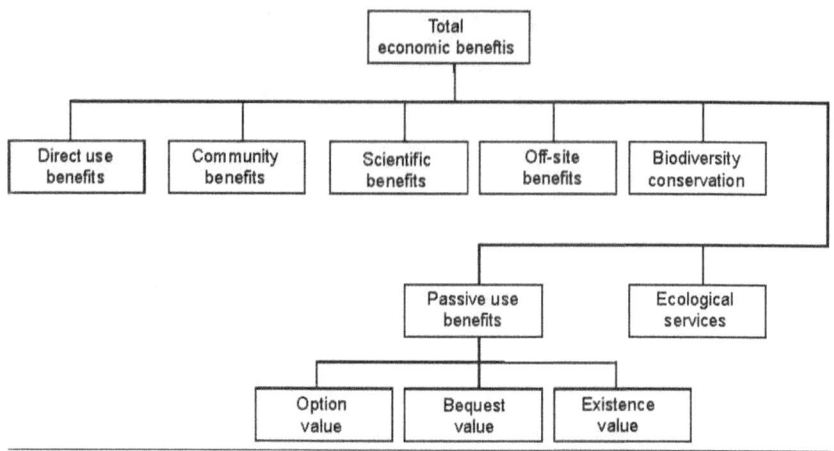

Figure 3—Morton's value classification schematic for wilderness areas (adapted from Morton 1999).

- People may derive **community benefits** from natural systems as they support jobs, whether these jobs are recreation and tourism-based or resource extraction-based, and other contributions to the quality of a place to live and/or do business.

- People may derive benefits from the **scientific values** of natural systems in the form of research areas, educational tools, and evaluation of management outcomes (an important component to adaptive management).

- Natural areas may provide **off-site benefits** to people in the form of off-site hunting and fishing, off-site recreation, scenic viewsheds, enhanced property values, and other non-consumptive uses (photos, books, stories about areas, history, etc.).

- Natural areas may provide **biodiversity conservation benefits** that include preserving genetic diversity. Biodiversity conservation also sustains passive use values by providing sanctuaries for rare or endangered species.

- Protected natural areas and managed natural areas may provide benefits through sustaining **ecological services** such as the protection of watersheds, nutrient recycling, natural pest control, and carbon storage.

- People may derive **option value benefits** from natural areas for future active use of the areas both on-site and off-site.

- People may derive **bequest value benefits** by knowing that certain areas and all they contain will be there for future generations' benefits.

- And people may derive **existence value benefits** from knowing that protected natural areas will exist into the future, independent of any human active use of the resources.

Loomis and Richardson (2000) estimated recreation benefits, passive use benefits and jobs supported by the 42 million acres of roadless natural areas in the coterminous 48-states. They estimated recreation benefits supported by these areas at almost $600 million annually and the passive use benefits of these areas at about $280 million annually.

They also estimated these roadless areas support almost 24,000 jobs in the continental United States. In the Western United States, these values were estimated to be $535 million, $274 million, and 21,000 jobs for recreation benefits, passive use benefits, and supported employment, respectively. Carbon sequestration benefits derived from roadless areas were estimated to range from nearly $500 million to $1 billion annually.

Krieger (2001: iii) reviewed economic values for forest ecosystem services in the United States. He notes:

> Globally, Costanza et al. (1997) estimated the total value of forest ecosystem goods and services at $4.7 trillion annually and the total annual value of all temperate/boreal forests at $894 billion. There are about 520 million acres of temperate/boreal forest in the United States (Pimentel et al. 1997), with an implied annual value for services of about $63.6 billion, using Costanza's estimates. Climate regulation, waste treatment and food production account for approximately 75 percent of this total.

Table 1 summarizes evidence provided in this report and elsewhere under the structure of the values matrix provided in figure 3. Based on this matrix we can identify where we have information along with where data are lacking. In general, we have more information and are relatively more certain regarding the impacts of climate change on commercial activities (agriculture, timber, water, energy, and coastal property) than impacts on other value types. How people are likely to respond to climate change is less certain, especially about changes in recreation resources, community benefits, scientific benefits, biodiversity conservation, ecological services, and passive use values. The spatial scale of analyses further exacerbates the problem of modeling climate change impacts in an uncertain future as we move from global scale models to local scale models.

The consequences of climate change are not to be taken lightly. While the impacts of climate change are expected to be greater for unmanaged natural environments (wilderness and other protected reserves) than for either social, economic or managed natural systems (agriculture, timber, water resources) in the United States (Smith 2004), the degree of impact and difficulty in measuring impacts of climate change are compounded by social and economic trends such as land-use changes, population growth, and changes in income distribution, human values and consumer preferences (IPCC 2001, Joyce et al. 2000). Social and economic uncertainties associated with population growth and migration, consumption rates, technology, policies and preferences dominate uncertainties regarding biophysical and ecological changes due to climate change (NRC 1999). Therefore, our ability to precisely predict impacts of climate change on social and economic systems depends on our ability to predict how people will respond to a changing climate, where we have our greatest uncertainty. Nonetheless, we do know that a changing climate will affect ecological, social and economic systems, which in turn will ultimately affect human well-being as we know it.

How people are likely to respond to climate change is less certain, especially about changes in recreation resources, community benefits, scientific benefits, biodiversity conservation, ecological services, and passive use values.

…our ability to precisely predict impacts of climate change on social and economic systems depends on our ability to predict how people will respond to a changing climate…

alue y e	e t r	m a ts[a]
Direct use Benefits	Agriculture	Southwest medium confidence in some net benefits, some net costs; Northwest medium confidence in net benefits (Smith 2004)
	Forestry	Uncertain direction of change (Smith 2004)
	Recreation	Medium confidence of net benefits across all regions (Mendelsohn and Markowski 1999; Loomis and Crespi 1999).High confidence of net damages to snow-related activities (Wagner 2003; Mendelsohn and Markowski 1999; Loomis and Crespi 1999)
	Water	Southwest low confidence in net damages; Northwest low confidence in some net benefits, some net damages (Smith 2004)
	Health	Medium confidence in some net benefits, some net damages (Smith 2004)
	Energy	Low confidence in energy savings in Northwest and energy costs in the Southwest (Mendelsohn 2001)
Community Benefits		Resource-dependent and nature-based tourism-dependent communities at greater risk of climate change (Wagner 2003). Diversified communities at less risk of climate change (Wagner 2003)
Scientific Benefits		Climate change effects will be ubiquitous, providing many natural labs for evaluating the effect of climate change on natural, social and economic systems. However, places representing pre-climate change conditions may not exist. (No studies known)
Off-Site Benefits	Coastal Communities	High confidence in small net damages to coastal properties (Smith 2004; Mendelsohn 2001)
	Property Values	Changes in natural amenities, migration of natural areas, economic sectors (skiing, forestry, agriculture), and changing landscapes and viewsheds could lead to increases or decreases in property values (Wagner 2003)
Biodiversity Conservation		Medium confidence in net damages to terrestrial biodiversity, in particular loss of alpine areas (Smith 2004). Low to medium confidence in net damages to freshwater aquatic biodiversity, in particular displacement of coldwater species with warmwater species (Smith 2004). Protected natural areas are particularly at risk of climate change (Hardy 2003)
Ecological Services		Low confidence in some net benefits, some net damages (Smith 2004)
Passive Use Values		Little evidence. Values transcend space and time. Extinction of ecosystems (alpine areas), species (salmon and other currently endangered species), or industries (salmon fishery, snow skiing) may trigger passive use value responses from people (Hardy 2003; Smith2004)

[a]Most references cited regarding impacts are syntheses of past research.

Table 1—Summary of likely impacts from climate change by value type for the Western United States.

What Can We Do About Climate Change?

Many sectors in the U.S. economy are sensitive to climate changes (Smith 2004), but they are not necessarily vulnerable to these changes. Vulnerability to climate change is a function of three factors—the degree of **exposure** to climate; **sensitivity** to effects of climate change on ecological, social and economic systems; and **adaptive capacity** (the ability to adapt to a changing climate) (McCarthy et al. 2001). Adaptive capacity depends on a community's wealth, access to technology, effective and stable institutions, efficient mechanisms for disseminating information, an equitable distribution of power, and a well-functioning social system (Smith et al. 2003). While many sectors in the U.S. economy are resilient and have a high capacity to adapt resulting in low impacts from climate change, sectors with long-lived infrastructure (water and coastal resources) are not able to adapt quickly to a changing climate (Smith 2004).

There are three general categories of responses to climate change—indirect policy options, mitigation options and adaptation options (Jepma et al. 1996). Indirect policy options target those social and economic trends that contribute to the climate change problem—population growth, resource demands and supply, and technology. While indirect policy options do not directly target factors associated with climate change, they can have a substantial impact on the concentration of greenhouse gases in the atmosphere by indirectly affecting greenhouse gas emissions or greenhouse gas uptake in sinks (Jepma et al. 1996).

Adaptive capacity depends on a community's wealth, access to technology, effective and stable institutions, efficient mechanisms for disseminating information, an equitable distribution of power, and a well-functioning social system...

Mitigation Strategies

Mitigation strategies target greenhouse gases that contribute to global warming by reducing the amount of gases being emitted by our economic system or through lowering the atmospheric concentrations of gases by sequestering them in forests, soils and oceans (IPCC 2001, Klein and Smith 2003, Smit et al. 2000). The IPCC's Third Assessment Report identified various levels of mitigation potential and provided some barriers to realizing these potential levels (IPCC 2001):

- **Market potential**—This is the level of potential that we have actually achieved and is a function of the amount of environmentally sound technologies and practices we actually use today.

- **Economic potential**—This is the level we can approach through the creation of markets, the reduction of market failures, and increases in financial and technology transfers. Barriers associated with reaching this potential include a lack of competitive markets, barriers to trade, ill-defined or undefined property rights, and a lack of adequate information.

- **Socio-economic potential**—This is the level we could achieve through the adoption of changes in behavior, lifestyles, social structures and institutions. Barriers associated with reaching this level include our social norms, individual habits, attitudes, values, and vested interests.

- **Technological potential**–This is the level we could achieve through implementation of technology with demonstrated success in combating the effects of climate change. Barriers to achieving this level include limited availability and knowledge about new technologies.
- **Physical potential**–This is the theoretical upper bound to what we could achieve through mitigation strategies.

Actualizing our mitigation potential rests on overcoming barriers in all levels of potential adoption of mitigation strategies. E.g., energy production from nuclear power plants is a demonstrated technology that may be underutilized, mostly due to socio-economic barriers that show an unwillingness to trade climate risk with the perceived risks of nuclear power plants (Burgman 2005).

There are several approaches that we could take to reduce or mitigate climate change (Hardy 2003):

- Capture or sequester carbon emissions;
- Reduce global warming or its effects through geo-engineering;
- Enhance natural carbon sinks;
- Convert to carbon-free and renewable energy technologies; or
- Conserve energy and use it more efficiently.

Within each of these mitigation approaches, there are several options. E.g., forestry practices that increase the sequestration of carbon on forestland (Richards and Stokes 2004: 6) include (1) afforestation of agricultural land; (2) reforestation of harvested or burned timberland; (3) change of forestry management practices to emphasize carbon storage; (4) adoption of low impact harvesting methods to decrease carbon release; (5) lengthening forest rotation cycles; (6) preservation of forestland from conversion; (7) adoption of agroforestry practices; (8) establishment of short-rotation woody biomass plantations; and (9) urban forestry practices. While mitigation strategies will not reverse the climate change trend, they may at least slow it down (McCarthy et al. 2001) and help avoid its worst effects (Smith et al. 2003). E.g., although conserving and sequestering carbon is not necessarily permanent, it may provide more time to develop other options by delaying climate change (IPCC 2001). Regardless, there will likely be effects from climate change on ecological, social and economic systems. We will have to adapt to these changes.

Adaptation

Adaptation is a necessary component to any response to climate change (Smith et al. 2003). It is not a new concept in that we are continually adapting to our changing surroundings. Adaptation is a "conscious ongoing process of monitoring, evaluating, and learning to make decisions. These decisions might involve changes to processes, practices, or structures to reduce potential vulnerabilities and damages, or to take advantage of new opportunities that may emerge" (Cohen et al. 2004: 152). In other words, adaptation is "any adjustment in natural or human systems that moderates harm and exploits beneficial opportunities

Actualizing our mitigation potential rests on overcoming barriers in all levels of potential adoption of mitigation strategies.

While mitigation strategies will not reverse the climate change trend, they may at least slow it down…and help avoid its worst effects…

associated with observed or expected impacts of climate change" (Klein and Smith 2003: 317). The adaptive capacity of a system depends on its resilience, stability, robustness, flexibility and other characteristics (Smit and Pilifosova 2003: 22).

While mitigation strategies may be implemented at the local level, they target the broader issue of greenhouse gas concentrations in the atmosphere. Adaptation, on the other hand, addresses localized impacts of climate change (IPCC 2001). What might work in one area or for a particular group may not work elsewhere (Smit and Pilifosova 2003). Therefore, even though we might conclude that society can adapt to climate change does not mean there will be no localized losses.

Even where regions on the whole may be able to successfully adapt to a limited climate change, specific individuals and communities could still be displaced and harmed by climate change. Of particular concern are those communities that have strong ties and associations with specific areas and resources that are exposed and sensitive to climate change (e.g., through sea-level rise, increased drought, extreme heat), derive a high share of their income from climate sensitive activities such as agriculture or fishing, and lack financial and other means to adapt to change (Easterling et al. 2004: 19).

Cohen et al. (2004: 153) identified several characteristics of adaptation to climate change:

- It can be undertaken by individuals, communities, government, private sector;
- It can be either autonomous or planned;
- It can be either proactive (anticipatory) or reactive (responsive);
- It can be implemented at the local, regional, national and international scales; and
- It can be market-based, behavioral, legislative, institutional, structural, operational, or technological.

Three primary approaches to tailoring adaptive measures to local needs have been identified (Smit and Pilifosova 2003: 24). First, we need to "address real local vulnerabilities, so that stakeholders buy into the issue and are interested in reducing vulnerabilities of which they are well aware." Second, we need to "involve real stakeholders early and substantively, so that any assistance is directed at known vulnerabilities, and adaptation initiatives are realistic and designed to be consistent with existing institutions and decision processes." And third, we need to "connect with local decision-making processes, so that adaptation initiatives are developed relative to other conditions, are 'mainstreamed,' to the extent possible, and have the best possible chance of actually being implemented."

Adaptation plays a central role in the overall damages incurred by social and economic systems due to climate change. Economic studies that did not account for adaptation estimated net losses associated with climate change for the United States. However, when adaptation is incorporated into economic models, results have tended to show small net

Even where regions on the whole may be able to successfully adapt to a limited climate change, specific individuals and communities could still be displaced and harmed by climate change.

81

gains from moderate climate changes over the next century (Mendelsohn 2000, Smith 2004). In Mendelsohn (2000: 584), several market sector adaptations to climate change are identified, including:

- Agriculture–private strategies
  - Alter crop species, alter timing, improve or extend irrigation
- Agriculture–public strategies
  - Engineer resistant/tolerant plants
- Sea level rise–private strategies
  - Depreciate vulnerable buildings
- Sea level rise–public strategies
  - Build sea walls as needed, enrich beaches as needed
- Forestry–private strategies
  - Harvest vulnerable trees, plant new tree varieties, intensify management
- Energy–private strategies
  - Expand cooling capacity, improve insulation, develop cool building designs
- Energy–public strategies
  - Develop new building codes
- Water–private strategies
  - Invest in water efficiency
- Water–public strategies
  - Shift water to high value uses, divert/store more water, re-assess flood zoning
- Biodiversity–public strategies
  - Move endangered species, manage landscapes, plant adapted species
- Health–private strategies
  - Prepare for extreme weather events, avoid insect bites
- Health–public strategies
  - Control disease carriers, treat infected people, control diseased ecosystems
- Aesthetics–private strategies
  - Adapt behavior (e.g., recreation)
- Aesthetics–public strategies
  - Educate people of adaptive options

Mitigation and adaptation are complementary approaches that need to be considered jointly with a changing climate (Easterling et al. 2004). If mitigation and adaptation are treated as substitutes for one another, then the costs of policies and programs targeting climate change are likely to increase with little change in climate risks and the benefits derived from reducing these risks (Kane and Yohe 2000). Regardless of our approach

Mitigation and adaptation are complementary approaches that need to be considered jointly with a changing climate…

to climate change, there will be costs associated with it (Easterling et al. 2004, Mendelsohn et al. 1999, Smit and Pilifosova 2003).

Areas of Further Research

Four research themes that are relevant to the climate change problem include policy-relevant science, micro-scale analyses, valuation of non-market changes, and local adaptation.

Policy-Relevant Science

Scientific understanding could be more effective in its role in the decision making process. In particular, the lack of knowledge regarding localized impacts from climate change leaves decision makers on the outside looking in, or attempting to make locally relevant decisions based on globally or nationally defined trends (NRC 1999). Therefore,

> research should pursue three related aims: improving methods for valuing nonmarket goods; improving analytical methods for integrating multiple types of decision-relevant information (e.g., integrated assessment models, cost-benefit analyses); and developing decision processes that effectively combine analytical, deliberative, and participatory approaches to understanding environmental choices and thus guide scientists toward generating decision-relevant information (NRC 1999: 59).

Risk and uncertainty of events occurring and their relative impacts need to be better conveyed to decision makers and the public, in particular concepts of likelihoods, confidences, and ranges of uncertainty (IPCC 2001). It is well-known that scientific measures of risk and lay perceptions of risk often diverge. Both expert and lay perceptions of risk are affected by psychological, social, cultural and political factors, including uncertainty regarding the consequences of climate change and how risks are distributed among affected populations (Burgman 2005, Slovic 1999). Uncertainties about the risks of climate change are compounded by uncertainty due to climate variability.

Better means of communicating risks to lay audiences seems appropriate if public discourse is to be informed by scientific findings (which includes measures of risk and probabilities). This discourse on climate change and its associated risks is important if perceptions of risk are socially constructed. Slovic (1999) argues that public participation, especially for those people most affected by climate change, in risk assessment and risk decision making is critical to defining strategies to deal with hazards and risks. Public participation at all levels of risk assessment and decision making would make "the decision process more democratic, improve the relevance and quality of technical analysis, and increase the legitimacy and public acceptance of the resulting decisions" (Slovic 1999: 689).

Most studies estimating long-term impacts of climate change assume risk neutrality of decision makers. Research on risk-averse behavior in environmental decision-making in the context of climate change may

...the lack of knowledge regarding localized impacts from climate change leaves decision makers on the outside looking in, or attempting to make locally relevant decisions based on globally or nationally defined trends...

Better means of communicating risks to lay audiences seems appropriate if public discourse is to be informed by scientific findings...

result in different strategies to deal with climate change and how to package climate change policies (Davidson et al. 2003, Mendelsohn 2001). A good starting point for assessing strategies to deal with risks from environmental change is the natural hazards literature (Smit et al. 2000).

Micro-Scale Analyses

Most research on climate change is at a macro-scale (i.e., global, national, or regional scale). These broad-scale efforts should continue as models are refined, additional data are gathered or become available, and trends in climate patterns become realized. However, more information at local levels (micro-scale analyses) is needed. Some social groups may be at greater risk, not solely because of their geographic location in a region of high climate sensitivity, but also because of economic, political and cultural characteristics (Davidson et al. 2003). Thus, at the regional or local scale, uncertainty regarding potential impacts of climate change increases (Mendelsohn 2001, Miller and Gloss 2003, Shugart et al. 2003, Smith 2004, Travis 2003, Wallentine and Matthews 2003). E.g., Mendelsohn (2001: 198) notes that

> climate change itself is not likely to be uniform. Changes in precipitation especially could vary widely on a local scale. Ecological impacts may be different in the southern edge of a region than in the northern edge. Economic activity and populations vary widely across regions. For all these reasons, one should expect that the experience of every household could vary within a region.

However, micro-scale analyses should be conducted with recognition that they are nested within a larger scale. Sustainable management involves multiple values and temporal and spatial scales. Only within the appropriate scale can sustainable management balance the needs of ecosystems with economic efficiency and distributional equity.

Non-market Valuation

Several authors have identified a need for climate change and policy-relevant measures of the effects on non-market resources such as health, aesthetics, recreation, and species losses (Loomis and Crespi 1999, Mendelsohn 2001, Mendelsohn et al. 1999, Mendelsohn and Neumann 1999, NRC 1999, Pearce et al. 1996, Smith 2004). Most scientific evidence regarding the likely impacts of climate change are for sectors with markets (see table 1). Estimates of non-market impacts of climate change are needed to help guide decision making through use of informative tools such as integrative models and cost-benefit analyses (Chee 2004, NRC 2005). Economic estimates of non-market impacts would aid decision makers as they evaluate climate change policies by elaborating on the trade-offs associated with their choices. Climate change may be a good proving ground for many of the well-established economic valuation methods and newly emerging approaches, in particular due to its complexity, uncertainty and potentially non-linear nature of impacts (NRC 2005).

Recreation is likely the primary means through which most people will directly experience climate change (Wagner 2003). How people

Climate change may be a good proving ground for many of the well-established economic valuation methods and newly emerging approaches, in particular due to its complexity, uncertainty and potentially non-linear nature of impacts...

respond in their recreation behavior may be a strong indicator of their knowledge of and attitudes toward climate change (Irland et al. 2001). In particular, will people support the relocation of recreation opportunities and facilities, especially when relocation is subject to significant costs (Loomis and Crespi 1999)? E.g., the ski industry may be sustained in the short-term by relocating facilities either higher in elevation or to another area where adequate snow is expected.

The loss of species and termination of ecosystem services may be a critical threshold that we are unwilling to cross (Farber et al. 2002). E.g., if a certain species requires a minimum amount of habitat to survive and changes in climate reduce habitat below the critical threshold, then a non-linear response (i.e., extinction) is likely to happen. Is this an acceptable outcome, especially if the risk of it occurring can be reduced through proactive management? What types of values and how much are they willing to trade for a reduction in the risk (probability) of an irreversible event? Are there critical thresholds that we need to manage against regardless of public opinion? How will people and communities respond to worst-case scenarios (NRC 1999, Smith 2004)?

Local Adaptation

We also need more applied research on how adaptation could occur (Davidson et al. 2003, Joyce et al. 2000, Mendelsohn and Markowski 1999, NRC 1999, Smith 2004). Potential adaptation responses to recent and historical events may provide important insights into likely adaptation responses to climate change at the local level. People have adapted their behavior due to other environmental events such as fish consumption advisories, smog alerts, beach closures and fish catch rates (Joyce et al. 2000, NRC 1999). A changing landscape due to climate change is important given evidence that migration patterns into rural areas are linked to the spatial distribution of natural amenities over the past two centuries (Deller et al. 2001, Rosenberger and English [In press]). What are the likely future migration patterns due to climate change, and how might these patterns affect efforts to reduce climate change or their impacts on social, economic and ecological systems?Most research to date is concerned with macro-scale models of climate change and economic systems. More localized studies with disaggregated data are needed since adaptation will occur at the local level (Davidson et al. 2003, Mendelsohn and Markowski 1999, Smith 2004). Adaptation is place and culture specific and can only be identified through place and culture specific research (Smit and Pilifosova 2003). Research on local adaptation should include those most affected by climate change and those with decision making responsibilities (Klein and Smith 2003).

What are the likely future migration patterns due to climate change, and how might these patterns affect efforts to reduce climate change or their impacts on social, economic and ecological systems?

Conclusions

There is little doubt that as climate continues to change we will see changes in our ecological, social and economic systems as a result. However uncertain we are regarding changes in ecological systems due to a changing climate, uncertainties about our social and economic systems are greater. This is important given humans are motivated by those values

The future is not bleak; there are other reasons to act now, regardless of whether climate change is perceived to be real.

Environmental quality improves through better air quality, lower environmental costs associated with air pollution, improved water quality from reduced nitrogen deposition, along with a reduction in the effects of climate change on ecological systems.

they hold. As climate change threatens these values, we ought to see people respond in an effort to protect them. Other human activities, such as deforestation and energy consumption are influenced by population growth, economic growth, values and belief systems, institutions and policies, and the dynamic interaction among them (NRC 1999). Not only are these factors intimately linked to the climate change problem, but they also create barriers to solutions for the problem (IPCC 2001). Human responses to climate change may not be effective or efficient, especially without full information (Hanemann 2000).

The future is not bleak; there are other reasons to act now, regardless of whether climate change is perceived to be real. Responding to climate change can result in significant benefits. The US EPA (2002) summarized several benefits we can expect from reducing greenhouse gas emissions. Public health benefits from reducing fossil fuel use leads to less air pollution and associated respiratory problems. Environmental quality improves through better air quality, lower environmental costs associated with air pollution, improved water quality from reduced nitrogen deposition, along with a reduction in the effects of climate change on ecological systems. Our economy benefits by reducing energy costs to households through increasing energy efficiency, lower material and disposal costs associated with increased recycling, greater reliability of alternative energy sources, and increased profits and jobs associated with businesses that incorporate energy efficient technologies in their production process and products and provide alternative energy sources. Land use changes result in more walkable cities and more efficient use of land including conservation of open space around cities, which directly contribute to human health and well-being (Rosenberger et al. 2005).

Urban forestry benefits include greener cities through tree planting programs that sequester carbon, filter air pollution and water runoff, reduce summer cooling costs, and result in more attractive communities. Managed forest benefits result from sustainably managing forests for long-term carbon storage, a sustained wood supply, and increased ecological benefits associated with sustainable forestry practices. Agriculture benefits by reducing energy costs to farmers from improved energy efficiency in operations and equipment, conservation tillage, and alternative practices such as strategic fertilizer applications. New sources of income for farmers may be realized through the supply of crops for biofuels and energy production from livestock waste. In many ways, several mitigation and adaptation strategies are win-win propositions. The challenge is to derive broad support for policies and programs targeting climate change.

Acknowledgments

This paper was presented at the Bringing Climate into Natural Resource Management Conference, Portland, OR, June 28-30, 2005. This research was supported in part by funds provided by the Pacific Northwest Research Station, Forest Service, U.S. Department of Agriculture. This paper benefited from comments on an earlier draft by Richard Haynes and Mark Sperow. Any remaining errors are the sole responsibility of the author.

References

Adams, R.M.; Hurd, B.H.; Reilly, J. 1999. Agriculture and global climate change. Arlington, VA; Pew Center on Global Climate Change. 36 p.

Burgman, M. 2005. Risks and decisions for conservation and environmental management. Cambridge, UK: Cambridge University Press. 488 p.

Chee, Y.E. 2004. An ecological perspective on the valuation of ecosystem services. Biological Conservation. 120: 549-565.

Cohen, S.; Bass, B.; Etkin, D.; Mortsch, L.; Scott, D.; van Kooten, G.K. 2004. Regional adaptation strategies. In: Coward, H.; Weaver, A.J., eds. Hard choices: climate change in Canada. Waterloo, ON, Canada: Wilfrid Laurier University Press: 151-178.

Costanza, R.; d'Arge, R.; de Groot, R.; Farber, S.; Grasso, M.; Hannon, B.; Limburg, K.; Naeem, S.; O'Neill, R.V.; Paruelo, J.; Ruskins, R.G.; Sutton, P.; van den Belt, M. 1997. The value of the world's ecosystem services and natural capital. Nature. 387: 253-260.

Davidson, D.J.; Williamson, T.; Parkins, J.R. 2003. Understanding climate change risk and vulnerability in northern forest-based communities. Canadian Journal of Forest Research. 33: 2252-2261.

de Groot, R.S.; Wilson, M.A.; Boumans, R.M.J. 2002. A typology for the classification, description and valuation of ecosystem functions, goods and services. Ecological Economics. 41: 393-408.

Deller, S.C.; Tsai, T.H; Marcoullier, D.W.; English, D.B.K. 2001. The role of amenities and quality of life in rural economic growth. American Journal of Agricultural Economics. 83(2): 352-365.

Easterling, W.E., III; Hurd, B.H.; Smith, J.B. 2004. Coping with global climate change: the role of adaptation in the United States. Arlington, VA: Pew Center on Global Climate Change. 40 p.

Farber, S.C.; Costanza, R.; Wilson, M.A. 2002. Economic and ecological concepts for valuing ecosystem services. Ecological Economics. 41: 375-392.

Hamlet, A.F.; Lettenmaier, D.P. 1999. Effects of climate change on hydrology and water resources in the Columbia River Basin. Journal of the American Water Resources Association. 35(6): 1597-1623.

Hanemann, W.M. 2000. Adaptation and its measurement. Climatic Change. 45: 571-581.

Hardy, J.T. 2003. Climate change: causes, effects, and solutions. Hoboken, NJ: Wiley. 260 p.

Houghton, J.T.; Ding, Y.; Griggs, D.J.; Noguer, M.; van der Linden, R.J.; Xiasou, D., eds. 2001. Climate change 2001: the scientific basis. Cambridge, England: Cambridge University Press. 944 p.

Hurd, B.H.; Leary, N.; Jones, R.; Smith, J.B. 1999. Relative regional vulnerability of water resources to climate change. Journal of the American Water Resources Association. 35(6): 1399-1410.

IPCC. 2001. Climate change 2001: synthesis report. A contribution of working groups I, II, and III to the third assessment report of the Intergovernmental Panel on Climate Change (R.T. Watson and the Core Writing Team, eds.). Cambridge, England: Cambridge University Press. 398 p.

Irland, L.C.; Adams, D.; Alig, R.; Betz, C.J.; Chi-Chung, C.; Hutchins, M.; McCarl, B.; Skog, K. 2001. Assessing socioeconomic impacts of climate change on US forests, wood-product markets, and forest recreation. BioScience. 51(9): 753-764.

Jepma, C.J.; Asaduzzaman, M.; Mintzer, I.; Maya, R.S.; Al-Moneef, M. 1996. A generic assessment of response options. In: Bruce, J.P.; Lee, H.; Haites, E.F., eds. IPCC. Climate change 1995: economic and social dimensions of climate change. Cambridge, England: Cambridge University Press: 225-262.

Joyce, L.; Aber, J.; McNulty, S.; Dale, V.; Hansen, A.; Irland, L.; Neilson, R.; Skog, K. 2000. Potential consequences of climate variability and change for the forests of the United States. In: National assessment synthesis team, eds. Climate change impacts on the United States: the potential consequences of climate variability and change: foundation. Washington, DC: US Global Change Research Program: 489-522.

Kane, S.; Yohe, G. 2000. Societal adaptation to climate variability and change: an introduction. Climatic Change. 45(1): 1-4.

Klein, R.J.T.; Smith, J.B. 2003. Enhancing the capacity of developing countries to adapt to climate change: a policy relevant research agenda. In: Smith, J.B.; Klein, R.J.T.; Huq, S., eds. Climate change, adaptive capacity and development. London, England: Imperial College Press: 317 – 334.

Kolbert, E. 2005. The climate of man-III: What can be done? The New Yorker. (May 9).

Krieger, D.J. 2001. Economic value of forest ecosystem services: a review. Washington, DC: The Wilderness Society. 30 p.

Lewis, B.J. 1995. Value and valuation methodology in forestry and natural resource management contexts. Minneapolis, MN: University of Minnesota. 176 p.

Loomis, J.; Crespi, J. 1999. Estimated effects of climate change on selected outdoor recreation activities in the United States. In: Mendelsohn, R.; Neumann, J.E., eds. The impact of climate change on the United States economy. Cambridge, England: Cambridge University Press: 289-314.

Loomis, J.B.; Richardson, R. 2000. Economic values of protecting roadless areas in the United States. Washington, DC: The Wilderness Society. 43 p.

McCarthy, J.; Canziana, O.; Leary, N.; Dokken, D.J.; White, K.S., eds. 2001. Climate change 2001: impacts, adaptation, and vulnerability. Cambridge, England: Cambridge University Press. 1,000 p.

Mendelsohn, R. 2000. Efficient adaptation to climate change. Climatic Change. 45: 583-600.

Mendelsohn, R., ed. 2001. Global warming and the American economy: a regional assessment of climate change impacts. Cheltenham, England: Edward Elgar Publishing. 209 p. [plus maps].

Mendelsohn, R.; Markowski, M. 1999. The impact of climate change on outdoor recreation. In: Mendelsohn, R.; Neumann, J.E., eds. The impact of climate change on the United States economy. Cambridge, England: Cambridge University Press: 267–288.

Mendelsohn, R.; Neumann, J.E. 1999. Synthesis and conclusions. In: Mendelsohn, R.; Neumann, J.E., eds. The impact of climate change on the United States economy. Cambridge, England: Cambridge University Press: 315-331.

Mendelsohn, R.; Smith, J.B.; Neumann, J.E. 1999. Introduction. In: Mendelsohn, R.; Neumann, J.E., eds. The impact of climate change on the United States economy. Cambridge, England: Cambridge University Press: 1-17.

Miller, K.; Gloss, S. 2003. Climate variability: social, policy, and institutional issues. In: Lewis, W.M., Jr., ed. Water and climate in the western United States. Boulder, CO: University Press of Colorado: 251-269.

Morton, P. 1999. The economic benefits of wilderness: theory and practice. University of Denver Law Review. 76(2): 465-518.

National Research Council. 1999. Human dimensions of global environmental change: research pathways for the next decade. Washington, DC: National Academy Press. 100 p.

National Research Council. 2005. Valuing ecosystem services: toward better environmental decision-making. Washington, DC: National Academy Press. 278 p.

Neilson, R.P.; Drapek, R.J. 1998. Potentially complex biosphere responses to transient global warming. Global Change Biology. 4: 132-148.

Oreskes, N. 2004. The scientific consensus of climate change. Science. 306(5702): 1686.

Parmesan, C.; Galbraith, H. 2004. Observed impacts of global climate change in the U.S. Arlington, VA: Pew Center on Global Climate Change. 56 p.

Pearce, D.W.; Cline, W.R.; Achanta, A.N.; Huang, R.; Dwen, P.; Flack, J.; Tran, Q.; Salman, T.; Cliff, B. 1996. The social costs of climate change: greenhouse damage and the benefits of control. In: Bruce, J.P.; Lee, H.; Haites, E.F., eds. IPCC. Climate change 1995: economic and social dimensions of climate change. Cambridge, UK: Cambridge University Press: 179-224.

Pimentel, D.; Wilson, C.; McCullum, C. [et al.]. 1997. Economic and environmental benefits of biodiversity. BioScience. 47(11): 747-757.

Randall, A. 1984. The conceptual basis of benefit cost analysis. In: Peterson, G.L.; Randall, A., eds. Valuation of wildland resource benefits. Boulder, CO: Westview Press: 53-63.

Richards, K.R.; Stokes, C. 2004. A review of carbon sequestration cost studies: a dozen years of research. Climatic Change. 63: 1-48.

Rolston, H., III. 1985. Valuing wildlands. Environmental Ethics. 7(1): 23-48.

Rosenberger, R.S.; English, D.B.K. [In press]. Impacts of wilderness on local economic development. In: Cordell, H.K.; Bergstrom, J.C.; Bowker, J.M., eds. The multiple values of wilderness. State College, PA: Venture Publishing.

Rosenberger, R.S.; Sneh, Y.; Phipps, T.T.; Gurvitch, R. 2005. A spatial analysis of the linkages between health care expenditures, physical inactivity, obesity and recreation supply. Journal of Leisure Research. 37(2): 216-235.

Shugart, H.; Sedjo, R.; Sohngen, B. 2003. Forests and global climate change: potential impacts on U.S. forest resources. Arlington, VA: Pew Center on Global Climate Change. 52 p.

Slovic, P. 1999. Trust, emotion, sex, politics, and science: surveying the risk-assessment battlefield. Risk Analysis. 19(4): 689-701.

Smit, B.; Burton, I.; Klein, R.J.T.; Wandel, J. 2000. An anatomy of adaptation to climate change and variability. Climatic Change. 45(1): 223-251.

Smit, B.; Pilifosova, O. 2003. From adaptation to adaptive capacity and vulnerability reduction. In: Smith, J.B.; Klein, R.J.T.; Huq, S., eds. Climate change, adaptive capacity and development. London, England: Imperial College Press: 9-28.

Smith, J.B. 2004. A synthesis of potential climate change impacts on the U.S. Arlington, VA: Pew Center on Global Climate Change. 44 p.

Smith, J.B.; Klein, R.J.T.; Huq, S. 2003. Introduction. In: Smith, J.B.; Klein, R.J.T.; Huq, S., eds. Climate change, adaptive capacity and development. London, England: Imperial College Press: 1-7.

Sohngen, B.L.; Mendelsohn, R. 1999. The impacts of climate change on the US timber market. In: Mendelsohn, R.; Neumann, J.E., eds. The impact of climate change on the United States economy. Cambridge, England: Cambridge University Press: 94-132.

Travis, W.R. 2003. A changing geography: growth, land use, and water in the interior west. In: Lewis, W.M., Jr., ed. Water and climate in the western United States. Boulder, CO: University Press of Colorado: 171-181.

Turner, R.K.; van den Bergh, J.C.J.M.; Soderqvist, T. Barendregt, A.; van der Straaten, J.; Maltby, E.; van Ierland, E.C. 2000. Ecological-economic analysis of wetlands: scientific integration for management and policy. Ecological Economics. 35(1): 7-23.

U.S. Department of Agriculture, Forest Service. 2005. Monitoring for sustainability. http://www.fs.fed.us/institute/monitoring/Sustainability_monitoring.htm. (6/13/2005)

U.S. Environmental Protection Agency. 2002. Partnerships and progress: EPA state and local climate change program: 2001 progress report. Washington, DC: Government Publishing Office. 28 p.

Wagner, F.H., ed. 2003. Rocky Mountain/Great Basin regional climate-change assessment. Report for the U.S. Global Change Research Program. Logan, UT: Utah State University. 240 p.

Wallentine, C.B.; Matthews, D. 2003. Can climate predictions be of practical use in western water management? In: Lewis, W.M., Jr., ed. Water and climate in the western United States. Boulder, CO: University Press of Colorado: 161-168.

Wigley, T.M.L. 1999. The science of climate change: global and U.S. perspectives. Arlington, VA: Pew Center on Global Climate Change. 48 p.

The Challenges of Bringing Climate into Natural Resource Management: A Synthesis

Linda Joyce[1] and Richard Haynes[2]

Tom Iraci, USDA Forest Service

Gary Kramer
U.S. Fish and Wildlife Service

James C. Leupold
U.S. Fish and Wildlife Service

[1] Research Project Leader, USDA Forest Service, Rocky Mountain Research Station, 240 West Prospect, Fort Collins, CO 80526. Email: ljoyce@fs.fed.us

[2] Program Manager, USDA Forest Service, Pacific Northwest Research Station, P.O. Box 3890, Portland, OR. Email: rhaynes@fs.fed.us

Abstract

Here we synthesize and extend observations and recommendations from the speakers at the 2005 workshop titled "Implications of Bringing Climate into Natural Resource Management in the Western United States." Discussions there illustrated the complexity of global climate change and the need for managers to consider how the impacts of climate change will unfold across regional and local landscapes. The geographical, ecological, political, and socio-economic differences between the West and the East suggest that approaches to bringing climate into natural resource management will be unique to the West. These approaches will vary reflecting differences in threat perceptions among scientists, land managers, landowners, interested stakeholders and the public all who play different roles in governing actions across forested ecosystems. The various discussions revealed that there are many potential solutions but none are simple. Managers, however, are already responding to those aspects of global climate change that they can see or perceive. Eventually the accumulation of these local actions will shape our future.

Keywords: Climate change, forest and range management

Introduction

The Western United States is a rich diverse land of wide open spaces, ranging from the Great Plains grasslands to the Rocky Mountain forests to the Intermountain shrublands and deserts to the rich valleys of California and Oregon, to the coastal forests of the Pacific Northwest. Through exploration, industrial development and human population expansion, humans have capitalized on the natural resources of the western environment. Early settlers exploited small-scale opportunities such as hunting and trapping. Mining pulled rich ores from the earth and modified the landscape through wood harvest for mining—altering stream bed structure and riparian areas all over the West—and energy uses. The wide open spaces brought the livestock industry, sheep and cattle herds, cattle drives, and alterations in native vegetation and the introduction of exotic plant species. Agricultural expansion capitalized on spring time mountain runoff, developed large irrigation systems, and reservoirs to serve the expanding human populations as well as the agricultural industry. Forest products industries quickly developed as railroads opened access to vast mature softwood stands and connected domestic and international markets. The industry, initially based on private timber, evolved on a large scale to one increasingly reliant on public timber, following World War II. It was an early adopter of advanced materials handling and processing technologies. Post World War II also brought new demands by an increasingly wealthy society for increased recreational opportunities, such as winter skiing, summer tourism, and second homes in scenic areas. In the late 20th century, attention focused on natural resources, and past examples of western land management were often the basis for a rethinking of land management on public and private lands (see Wilkinson 1992 for a discussion of these changes).

Through exploration, industrial development and human population expansion, humans have capitalized on the natural resources of the western environment.

Today, the rural nature of the western landscape continues to change: scenic mountain valleys are being developed, urban areas are expanding into the deserts and grasslands around the major metropolitan centers, and settlements in the Great Plains and the Interior West are declining. The relationship between the humans and the western environment has changed over time as settlers became aware of their impact on the landscape, coupled with reoccurring droughts, potential for wildfire, and the periodic outbreaks of insects on forests and grasslands. That relationship and understanding will likely be challenged as the West faces potential changes in its climate.

Natural resource managers, scientists and policy makers from private and governmental agencies gathered for 2½ days in June 2005 to explore the implications of bringing climate into natural resource management in the western United States. In this paper, we synthesize observations and recommendations of speakers for resource management approaches to climate change, and our own thoughts on this challenge.

In the United States, the West is Different from the East

The Western United States was repeatedly described in this workshop as very different from the Eastern United States. In terms of forestland ownership, 81 percent of the West is in federal land management versus only 19 percent in the East. In the West, elevation often fragments the landscape with higher elevations mostly in federal ownership and the valleys are privately owned where agriculture is feasible. In terms of land cover, 38 percent of forests in the United States are found in the West. Rangeland accounts for one third of the land in the United States, but the Western United States holds the majority of that rangeland, 80 percent. These ecosystems include the Great Plains grasslands, the savannas in Texas, sagebrush steppe and shrublands in the Great Basin, alpine meadows, wetlands, and southwestern deserts.

The highest mountains ranges in the United States occur in the West with the Rocky Mountains and the Pacific Coastal Ranges reaching more than 14,000 feet above sea level. The West also holds the lowest elevation with Death Valley at 282 feet below sea level. The terrain of the West strongly influences the environment, the vegetation and the habitats of animals. In the mountains, north facing slopes often have a forested vegetation whereas the south facing slopes may have only shrubs and grasses. Distances between cool moist environments and warm dry environments can be remarkably short.

The social and economic conditions in the West are often described in terms different than those for the East. In 2000, the West accounted for 23 percent of the United States population but 53 percent of those people lived in California. It is often thought of as a place of wide open spaces yet 82 percent of its population lives in urban areas (as opposed to 77 percent of the population in the East). It contains rapidly growing metropolitan areas like Phoenix or Las Vegas that attract both economic as well as lifestyle migrants. It also contains an emerging frontier where population

The relationship between the humans and the western environment has changed over time as settlers became aware of their impact on the landscape, coupled with reoccurring droughts, potential for wildfire, and the periodic outbreaks of insects on forests and grasslands.

93

densities are less than 6 people per square mile. Western states account of 24 percent of the U.S. economic activity in 2004. The diversities of western economies mirrors that for the United States but with a slightly higher proportion of some states economies being accounted for by softwood lumber manufacturing and mining than Eastern States. In addition, the services sector is slightly large in the West than in the East.

These geographical, ecological, political, and socio-economic differences between the West and the East suggest that approaches to bringing climate into natural resource management will be unique to the West. For example, the complex terrain makes it challenging to model fine scale climate change using the current large scale climate models. Additionally, this complex geography and the difficulty of access in remote areas of the West have limited adequate monitoring of weather and ecological phenomena. The intermingling of public and private land raises challenges to managing the large diverse landscapes.

Past and Future Climates in Western United States

Weather is the short-term variation in temperature, precipitation, humidity, wind, and cloudiness. Climate is the long-term description of weather. Plants and animals adapt to local climates, to the summer rains, snowfall, snow depth, the direction of wind and wind speed, the timing of last frost in spring or the first in fall, and soil temperature and moisture. Western climates are variable across space and time, much more so than eastern climates.

Observations of climate in the West for the last 100 years indicate that we may be seeing a warming trend already (see Redmond, this report, for an extensive discussion of western climate). Western winter and spring temperatures show the strongest trend in warming, a point also stressed by Phil Mote in his presentation (see figs. 1 and 3, Redmond, this report). Climate models suggest that these warming trends will likely continue into the 21st century, see figure 4 in Redmond (this report). Precipitation over the last 100 years in the west shows little trends and great variability (fig. 7, Redmond, this report). Across several climate models scenarios, potential future precipitation in the West shows no trend up or down, but does exhibit more variability, interannual as well as multi-year variability.

Observed Changes in Western Ecosystems in Relation to Climate

The human influence on climate and water resources in the West is emerging from numerous studies (fig. 1). Phil Mote described studies of changes in western watersheds. From 1950 to 1997, snowpack on April 1 showed a decline throughout most of the western watersheds. These snowpack changes led to documented earlier springtime flows and lower summer time flows in streams from mountainous areas. Spring time runoff is critical to water needs for agriculture and urban areas in the West. Phil Mote also showed the West is very vulnerable, with modest

These geographical, ecological, political, and socio-economic differences between the West and the East suggest that approaches to bringing climate into natural resource management will be unique to the West.

The human influence on climate and water resources in the West is emerging from numerous studies...

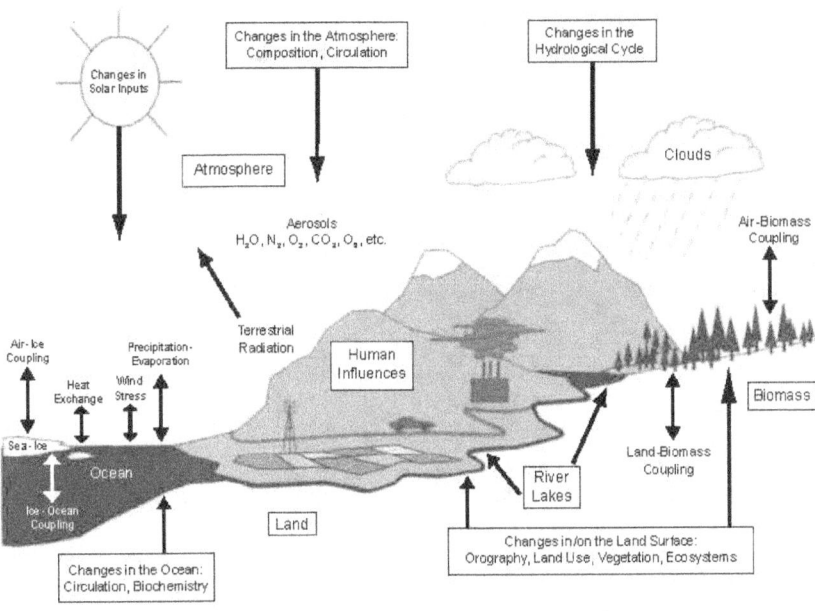

Figure 1—A diagram of the atmospheric-biospheric interactions. Source: Trenberth et al. 1996, p. 55.

winter temperature increases of only 2-4°F, to shifts in snow to rain events. Both Redmond (this report) and Mote showed future projections under several different possible climate scenarios where warming temperatures led to declines in the western snowpack.

Joel Smith presented recent research focused on the climate-sensitive behaviors of plants and animals, such as breeding, emergence from hibernation, seasonal migration, productivity, and changes in species ranges. Many of these changes (fig. 2) have been documented in the Western United States. Examples include earlier egg laying of the first clutches in Mexican Jays, earlier emergence from hibernation by marmots, northern expansion of the Sachem Skipper butterfly, and the rising dominance of warm-water species in Monterey inter-tidal community. In each case, a climate indicator tied to the behavior or the plant or animal species also had changed. For example, water temperature in Monterey Bay has increased by 2°F over the 1939-1990 period, bringing about a corresponding shift in species dominance. Yet, with these individual examples, can we conclude climate change is responsible for these observed impacts at the scale of the Western United States? Joel Smith described large scale studies of thousands of species where the scientists concluded that climate changes can be linked to the observed global biological changes and the changes in North American plants and animals. However, meta-studies at the scale of the Western United States are needed to definitely conclude that the impacts in this region are clearly attributable to climate change. The West is experiencing other factors that affect regional climate and the landscapes, but, the observed changes on the western landscape are consistent with projected climate changes.

…meta-studies at the scale of the Western United States are needed to definitely conclude that the impacts in this region are clearly attributable to climate change.

Examples of Climate Sensitive Behaviors of Plants and Animals

Plants

First leaf out in spring

Flowering

Senescence at the end of the growing season, arrival of fall colors

Plant productivity

Dominance of particular plant species in plant communities

Extension of geographic ranges through more favorable climate

Animals

Breeding, courtship, nesting, egg laying

Life cycles of insects, from two year to adult stage to one year

Seasonal migration

Emergence from hibernation

Animal productivity

Extension of ranges through more favorable climate

Ecosystem Dynamics

Nutrient availability

Decomposition in the soil

Figure 2—Examples of climate-sensitive behaviors of plants and animals.

Potential Changes in Western Ecosystems and Economies Under Climate Change

Scientists have explored potential changes in western ecosystems and economies through the use of simulation models and different projected future climates. Global general circulation models project different future climate scenarios as a function of assumptions about future emissions of trace gases such as carbon dioxide, methane, and nitrous oxides. Redmond (this report) described some of those future scenarios. As the amount of carbon dioxide is likely to double over the next century, scientists have also studied the responses of plants to higher amounts of carbon dioxide.

The impact of higher atmospheric concentrations of carbon dioxide on plants is the focus of Jack Morgan's research at the Agricultural Research Service. While plant production increases when plants are grown under higher levels of carbon dioxide, the response varies by climate, plant community, and soil fertility of the grassland ecosystem. The increased response in plant production was seen only in the dry years at a sub-humid grassland of Kansas, across dry, normal and wet years on the semi-arid grassland in Colorado, and only in wet years in the arid grassland of Nevada. Across individual species, the response could be increased biomass production, greater seedling response, or increased seed production. For these grasslands, a more disconcerting response was a decline in the quality of the vegetation as forage, less nutritious and lower digestibility of the forage. This decline in forage quality has implications to both domestic livestock and wildlife.

Lewis Ziska described relationships between climate, carbon dioxide, and invasive plants. In one experiment, he explored the response of six invasive weeds—Canada thistle (*Cirsium arvense* (L.) Scop.), field bindweed (*Convolvulus arvensis* L.), leafy spurge (*Euphorbia esula* L.), perennial sowthistle (*Sonchus* L.), spotted knapweed (*Centaurea stoebe* L.), and yellow star-thistle (*Centaurea solstitialis* L.)—to concentrations of carbon dioxide that corresponded to the beginning of the 20th century, current levels, and concentrations projected for the end of the 21st century. The likely future concentrations stimulated plant biomass on the average by 46 percent with the largest response observed for Canada thistle (fig. 3). Perhaps even more intriguing was the response from the early 20th century to present, 110 percent. This study suggests the possibility that recent increases in atmospheric carbon dioxide during the 20th century may have been a factor in the growth of these invasives. Lewis Ziska also described an experiment along the rural to urban gradient where temperature and atmospheric carbon dioxide concentrations reflect what the future might be—urban areas currently reflecting warmer climate and higher carbon dioxide concentrations than rural areas. Early results suggest the warmer environment with higher levels of carbon dioxide is an excellent environment for weedy species.

Scientists exploring the potential impacts of future climate change on ecosystems and economies have used large scale models to simulate different future climates. Neilson (this report) describes the potential futures of North American ecosystems under climate change using the MC1 Dynamic General Vegetation Model (DGVM) and six future climate scenarios (3 General Circulation Models X 2 emission scenarios). His results show an increase in carbon sequestration in the late 20th century and briefly early in the 21st century, the result of increased precipitation, enhanced water-use efficiency and mild temperature increases. He shows that these 'greening' processes were overtaken by the exponential effects of increasing temperature on evaporative demand and respiration, producing a subsequent decline in ecosystem productivity (Neilson, this report).

There has been limited work describing the potential western socio-economic impacts of changing climate (Rosenberger, this report). Much of this work is very general given the lack of specificity in possible impacts to determinants of social and economic activities. At the same time land managers and others are responding to changing climate by adapting or modifying their management actions. For example, some ski areas are considering or have added snow making machines to both extend seasons and to adapt to perceived variability in snow fall. At the same time we are seeing increased amenity based migration to places previously considered too remote or inhospitable (such as Prince of Wales Island, Alaska) as either perceptions or mitigation activities change. Rosenberger (in this report) described that the biggest winners from climate change are likely to be agriculture and summer recreation while the biggest losers are likely to be water resources and energy sectors.

Early results suggest the warmer environment with higher levels of carbon dioxide is an excellent environment for weedy species.

...land managers and others are responding to changing climate by adapting or modifying their management actions.

97

Norman E. Rees
USDA Agricultural Research Service
www.forestryimages.org
leafy spurge

Peggy Greb, USDA
Agricultural Research Service,
www.ipmimages.org
yellow star-thistle

Mary Ellen (Mel) Harte
www.forestryimages.org
field bindweed

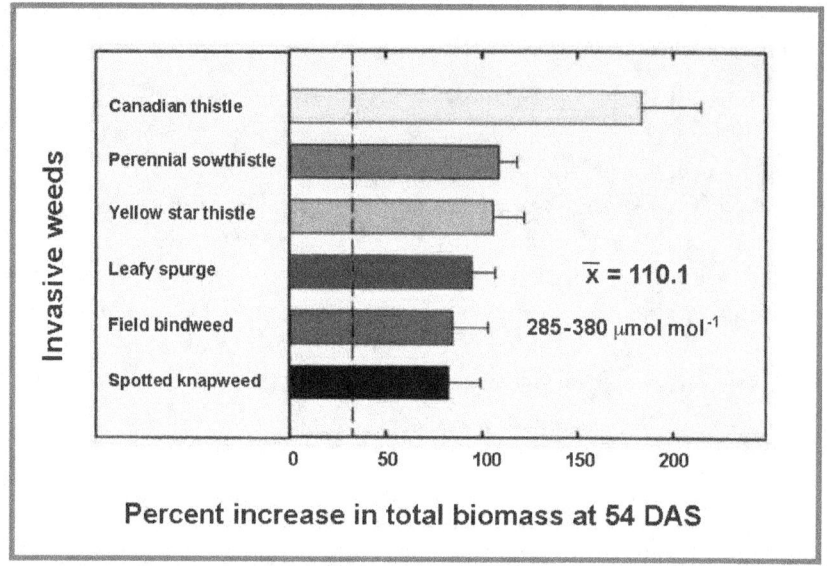

Percent increase in total biomass at 54 DAS

Figure 3—Six invasive weeds, Canada thistle, field bindweed, leafy spurge, perennial sowthistle, spotted knapweed, and yellow star thistle were grown from seed at either 284, 380 or 719 μmol mol-1 carbon dioxide through the vegetative period. The concentration of 284 reflects the atmospheric concentration of carbon dioxide in the early 20th century, and the 380 reflect the current concentration. At 54 days, the average stimulation of plant biomass among invasive species during the 20th century was 110 percent. The response to future concentrations of carbon dioxide (not shown here) was an average of 46 percent (Ziska 2003).

Steve Sutherland
spotted knapweed

Since 1995, the various RPA timber Assessments have included different scenarios examining the effects of climate change on U.S. forests and forest products markets (see Haynes 2003, Haynes and others 1995, Haynes and others, in prep.; Joyce and others 1995). In these scenarios climate change is expected to involve temperature increases 3 to 5°F in the East and up to 7°F in the West and increased precipitation, except for the Gulf Coast and the Pacific Northwest. The effects of climate change are modeled by modifying the growth rates of different forest types. In general these scenarios have shown that climate and elevated carbon dioxide act to augment growth in nearly all regions. Both softwood and hardwood growth on private lands expand steadily with particularly large percentage changes in the western regions. As in previous climate impact analyses, the regional impacts vary geographically and can be quite different from the national average results, reflecting regional climate changes. Because the inventory changes are gradual, their impacts on private timber harvest, timber prices and ultimately on product markets and prices in both scenarios are relatively small. For example, total U.S. softwood sawtimber harvest and annual softwood lumber production both increase by about +0.1 to 0.4 percent. Impacts in national product markets are muted given extensive inter-regional and international substitution (for more details see Haynes and others, in prep.).

Current Challenges of Natural Resource Management

Within the last 20 years, western land managers have not only faced increases in invasive plants but many other seemingly unprecedented natural disturbances. Recent catastrophic fires have been described as outside of the known behavior, intensity, and extent of past fires. Managers have also faced droughts in the Southwest that appear to rival past droughts. Water and aquatics management has had to respond to the reduced snowpack throughout the West. Insect patterns appear to represent significant change from historical records. The question was raised as to whether these disturbances are symptoms of the underlying changes associated with climate.

Jesse Logan described the implications for bark beetle management under a changing climate. Jesse reviewed the current large outbreaks of spruce beetle (*Dendroctonus rufipennis* Kirby) in North America, the pinyon ips (*Ips* spp.) in the Southwest, and mountain pine beetle (*Dendroctonus ponderosae Hopkins)* throughout Western United States. Building on his extensive research on the relationship of climate and beetle biology, he described simulations showing that increasing temperatures enhances beetle populations. He also presented results showing beetles occurring at higher elevations than previously seen—the range expansion of mountain pine beetle into high elevation white pines. He concluded that we are beyond demonstrating that something (climate-related) is occurring and that it is time to start formulating a management response to this changing environment in western high-elevation forests.

Mike Pellant described the challenges of managing Great Basin rangelands that have been dramatically altered by invasive plant species. The exotic annual grasses have altered the vegetation composition and the fire frequency in the Great Basin. Wildfires are now a common event in the Great Basin, and given the nature of the vegetation changes, wildfires will continue to increase in size and frequency, with or without climate change. Thus, without restoration, the ecosystems dominated by these annual grasses will continue to increase and the values associated with native plant communities, such as wildlife habitat, and the uses of these communities will continue to decline. He referred to this situation as the downward spiral from native plant communities to communities with cheatgrass (*Bromus tectorum* L.) and perennial invasive forbs, and ultimately to an endpoint of degradation unknown yet (fig. 4). The ecological integrity of the Great Basin is rapidly changing as a result the combination of invasive species, wildfires and increasing human-related disturbances. Restoration of altered western rangeland ecosystems is currently costly, yet if land management does not begin to restore these altered ecosystems and maintain healthy plant communities, weeds and wildfires will continue to control the ecological and economic health of the Great Basin. And the challenges could be even greater under an altered climate. But restoration is made difficult because species selected need to be adapted to potentially warmer or drier future environments.

Within the last 20 years, western land managers have not only faced increases in invasive plants but many other seemingly unprecedented natural disturbances.

The ecological integrity of the Great Basin is rapidly changing as a result the combination of invasive species, wildfires and increasing human-related disturbances.

Will downward spiral of rangeland ecological integrity be accelerated?

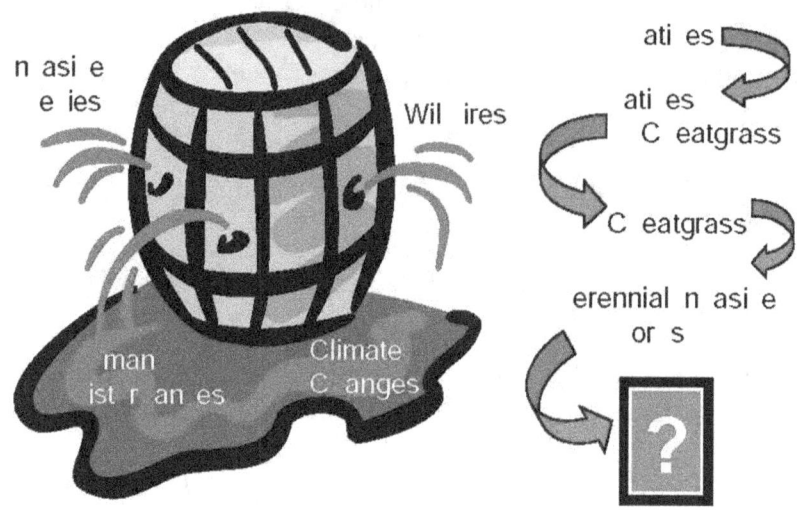

Figure 4—Downward spiral of rangeland ecological integrity from invasive species, wildfire, climate change and other human disturbances (from Pellant's presentation at the Conference).

Can Current Goals of Resource Institutions be Sustained Under Climate Change?

In the broader community of natural resource management, institutions set goals and strategies for their resources based on interest or legal mandate. Institutional objectives are likely set without regard to climate or with assumptions that climate, though variable is not changing. Several speakers identified the challenge of whether and how to readjust institutional goals under a changing climate.

Steve Malloch used metaphors to describe how institutions might face a potential change in their objectives: brakes, seat belts, and chickens. Brakes were the metaphor for prevention and mitigation, keep the institutional objectives but bring a focus on how to stop the change from occurring or going further. Seat belts were the metaphor for adaptation, recognize the changing climate and seek ways in natural resource management to adapt to those changes. Speakers gave examples where a United States institution may focus on the conservation of a species that, under a changing climate, may no longer find habitat in the lower 48 states. Does the United States institution broaden to North American objectives and focus on the species in Canada? In discussing preservation, the question was raised as to what can really be preserved? Many participants in the workshop responded that preservation may not be a solution under a changing climate. The last metaphor referred to an event or issue that disrupts the chickens in the barnyard, tossing the chickens in the air. This scattering of the barnyard would force a total reconsideration of options such as current discussions about changing from a fossil fuel economy raises reconsideration of nuclear power. The question of how to face changes in institutional and organizational objectives were seen as

Many participants in the workshop responded that preservation may not be a solution under a changing climate.

even more critical for organizations and institutions that focus on more local landscapes than regional or national groups.

Institutions or owners tied to a particular landscape face other management problems. Kyle Martin discussed climate data needs on tribal lands and the different risks associated with different tribal lands under a changing climate. The West is a mix of multiple ownerships and land managers each with unique management objectives and perceptions of risk. These differing resource management goals challenge management of vegetation and hydrological changes across ownerships.

The broad scale nature of climate change and how human perception of and response to it varies complicates governance efforts. For example, discussions of how to manage potential changes to river flow from climate change will eventually involve managers of various ecosystem components such as fish, rivers, land use, and will raise questions about who has the authority to make management decisions. In addition there already is a mix of market and regulatory functions that have evolved to guide land management activities. These include very formal processes for federal forestlands that involve stakeholder participation and few apparent processes for privately owned forestland other than for being compliant with state forest practice acts that influence the design and applications of forest management practices. All of this raises questions about the necessity of policy intervention, how to accomplish it, and the form it needs to take to address climate change.

> Since public lands dominate much of the western landscape, management activities are in the public eye...

Institutional and Individual Perceptions of Adaptation, Mitigation, and Risk

The conference included managers and land owners who manage for a diversity of objectives from relatively intensive to custodial. The land managers represented a variety of institutions and organizations, some where only a few individuals are involved in decision-making to institutions where planning is a public process. Since public lands dominate much of the western landscape, management activities are in the public eye and changing objectives and management on public lands to respond to a changing climate involves the acceptance of the relevant publics.

Discussions revealed differences in various perceptions of the threat of a changing climate, proposed management responses, associated costs, and the calculation of risks associated with potential threats of climate change. Public and institutional perceptions of environmental change influence efforts to deal with that change. There is public skepticism of the science associated with climate change—many individuals in the public want to see environmental changes before deciding how to act. Part of the issue is that managers and scientists communicate risks in terms of threats to safety and property but many in the public react to broader threats such as impacts on community or ecological well-being. Another way to consider this is that many people do not put climate into their problem framing.

> There is public skepticism of the science associated with climate change—many individuals in the public want to see environmental changes before deciding how to act.

Courtney Flint described one situation (the Spruce Bark Beetle outbreak on the Kenai Peninsula, Alaska) where the public does perceive the link between changing climate and the loss of local forests to increased disturbances. There the threat of changing climate has manifested itself in large scale forest die-off and management responses are now being framed that consider climate.

Several aspects of the discussion suggested that managers are starting to reframe their management problems to include climate. Currently much of this reframing is reactive but more proactive approaches are possible as forest or range managers include climate in their management frameworks. For example, forest managers could do this by developing yield functions that are sensitive to climate.

Jim Stevens described the active management regimes characteristic of a timber investment organization where the challenges and risks to the timber inventory were constantly being recalibrated in order for the company to take action to maintain their investment. Companies approach risk by diversification of their portfolios, and through geographic diversification and species mix. He described potential climate change impacts to forestry and their related costs—higher extreme events such as fire danger and the higher costs of fire monitoring and suppression, insect damage, drought, invasive species, shorter dormancy and potential increases in reforestation problems, shorter dormancy. These approaches do not yet incorporate climate variables—precipitation, temperature, soil water—so managers are unable to estimate the impact of climate change on net returns to forest management investments.

Institutions and organizations may also have to address new policy and management objectives, such as fuels management, carbon sequestration, and biomass energy. These represent a possible suite of changing or additional objectives for natural resource management in the Western United States. Darius Adams described forest management activities that could increase the carbon storage in forests (fig. 5). Matt Delaney described the international and national policies with respect to carbon sequestration and the carbon accounting activities, such as carbon sequestration in forests. Most of this activity has been in the East or Midwest. Overwhelmingly there was a lack of knowledge among the participants about how energy policy and climate change policy were moving, particularly in terms of carbon sequestration, what role forests might play and what the benefits might be to land owners. Bill Carlson described the biomass energy arena, the current challenges to developing biomass energy as well as the current possibilities. In the course of managing forests and rangelands, Bill Carlson noted that managers can contribute to the reduction in greenhouse gas generation by the management methods chosen. Biomass growth, utilization and disposal is theoretically greenhouse gas neutral, but some disposal methods generate large quantities of methane and other hydrocarbons, upsetting the balance and increasing global warming potential. For biomass power, Bill described the outlook is best in 15 years, as fossil fuel prices are increasing, renewables (solar, wind) in favor (19 states with renewable portfolio standards), tax credits are being enacted, and forest fuel subsidies

Overwhelmingly there was a lack of knowledge among the participants about how energy policy and climate change policy were moving, particularly in terms of carbon sequestration, what role forests might play and what the benefits might be to land owners.

— Options for Raising Net Forest Carbon Flux —

- ■ Regulating Forest Area
  - ❑ Afforestation Of Agricultural Lands
    - ● Major Source Of Large, Long-Term Increments
    - ● Restricted Time Pattern Of Flux Changes
    - ● Difficulties Tracing Carbon In Use Changes
  - ❑ Reducing Forest Land Losses To Other Uses
    - ● Large Potential
    - ● Can Have Immediate Impact—Carbon Losses Averted
- ■ Altering Management In Currently Forested Areas
  - ❑ Existing Stands (Rotation Age, Intermediate Practices)
  - ❑ New Stands (Regeneration Practices, Intermediate Treatments And Rotation
  - ❑ Can Provide Large, Near-Term Carbon Increments
  - ❑ Analytical Problems
    - ● Establishing A Credible Baseline
    - ● Simulating Policy Instruments

Figure 5—Activities to increase carbon storage in forests (from Adams Presentation at the Conference)

are being considered in energy policy. Land managers have tools to lower greenhouse gas emissions in forest management activities while preserving carbon inventory and preparing the land for an increased rate of carbon sequestration, but Bill cautioned that managers must be aware of the methods and conditions that will allow them to attract the infrastructure necessary to accomplish this management objective.

Regulations that companies deal with may change, such as climate warming the stream temperatures and then regulations in forestry changing to deal with this management issue for fisheries. Most land managers are concerned about the regulatory risks from climate change effects.

In the presentations and in the discussion period, it was clear that the terms participants used had different definitions depending upon the context in which they operated—disciplines, careers, and perspectives. Common definitions may not be possible, so it is very important to state the context out of which a person comes. Adaptation, mitigation, and restoration were some terms that had different definitions depending upon if the proponent was an ecologist or a social scientist. Short versus long terms was also in the observer's eye. Risks and uncertainty were commonly misunderstood across a diverse set of participants. For example, Benjamin Harding offered a clarification of the definition of variability—the effect of change, and uncertainty—imperfections in the state of our knowledge. He suggested that there are two components to uncertainty: measurement error and what we don't actually know (such as being surprised by something that was not considered).

> Most land managers are concerned about the regulatory risks from climate change effects.

Finally, there is confusion about who in the West is in charge of broad scale environmental issues. While there is general agreement that individual actions contribute to environmental issues globally and locally, there are diverse viewpoints about how to govern cross boundary problems. Benjamin Harding offered that climate change issues might be addressed through the wisdom of crowds where a diversity of opinions from individuals who are independent from one and other could be aggregated efficiently to develop a management or policy solution. There was agreement that there are many solutions to addressing climate change in natural resource management and that encouraging a diversity of responses is very important for ecological as well as economic resilience.

Participant Reflections About Resource Management Under a Changing Climate

The question for managers is how to plan strategies today for the world of tomorrow. Participants suggested a number of concepts for future management of natural resources under a changing climate.

Recognize a Changing Relationship Between Climate and Ecosystems

Management must look forward to an uncertain context, rather than backward to a presumed certain historical potential natural vegetation. Much effort has gone into determining the range of natural variability in western ecosystems. This effort has given a detailed picture of the past relationship of climate and ecosystems, how ecosystems respond to the variability in climate and other natural disturbances. It is not clear how well past climate will adequately predict future climate. If climate is changing, then the past relationship between climate and ecosystems will change. Ecosystems, plants and animals have adapted to these local climates and will respond to changes in climate.

Ron Neilson identified the need to improve resilience of ecosystems to rapid climate change. Future climates may be drier either through increased temperature and/or reduced precipitation. Given this possible change, his recommendation is to keep forest stand biomass below the water-limiting capacity, so that the stress is lessened. Looking at the water limiting capacity of a forest would be recognition of the changing relationship between climate and forests.

Manage Ecosystems as Dynamic Systems Not as Static Systems

Management must develop the ability to deal with variation; work with the dynamics in natural systems rather than managing the systems as static. In contrast, intensive management is a case where managers are trying to take advantage of existing dynamics. In many recent management approaches especially on public lands there is the assumption that extensive or custodial management of natural resources will help the ecosystem to restore itself. This works when the processes for resilience have not been disrupted, as potentially under a changing climate. In addition, Gordon Reeves pointed out that some systems like aquatics require periodic disturbance to maintain resilience.

Manage Ecosystems with Agility

Pete Holmberg stressed hedging and not over-reacting. Forests should be managed with an agility—making modest changes that do not limit management in the future—that recognizes various possible contingencies. Although Pacific Northwest forests have life spans indicating genetic resilience to historic climate change, forest health may still suffer through insect, diseases and fire. Proactive management and mixed stands is a prudent approach. He described forest health insurance as diversity plus agility plus vigor.

Bring Climate into the Planning and Management Processes

Climate change potentially has implications to many forest and rangeland uses: livestock grazing, water quantity and quality, recreation, hunting, social and economic uses. It also has implications to the success of any restoration treatment—will the result be as we expect or another vegetation type developing? Mike Pellant recommended these changes to land planning: (1) Incorporate climate change into long-term planning, (2) Emphasize flexibility in plan alternatives until science is more definitive and (3) Adaptive management. Research and monitoring western rangelands is important, as is education and outreach, to make the public aware of these potential changes in western rangelands.

Gary Lettman described the Oregon Department of Forestry focus on sustainability management and a policy of enhancing carbon storage in Oregon's forests. The 2010 Assessment of Oregon's forest included the consideration of climate change in the landscape analyses.

But several speakers emphasized that the real challenge was to get the science to the local planning level. How, they ask, can local managers respond to perspective changes without some indication of how the resources they manage be impacted?

Information Needs of Managers

Speakers and small group discussions suggested a number of information needs for resource managers in the Western United States. The information needs that evolved from the Roundtable Discussions are described in more detail (White and Barbour, this report). How these information needs were to be solved was not discussed. Recent observations of western natural resource management would suggest that resource agencies are pushing ahead to get this information internally or engaging researchers to work with them to obtain the needed information.

Local to subregional climate projections—Current climate models observe and project climate at very large simplified spatial scales. Nearly all resource managers identified the value and need for such information on the local scale. The utility of the large scale models is

Forests should be managed with an agility—making modest changes that do not limit management in the future…

…several speakers emphasized that the real challenge was to get the science to the local planning level.

particularly problematic for western resource managers where the West is topographically variable.

Hydrologic projections at appropriate scales—Water demand analyses utilize climate data. What is needed is the conversion of the climate scenario data into a format that can be readily used. Water managers in the Pacific Northwest worked with the Climate Impacts Group, University of Washington, to obtain such data for their future water demand analyses. Such information is needed by water managers in other parts of the western United States.

More local or locally adaptable models for forestry—Plants and animals adapt to the local climate. Models that reflected local conditions would enhance forest managers' ability to respond to these changes.

Vulnerability indices for ecosystems and for ecosystem components—An assessment of how vulnerable western ecosystems are to climate change would assist managers in prioritizing funds and tasks.

Monitoring protocols—What to monitor with respect to climate change was a question raised by resource managers. Identifying what to monitor and having a protocol to monitor would assist land managers in observing changes and developing management strategies for those changes. Participants also described the needs for both success and early warning indicators.

Clearing house for information at the regional scale—It was recognized by the conference participants that there is a wealth of information on climate and climate change impacts. A clearinghouse that would organize not just data on climate, and ecosystems, but also assessment studies and models was identified as an important need.

Conclusions

The presentations and discussions at the workshop illustrated the complexity of global climate change and they emphasized that the impacts of climate change will unfold on the regional and local stages. We were reminded repeatedly that little concerted action would take place until the issue could be described in relation to specific localities relevant to land managers. The discussions also revealed the wide spectrum of threat perceptions. There were scientists and managers who believed in the inevitability of climate change, there were managers who were willing to consider hedging future projections accepting climate change as one of many risks, and there were many who needed to perceive changes before forming perceptions about the threat. Finally, the broad scale nature of climate change complicates both the human perception of and response to it. One consequence of this is to consider how we govern forested ecosystems when forest management takes place across relatively large geographic spaces composed of many different landowners with a myriad of land management objectives. While no simple solutions emerged, there was an appreciation that policy complexity may exceed the science complexity.

Models that reflected local conditions would enhance forest managers' ability to respond to these changes.

We were reminded repeatedly that little concerted action would take place until the issue could be described in relation to specific localities relevant to land managers.

Finally, the workshop offered a glance of hope in that managers are already responding to those aspects of the global climate change that they can see or perceive. Eventually the accumulation of these local actions will shape our future. In this sense the workshop achieved its purpose in furthering the dialogue among early adopters of how individuals are addressing climate change in natural resource management. Through civic engagement, we can help reduce the complexity of the issue and increase the certainty of outcomes in the face of changing climate.

...managers are already responding to those aspects of the global climate change that they can see or perceive. Eventually the accumulation of these local actions will shape our future.

References

Haynes, R.W., tech. coord. 2003. An analysis of the timber situation in the United States: 1952 to 2050. Gen. Tech. Rep. PNW-GTR-560. Portland, OR: U.S. Department of Agriculture, Forest Service, Pacific Northwest Research Station. 254 p.

Haynes, R.W.; Adams, D.M.; Alig, R.J.; Ince, P.J.; Mills, J.R.; Zhou, X. [In prep.]. The 2005 RPA timber assessment update. Gen. Tech. Rep. PNW-GTR-xxx. On file with: Richard Haynes, Portland Forestry Sciences Laboratory, P.O. Box 3890, Portland, OR 97208.

Haynes, R.W.; Adams, D.M.; Mills, J.R. 1995. The 1993 RPA timber assessment update. Gen. Tech. Rep. RM-GTR-259. Fort Collins, CO: U.S. Department of Agriculture, Forest Service, Rocky Mountain Forest and Range Experiment Station. 66 p.

Joyce, L.A.; Mills, J.R.; Heath, L.S.; McGuire, A.D.; Haynes, R.W.; Birdsey, R.A. 1995. Forest sector impacts from changes in forest productivity under climate change. Journal of Biogeography. 22: 703-713.

Trenberth, K.E.; Houghton, J.T.; Filho, L.G. Meira. 1996. The climate system: an overview, Chapter 1. In: Houghton, J.T., Filho, L.G. Meira, Callander, B.A., Harris, N., Kattenberg, A., Maskell, K., eds. Climate Change 1995. Cambridge, England: Cambridge University Press: 51-64.

Wilkinson, C.F. 1992. Crossing the next meridian. Land, water, and the future of the West. Washington, DC: Island Press. 376 p.

Ziska, L.H. 2003. Evaluation of the growth response of six invasive species to past, present and future carbon dioxide concentrations. Journal of Experimental Botany 54:395-404.

The Roundtable Session

Rachel White[1] and Jamie Barbour[2]

USDA Forest Service

[1] Science Writer-Editor, USDA Forest Service, Pacific Northwest Research Station, P.O. Box 3890, Portland, OR 97208. Email: rachelwhite@fs.fed.us

[2] Program Manager, USDA Forest Service, Pacific Northwest Research Station, P.O. Box 3890, Portland, OR 97208. Email: jbarbour01@fs.fed.us

As Albert Einstein observed "You cannot solve current problems with current thinking. Current problems are the result of current thinking." In recognition of this, we wanted to try a more innovative way of presenting information. Most conferences are a combination of entertainment and education—they must promise topics interesting enough to pull people away from busy schedules, and they at least hold out the pretext of providing new information to the audience. But however you characterize most conferences, the audience is always a passive receptor. The Focused Science Delivery program is attempting to give the audience a voice; because although it is true that the presenters are considered the experts, we contend that the collective knowledge of the audience is probably as great as or greater than that of the presenters when the topic as a whole is considered. The "Bringing Climate Change into Natural Resource Management" conference was attended by 113 individuals representing 20 organizations, including government agencies, tribal organizations, conservation groups, and the timber industry. One of the goals of this workshop was to allow these practitioners to offer their ideas on the pressing problems they face in attempting to adapt management plans and policies in the face of a changing climate.

To this end, we set up a roundtable session, which got participants out of passive listening mode and into active brainstorming together. The roundtables were intended as the initial step in a problem framing process. This refers to the fact that different stakeholders have their own perspectives, interests, and priorities. The way an issue is "framed" reveals differences in the way stakeholders form interpretations of what is at stake and what approach should be taken. The importance of problem framing is being recognized in a small but growing literature (Bardwell 1991, Miller 1999, Stankey et al. 2005, Van Cleve et al. 2003).

We took 10 different topics relevant to current natural resource management—water, fisheries, silviculture, invasives, wildlife, preservation, management and policies for adaptation of western ecosystems, carbon policy, mitigation of human impacts, and science consistency—and assigned each topic to a table. Participants then selected their topic area of interest, and were given an hour to discuss their table's topic in light of the three following questions:

1. What information do you need in a natural resource management plan to address climate change?

2. What do you currently have that you could use to address the information needs identified in question 1?

3. What are the top 2 or 3 critical information needs and/or tools that you currently don't have that would help you make better decisions with respect to this management issue and adapting to climate change and variability?

Each group recorded major themes and ideas on a flip chart. Prior to the meeting the organizing committee had identified a leader for each table who was assigned the task of keeping the discussion focused on climate change. Each group also chose a "spokesperson," who reported back to the audience at large the main points discussed by their table.

...although it is true that the presenters are considered the experts, we contend that the collective knowledge of the audience is probably as great as or greater than that of the presenters when the topic as a whole is considered.

The purpose of the reports was twofold. First, to concisely summarize what was said, and second, to stimulate further conversation over the rest of the conference among the group members and others who did not participate in that particular group. Accordingly, each reporter was given two opportunities to report their findings. The first came at the end of the day the roundtable sessions were held. Each reporter was given 5 minutes to present the major points from the discussion, members of that group were given an opportunity to add missing information, and the general audience was encouraged to ask clarifying questions.

At the end of that day's session the audience was reminded to talk among themselves about what they had discussed at their respective tables and what they had heard during the initial set of summary reports. The second opportunity for reports came at the end of the conference when table reporters were asked to present a synthesis of the most important points of their roundtable discussions, the conversations they had after the first reporting, and any other related interactions with other conference participants. They were reminded that the intent of the exercise was to present the views of the audience not necessarily their own views.

We also included a note-taker at each table during the discussions. This person was instructed to be as unobtrusive as possible and to record the conversation as accurately as possible. The note-taker was allowed to ask clarifying questions but not to take part in the conversation itself. The note-taker's goal was to record what was said but not necessarily by whom.

Together these techniques provided three sources of information in addition to our own observations. They were: flip chart notes from each table, note-taker notes from the roundtable discussions, and notes from the table leader presentations. We compiled those bits of information into the narrative that follows.

The 10 tables covered topics big and small—from seed sources to public awareness to landscape connectivity—as participants confronted the uncertainties and challenges surrounding climate change. But around the room common topics began to emerge. The major themes we will emphasize in this narrative were distilled from these common threads, as we could not include all the ideas and issues brought up at all 10 tables.

Better information and better access

Participants identified a wealth of information that is currently available, such as the climate and ecological published literature, results from global studies, and results from ecological models. However, participants frequently mentioned the need for improved access to information and studies, in progress or completed. They said they find information to be scattered, or displayed as stand-alone scientific facts that are never translated into management implications. Because of this, knowing what's known and what might be useful is a problem. For example, there have been some regional risk assessments that address large scale changes in forest response to carbon and climate already. But it is unclear whether this information is finding its way into use, and some managers at the roundtable session mentioned it would be more useful if it could be made available at smaller scales.

> participants…said they find information to be scattered, or displayed as stand-alone scientific facts that are never translated into management implications.

Another area where participants need better access to information involves carbon sequestration, which has significant implications for forest management. In fact, there is growing recognition that land management strategies that aim at increasing the volume of carbon storage in forests could make a considerable impact on global CO_2 concentrations (Peterson et al. 2004). But managing for carbon storage can have complex and potentially unintended consequences. As one participant noted, sequestering carbon by letting trees grow generates fire hazard. Society has only relatively recently begun to recognize the impact on forest health and fire risk that a century of aggressive fire suppression has had, and that many fire-adapted forests need to be thinned or burned regularly. For forest managers, the tradeoffs between fuel treatments and carbon sequestration might become a serious management consideration.

Other information requests focused on expanding current understanding of natural resource dynamics and ecological systems by looking at the influence of climate variability on these systems. For example, information requests included identifying and mapping "sleeper" invasive species (ones that aren't a problem now but that might experience increased vigor and expansion with climate change variations); information on climate change impacts on growth and yield; and a synthesis of literature on ecosystem resilience under climate change. "We need to get at how to make communities as resilient as possible [given expected climate variation]," said one participant. "How do we build pools of biodiversity? How do you create a landscape with corridors and refugia that allows movement but so you don't lose the specialists?"

Data, models, projections

Climate change involves such unstable systems on such a grand scale that there is no way to conduct experiments on how the global climate changes. Because of this, climate science relies heavily on large sets of historical records of climate and other environmental data, and on computer models and simulations. Participants recognized the value of long-term records of temperature and precipitation and also the need for better access to these records. They also identified the need for long-term data on climate-related factors such as hydrological data and snow pack data, particularly for local conditions. Often a finer time scale is needed by managers, such as daily records. Sometimes this information exists, but inconsistently. For example, there are approximately 2,200 interagency Remote Automated Weather Stations across the U.S. that collect weather data. They provide a useful source of information, but because they are currently used mainly by the fire-fighting community, they don't operate in the winter. Year-round data collection at would make this information source even more valuable to managers.

Participants also recognized the need for reasonable projections and usable computer models in their work. For example, they want to know how precipitation will change in the next 50-100 years. Scientific projections showing increases in temperature are fairly robust, but there is greater variability in the precipitation projections. Participants identified a need for this projection information, especially at a scale relevant to management plans or models currently in use.

"How do we build pools of biodiversity? How do you create a landscape with corridors and refugia that allows movement but so you don't lose the specialists?"

Participants would also like localized projections of climate change impact on plant associations, insects, disease, fire risk, and adaptive plant movement zones; a better description of the interactions between climate change and other threats such as land use changes and human population changes; accurate species-based habitat models that could be used to monitor changes over time; and vulnerability maps that identify species most sensitive to climate change. There are models managers currently use that need to have climate added as a component, such as the growth and yield models used in silviculture, and in hydrological forecasting models. In general, better modeling of potential threats is crucial to constructing climate change response strategies in management plans. In the face of so much uncertainty, and without some precautionary help from models and projections, it is extremely difficult to balance the risks of either insufficient or excessive action.

Monitoring

Species have evolved adaptive mechanisms that allow them to adjust to, or at least tolerate, short-term fluctuations without serious damage. For example, many plants and animals can accommodate a week of record temperatures, or a few months of drought. But these adjustments create small impacts that accumulate over time, and in the face of longer or more extreme disturbances, the elasticity of these systems begins to wear thin (Pollack 2003). At a certain threshold, systems that had been adapting will begin to break down. Without monitoring this progression, it will be impossible to anticipate these thresholds and do anything to intervene. Participants grappled at length with this issue, and came up with several information gaps and questions.

For example, rather than trying to protect a single species, how do you protect the landscapes that can serve as habitat for multiple species? How do you then measure this? "We need a monitoring strategy of physical systems at a scale that matters," said one person. "It must be cheap and easy to measure, and it must be tailored to the resource." It must also be conducted with climate change in mind. One thing to remember is that climate change will certainly change habitat conditions, which may allow for migration or dispersal of some species, reduce the range of others, and create new interactions between native species and invasives. Given this potential for movement and habitat loss, it would probably be a good idea to monitor genetic heterogeneity of populations over time to measure whether they are becoming more genetically isolated and homogeneous. There is also a need to continue tracking changes in diseases, pathogens, and insects and their impacts. Finally, climate change will involve an increased need to monitor water supply, water storage, and soil moisture, because projections forecast changes in average precipitation in many regions.

Negotiating regulations

The ability to manage forests under future climate regimes rests heavily on a better understanding of the processes at work, and on better access to good scientific information. But it also rests on the policies

In the face of so much uncertainty, and without some precautionary help from models and projections, it is extremely difficult to balance the risks of either insufficient or excessive action.

...climate change will involve an increased need to monitor water supply, water storage, and soil moisture, because projections forecast changes in average precipitation in many regions.

and regulations that guide (and sometimes restrict) natural resource management planning. Regulations such as the Endangered Species Act (ESA), and the National Environmental Policy Act (NEPA), were founded on the assumption of static vegetative composition and don't incorporate flexibility. As a result, active management tends to be reactive as opposed to agile and adaptable. How can the ESA protect species under climate change if it doesn't include awareness of habitat changes?

Discussion at the roundtable session often led back to the need for a good sense of tactical options and solutions available under current policy structures. In other words, given the range of genetic variation in forest stands, and given what's likely to happen as climate changes, what silvicultural options are open to us? What treatment alternatives based on rotation length, rate of carbon storage and carbon expenditure are available? A potential approach would be to provide an array of options for forest managers and policy makers to consider, and to inspire more flexibility.

In addition, we heard from participants that it would be helpful to have some idea of how states differ in their energy policies and politics, and what direction energy policy may be headed in. For instance, with the current increase in gas prices will we still be using as much gasoline in the future? Will we rely more on wood to provide energy? Looking at energy, woody biofuel, carbon sequestration, and fire risk together could aid managers in formulating the multiple strategies that might go into a management plan that incorporates climate change. Another concern participants mentioned is the need for economically viable opportunities to deal with climate change, such as harvesting small diameter timber. Is there an accessible infrastructure (rails to move product)? There have been several studies exploring the relationships between timber markets and climate change, in fact there is a large amount of information available on carbon, climate change, and forests, but it is rarely addressed in management plans. Some of our participants admitted knowing that information exists, but find it difficult to keep up with it or even locate it. This suggests that assisting practitioners in finding information when they need it could be valuable.

Many managers acknowledged that the challenges of coping with climate change go beyond better information and better access to it. Actions are often constrained by current policies and local management practices. And it's difficult to motivate change in natural resource management based on potential future changes when there are many pressing issues facing managers already, such as fire risk, insect outbreaks, and increasing demand for water supply in the West. Still, even though it may be challenging to address climate change at a local project level, that's where many decisions are made, and all our participants agreed that the potential impacts of climate change on natural resources will need to be addressed at the local level. This task will involve viewing ecosystems as dynamic systems, synthesizing information across land ownerships, and evaluating risk based on climate change impacts and other disturbances.

Discussion at the roundtable session often led back to the need for a good sense of tactical options and solutions available under current policy structures.

…participants agreed that the potential impacts of climate change on natural resources will need to be addressed at the local level.

114

Summary

The deliberations of our roundtable participants formed a clearer idea of the management implications and information needs associated with climate change. After distilling the many comments and questions we heard at the roundtable sessions, we've summarized some of general recommendations we heard from participants for successful integration of science and management in coping with this issue.

Looking back

To put climate change into perspective, we need an understanding of historical context. Tracking historical data on how different vegetation has responded to variations in temperature and precipitation can provide insight into how we might anticipate future change. Similarly, understanding how different systems have responded to past disturbances provide clues as to what makes a system resilient.

Looking ahead

We need to continually improve the tools we have that can show what's going on and what's most likely to happen. We also need to make sure these tools are available and accessible. Computer models and projections may include a lot of uncertainty but can still help in guiding decisions. We might think of heading into the future as akin to driving at night: our computer models act as headlights, dimly illuminating the road ahead, and we may not be able to see much, but maybe we can at least stay on the right road. The more accurate and accessible our modeling tools are, the better able we are to maintain flexibility and adapt our management objectives as the future unfolds.

Collaboration

A common concern among our participants was the disconnection between research and management, and between various agencies and organizations. Many agencies manage as if they were islands and get overwhelmed when trying to view the uncertain path ahead from the vantage point of their resources, time, and energy alone. The task may become easier if we can join forces, work across agency boundaries, and pool information and resources. This would help in terms of consistency of data and better ability to identify trends, but also would enable groups to learn from each other's mistakes and triumphs. "We need a peer group so we can interact and share hypotheses and success stories," said one participant. "Are there any examples out there? Are there management plans out there that incorporate climate change that we can work from?"

Communication

There is no longer much scientific debate as to whether climate change is happening. But confusion about the potential consequences and what we should do to counteract or accommodate these consequences, along with an inability to fully grasp a phenomenon that operates on an entire planet on a time scale that exceeds life spans and even generations,

> Many agencies manage as if they were islands and get overwhelmed when trying to view the uncertain path ahead from the vantage point of their resources, time, and energy alone.

creates an aura of disbelief, hesitation, and doubt. To get the attention and support of a public immobilized by the uncertainties of climate change, managers need an interpretive tool, such as graphically displayed, distilled information. Scientists can respond by making this information easier for the public to understand and easier for managers to make use of.

Meanwhile, new international climate data indicates that 2005 is shaping up to be the hottest year on record, with 2002, 2003, and 2004 not far behind on the list. And sea surface temperatures in the Gulf of Mexico were higher in August of this year than at any time since 1890, which may have contributed to the intensity of the hurricane season there. And while we still can't attribute any single weather event to climate change, we can recognize that extreme weather events have been increasing in the past few decades. There is no reason to believe that climate change will disappear, and it may even become more difficult for natural resource managers to deal with in the future, especially if policy and implementation continue to lag behind scientific discovery. But identifying information gaps is crucial, and it is our hope that these roundtable discussions will result in an increased focus on the role of management in addressing climate change, and will improve the delivery of good science to the practitioners who need it. During our discussions there was a realistic and sobering acknowledgement of the uncertainties that lie ahead, and that there is often a tendency to succumb to hesitance or irresolution in the face of this confusion. But confusion is the beginning of knowledge, and we hope that we can turn information gaps into an opportunity, and use uncertainty as a stimulus for creativity.

> There is no reason to believe that climate change will disappear, and it may even become more difficult for natural resource managers to deal with in the future, especially if policy and implementation continue to lag behind scientific discovery.

References

Bardwell, L.V. 1991. Problem-framing: a perspective on environmental problem-solving. Environmental Management 15(5): 603-612.

Endangered Species Act of 1973 [ESA]; U.S.C. 16: 531-1536, 1538-1540.

Miller, A. 1999. Environmental problem solving: psychological barriers to adaptive change. New York: Springer-Verlag. 239 p.

National Environmental Policy Act of 1969 [NEPA]; 42 U.S.C. 4321 et seq.

Peterson, D.L.; Innes, J.L.; O'Brian, K. 2004. Climate change, carbon, and forestry in northwestern North America: Proceedings of a workshop. November 14-15, 2001, Orcas Island, Washington. Gen. Tech. Rep. PNW-GTR-614. U.S. Department of Agriculture, Forest Service, Pacific Northwest Research Station: Portland, OR.

Pollack, H. 2003. Uncertain science, Uncertain world. Cambridge, UK: Cambridge University Press. 243 p.

Stankey, G.H.; Clark, R.N.; Bormann, B.T. 2005. Adaptive management of natural resources: theory, concepts, and management institutions. Gen. Tech. Rep. PNW-GTR-654. Portland, OR: U.S. Department of Agriculture, Forest Service, Pacific Northwest Research Station. 73 p.

Van Cleve, F.B.; Simenstad, C.; Goetz, F.; Mumford, T. 2003. Application of "best available science" in ecosystem restoration: lessons learned from large-scale restoration efforts in the U.S. Puget Sound Nearshore Ecosystem Restoration Project. 38 p. http://www.pugetsoundnearshore.org.

The Potential for Widespread, Threshold Dieback of Forests in North America Under Rapid Global Warming

R.P. Neilson[1], J.M. Lenihan[1], D. Bachelet[2], R.J. Drapek[1], D. Price[3], D. Scott[4]

Erik Ackerson, EarthDesign, Ink

[1]Bioclimatologist, Ecosystem Modeler, Ecosystem Modeler/GIS Technician USDA Forest Service, PNW Research Station, 3200 S.W. Jefferson Way, Corvallis, OR 97331; Email: rneilson@fs.fed.us; jlenihan@fs.fed.us; rdrapek@fs.fed.us

[2]Associate Professor, Department of BioEngineering, Oregon State University, Corvallis, OR 97331; Email: bachelet@fsl.orst.edu

[3]Research Scientist, Integrative Climate Change Impacts Modelling, Canadian Forest Service, Northern Forestry Centre, 5320 - 122 Street, Edmonton, AB, T6H 3S5; Email: dprice@nrcan.gc.ca

[4]Canada Research Chair in Global Change and Tourism, Department of Geography, University of Waterloo, Waterloo, ON, N2L 3G1; Email: dj2scott@fes.uwaterloo.ca

Abstract

The MC1 Dynamic General Vegetation Model (DGVM) was used to assess the impacts of global warming on North American ecosystems, north of Mexico, under six future climate scenarios (three General Circulation Models X two emission scenarios). The simulations were begun in 1900 using observed climate and CO_2 until 2000, then transferring to the future scenarios to 2100. Carbon sequestration over the continent occurred in the late 20th century and for a short period into the 21st century, being fostered largely by increased precipitation, enhanced water-use efficiency and mild temperature increases. However, these 'greening' processes were overtaken by the exponential effects of increasing temperature on evaporative demand and respiration, producing a subsequent decline. Simulation experiments suggested that fire suppression could significantly mitigate the carbon losses, yet many ecosystems were still forced to a lower carrying capacity.

Keywords: Global warming, carbon balances, ecosystem dynamics.

Discussion

With the exception of the tundra, which is invaded by the boreal forest, all major forested ecosystems in North America exhibit carbon sequestration until the late 20th or early 21st century, followed by a drought-induced decline...

An assessment of North American carbon balance and ecosystem dynamics, including changing vegetation distribution and fire disturbance, in 'natural' ecosystems has been undertaken. The VINCERA project (Vulnerability and Impacts of North American forests to Climate: Ecosystem Responses and Adaptation) is an intercomparison among three dynamic general vegetation models (DGVMs) running under six new future climate scenarios. The scenarios were produced by three general circulation models (GCMs), each using two different future trace gas emissions scenarios, SRES A2 and B2. The GCM scenarios are from the Canadian Climate Centre (CGCM2), the Hadley Centre (HADCM3) and Australia (CSIRO-MK2). The three DGVMs are MC1, IBIS and SDGVM. All of the scenarios are near the warmer end of the Intergovernmental Panel on Climate Change's projected future temperature range.

We present here only the results from MC1 (Daly et al. 2000). With the exception of the tundra, which is invaded by the boreal forest, all major forested ecosystems in North America exhibit carbon sequestration until the late 20th or early 21st century, followed by a drought-induced decline and loss of carbon to levels below those at 1900 in the absence of fire suppression (fig. 1). By the end of the 21st century in the absence of fire suppression, the entire continent will have lost from 10 to 30 Pg of carbon, depending on the scenario. However, fire suppression can significantly mitigate carbon losses and ecosystem declines, producing a net change in carbon from a loss of about 5 Pg to a gain of about 8 Pg under the different scenarios (fig. 2). Most of the suppression benefits are obtained in the Western U.S. forests. However, suppression also mitigates carbon losses and conversions to savanna or grassland in the Eastern United States, but forest decline still occurs in the East under all scenarios.

ort   meri a
it   ire

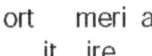

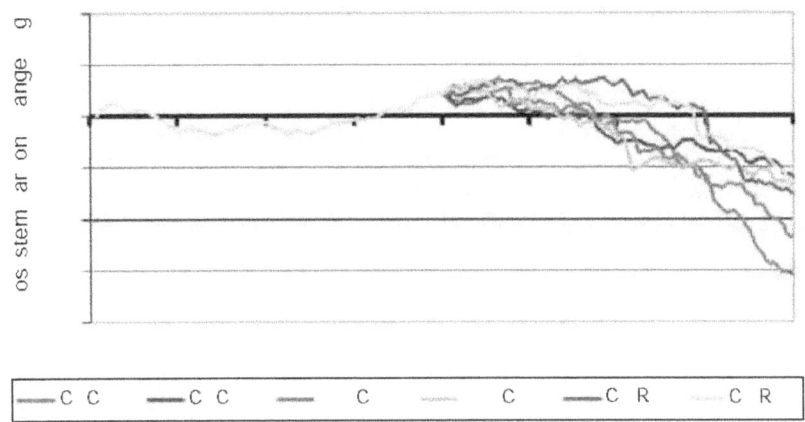

Figure 1—Net gain or loss of carbon from North American Ecosystems under climate change, without fire suppression.

Tom Iraci, USDA Forest Service

ort   meri a
ire s   ression

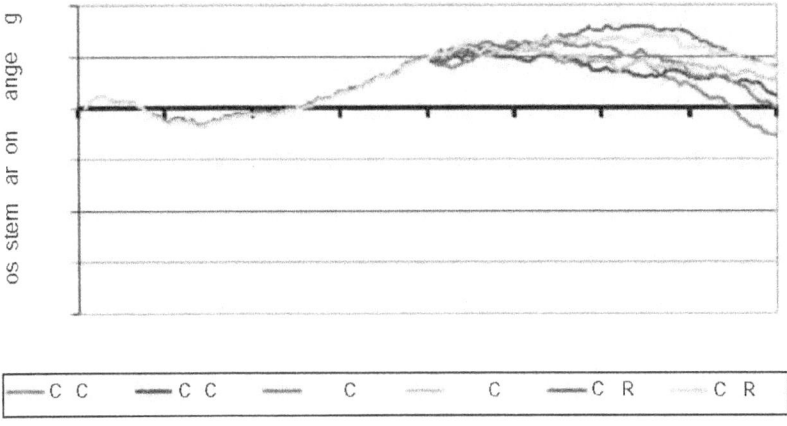

Figure 2—Net gain or loss of carbon from North American Ecosystems under climate change, with fire suppression.

The MC1 simulations produce a significant dieback in Eastern U.S. forests under all scenarios as well as excursions of the central grasslands into the boreal forest zone. Dieback is triggered under two mechanisms. Reduced regional precipitation patterns, variable among the scenarios, are one mechanism for dieback. However, a more insidious and more pervasive effect is due to the exponential influence of rising temperatures on evapotranspiration (ET). Even with the benefits of enhanced water use efficiency from elevated CO_2 and slight increases in precipitation, dramatic increases in temperature can produce widespread, very rapid forest dieback, followed by infestations and fires. The Eastern United States appears to be particularly vulnerable to this sequence of processes, as does the central boreal forest. The reason for the widespread sensitivity of these forests is the relative flatness of the climate gradients. If one locale is near a transition from forest to savanna, then so too are large neighboring locales.

Under some scenarios, dieback is driven by both increasing temperatures and decreasing precipitation in some regions, notably the Southeastern United States and the Northwestern United States. Following a period of gradual carbon sequestration, the enhanced ET appears to overtake the 'greening' processes producing a rapid dieback. The dieback occurs over North America within a few decades from now, initiating an extended period of rapid losses of ecosystem carbon.

Note added in Proof: Recent findings on the strength of the CO_2 effect have been incorporated in new simulations in the VINCERA project. The conclusions are not qualitatively changed. However, the strength of potential sequestration under fire suppression is increased in both eastern and western forests (figs. 3, 4). The level of dieback of eastern forests is somewhat reduced and can even be reversed with active fire suppression or exclusion, in some scenarios. Overall, the continent sequesters carbon, even with no fire suppression, with gains being greater under the hotter A2 scenarios due to the enhanced CO_2 effect (fig. 3, average 32 Pg compared to 16 Pg under B2). With active fire suppression or exclusion continental carbon sequestration by the end of the 21st century under the A2 scenarios averaged 63 Pg compared to 36 Pg under the B2 scenarios (fig. 4). It must be emphasized that there is still uncertainty as to whether the higher or more modest CO_2 effect will be more realistic in the long run, since the data come from relatively young stands.

e eren es

Daly, C.; Bachelet, D.; Lenihan, J.M.; Parton, W.; Neilson, R.P.; Ojima, D. 2000. Dynamic simulation of tree-grass interactions for global change studies. Ecological Applications. 10: 449-469.

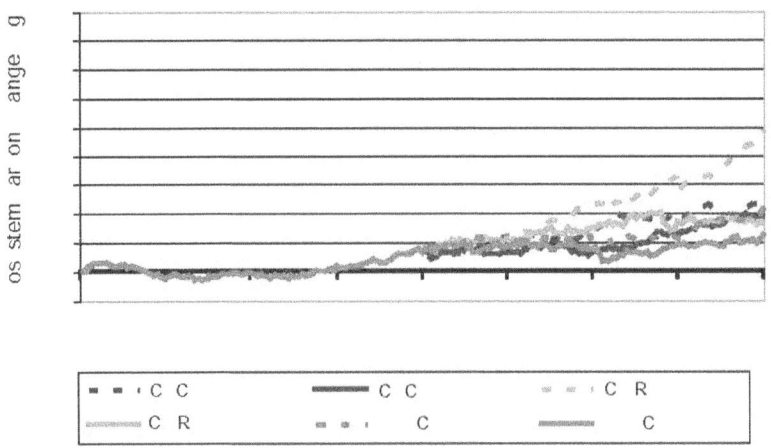

Figure 3—Net gain or loss of carbon from North American Ecosystems under climate change (using an enhanced effect of CO_2 on production and water use efficiency), without fire suppression.

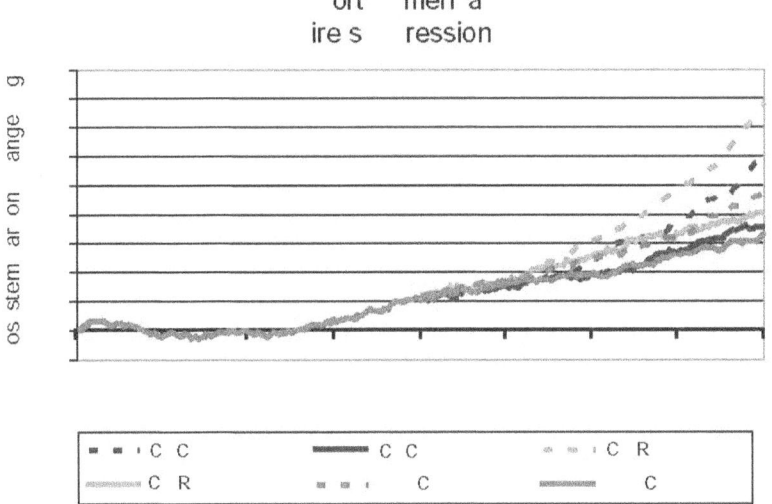

Figure 4—Net gain or loss of carbon from North American Ecosystems under climate change (using an enhanced effect of CO2 on production and water use efficiency), with fire suppression.

Erik Ackerson, EarthDesign, Ink

Predicting Climate-Induced Range Shifts for Mammals: How Good are the Models?

Joshua J. Lawler[1], Denis White[2], Ronald P. Neilson[3], Andrew R. Blaustein[4]

Gary Kramer, U.S. Fish and Wildlife Service

Robert Karges II, U.S. Fish and Wildlife Service

Brian Anderson, U.S. Fish and Wildlife Service

[1]David H. Smith Postdoctoral Fellow, Department of Zoology, Oregon State University, c/o U.S. Environmental Protection Agency, 200 SW 35th St., Corvallis, OR 97333; Email: Lawler.Joshua@epa.gov

[2]Geographer, U.S. Environmental Protection Agency, 200 SW 35th St., Corvallis, Corvallis, OR 97333; Email: white.denis@epa.gov

[3]USDA Forest Service, PNW Research Station, 3200 S.W. Jefferson Way, Corvallis, OR 97331; Email: rneilson@fs.fed.us

[4]Professor, Department of Zoology, Oregon State University, Corvallis, OR 97331; Email: blaustea@science.oregonstate.edu

Extended Abstract

Recent climatic changes have had clear impacts on biological systems (Parmesan and Yohe 2003, Root et al. 2003). Because changes in the earth's climate in the coming century are predicted to be at least twice as large as those seen in the past 100 years (Houghton et al. 2001), we are likely to see even more dramatic changes in ecological systems. One of the basic responses to climate change is a shift in species geographic ranges (Parmesan et al. 1999). In order to manage wildlife and conserve biodiversity in the coming century, it is critical that we understand the potential impacts of climate change on species distributions.

Several different approaches to predicting climate-induced geographic range shifts have been proposed to address this problem (Segurado and Araújo 2004). Unfortunately, no one approach has yet been found that consistently performs well for modeling a large number of species. We investigated the potential implications of using different bioclimatic modeling approaches for conclusions drawn about future climate-induced range shifts and extinctions. Using the current ranges of 100 mammal species found in the Western Hemisphere, we compared six methods for modeling their predicted future ranges including generalized linear models (McCullagh and Nelder 1989), classification trees (Breiman et al. 1984), generalized additive models (Hastie and Tibshirani 1990), random forest predictors (Breiman 2001), artificial neural networks (Ripley 1996), and genetic algorithms for rule-set prediction (GARP, Peterson et al. 2002).

All approaches modeled current ranges as a function of current climate and current land cover. Models were built with a subset of 80 percent of the data and tested using the reserved 20 percent of the data. Future ranges were predicted using predicted future climatic conditions and predicted future land cover. Future climate projections were taken from the Hadley Climate Centre's HADCM2SUL model (Johns et al. 1997) using Intergovernmental Panel on Climate Change (IPCC) predicted future greenhouse gas contributions (IS92a) for the years 2061-2090 (Kattenberg et al. 1996). Predicted future land cover was produced using the Mapped Atmospheric Plant-Soil-System model (MAPSS) (Neilson 1995).

Predicted future distributions differed markedly across the alternative modeling approaches (e.g., fig. 1). These differences resulted in estimates of extinction rates that ranged from 0 to 7 percent, depending on which modeling approach was used. Random Forest predictors, a model-averaging approach, consistently outperformed the other techniques (correctly predicting > 99 percent of current absences and 86 percent of current presences). Random forest models were the top-ranked model based on omission and commission error rates for 88 percent of the species.

Our results support previous studies that conclude that uncertainties in bioclimatic models can be large, often overshadowing the uncertainty in climate-change predictions from general circulation models (Thuiller et al. 2004). We conclude that the types of models used in a study can have

...to manage wildlife and conserve biodiversity in the coming century, it is critical that we understand the potential impacts of climate change on species distributions.

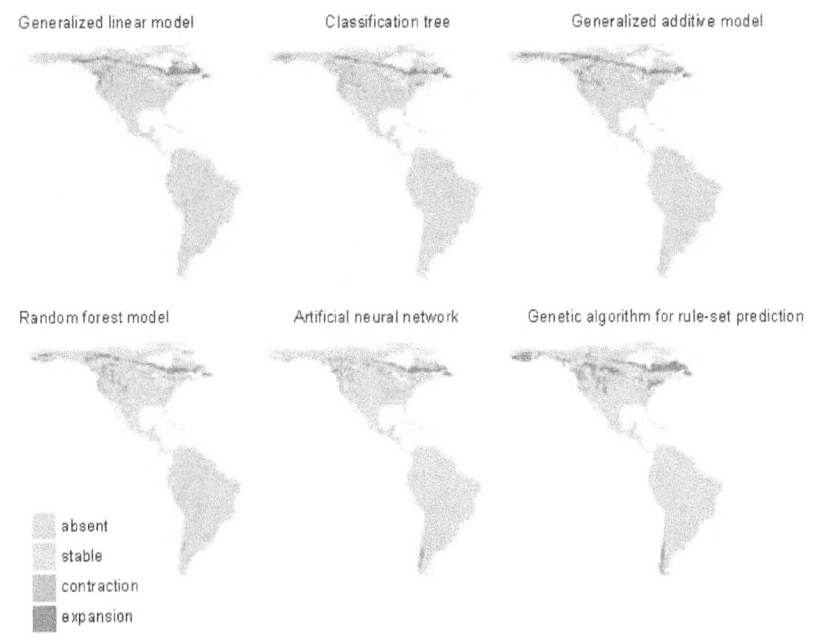

Figure 1—Predicted range shifts for the Fisher *Martes pennanti*. Maps depict range shifts as predicted by six different modeling approaches using the same data set. Predictions are based on climate data produced by the HADCM2SUL general circulation model using IPCC predicted future greenhouse gas contributions (IS92a) for the years 2061-2090.

dramatic effects on predicted range shifts and extinction rates. Our work demonstrates one potential method for greatly reducing the uncertainty in predicted future range shifts. Random Forest predictors and other model-averaging approaches will be important tools for accurately predicting range shifts in the face of climate change.

Keywords: Climate change, predictive modeling, climate-envelope, bioclimatic models, range shifts, species distributions.

References

Breiman, L. 2001. Random forests. Machine Learning. 45: 5-32.

Breiman, L.; Friedman, J.H.; Olshen, R.A.; Stone, C.J. 1984. Classification and regression trees. Monterey, CA: Wadsworth and Brooks/Cole. 358 p.

Hastie, T.J.; Tibshirani, R.J. 1990. Generalized additive models. London: Chapman and Hall. 335 p.

Houghton, J.T.; Ding, Y.; Griggs, D.J.; Noguer, M.; van der Linden, P.J.; Dai, X.; Maskell, K.; Johnson, C.A. 2001. Climate change 2001: the scientific basis. Intergovernmental panel on climate change third assessment report. Cambridge, England: Cambridge University Press. 944 p.

Johns, T.C.; Carnell, R.E.; Crossley, J.F.; Gregory, J.M.; Mitchell, J.F.B.; Senior, C.A.; Tett, S.F.B.; Wood, R.A. 1997. The second Hadley Centre coupled ocean-atmosphere GCM; model description, spinup and validation. Climate Dynamics. 13: 103-134.

Kattenberg, A.; Giorgi, F.; Grassl, H.; Meehl, G.A.; Mitchell, J.F.B.; Stouffer, R.J.; Tokioka, T.; Weaver, A.J.; Wigley, T.M.L. 1996. Climate models: projections of future climate. In: Houghton, H.T.; Meira Filho, L.G.; Gallander, B.A.; Harris, N.; Kattenberg, A.: Maskell, K., eds. Climate change 1995: the science of climate change. Contribution of working group 1 to the second assessment report of the intergovernmental panel on climate change. Cambridge, England: Cambridge University Press: 285-357.

McCullagh, P.; Nelder, J.A. 1989. Generalized linear models. 2nd edition. London: Chapman & Hall. 261 p.

Neilson, R.P. 1995. A model for predicting continental scale vegetation distributions and water balance. Ecological Applications. 5: 362-385.

Parmesan, C.; Ryrholm, N.; Stefanescu, C.; Hill, J.K.; Thomas, C.D.; Descimon, H.; Huntley, B.; Kaila, L.; Kullberg, J.; Tammaru, T.; Tennent, W.J.; Thomas, J.A.; Warren, M. 1999. Poleward shifts in geographical ranges of butterfly species associated with regional warming. Nature. 399: 579-583.

Parmesan, C.; Yohe, G. 2003. A globally coherent fingerprint of climate change impacts across natural systems. Nature. 421: 37-42.

Peterson, A.T.; Ortega-Huerta, M.A.; Bartley, J.; Sanchez-Cordero, V.; Soberon, J.; Buddemeier, R.H.; Stockwell, D.R.B. 2002. Future projections for Mexican faunas under global climate change scenarios. Nature. 416: 626-629.

Ripley, B.D. 1996. Pattern recognition and neural networks. Cambridge, England: Cambridge University Press. 416 p.

Root, T.L.; Price, J.T.; Hall, K.R.; Schneider, S.H.; Rosenzweig, C.; Pounds, J.A. 2003. Fingerprints of global warming on wild animals and plants. Nature. 421: 57-60.

Segurado, P.; Araújo, M.B. 2004. An evaluation of methods for modelling species distributions. Journal of Biogeography. 31: 1555-1568.

Thuiller, W.; Araújo, M.B.; Pearson, R.G.; Whittaker, R.J.; Brotons, L.; Lavorel, S. 2004. Biodiversity conservation: uncertainty in predictions of extinction risk. Nature. 430.

Community Response to Climate Change and Forest Disturbance

Courtney G. Flint[1]

U.S. Fish and Wildlife Service

Courtney G. Flint

[1]Assistant professor, Department of Natural Resources and Environmental Sciences, University of Illinois at Urbana-Champaign, W-503 Turner Hall, 1102 S. Goodwin Avenue, Urbana, IL 61801.

Introduction

Understanding climate change and its relationship with forest resources and communities involves a question of scale. Our understanding—or lack of understanding—of this interaction is complicated by a scale mismatch. We have global climate change models that provide scenarios with some regional and little local specificity (Cohen 1997, Wilbanks et al. 2003). At the regional scale, there are institutional structures and mechanisms for risk assessment and risk management related to environmental change (Haynes and Cleaves 1999). At the community scale, locality studies emerge that are less generalizable and subject to much variation (Wilbanks et al. 2003). But environmental change is most immediately experienced at the community scale and this is where adaptation and response really take place on an everyday basis (Berkes and Jolly 2001, Flint and Luloff 2005). The large gap between the scale of forecasting models and the scale where extreme conditions and climate change are actually experienced is deserving of more attention.

Alaska is acutely experiencing climate change as highlighted in recent publications with broad distribution such as the *New York Times* and *High Country News*. Berman et al. (1998) referred to a number of potential effects of climate change on Alaskan forest environments. These included: increased risk of wildfires; increased insect epidemics, increased windthrow; hydrological changes; reforestation failures; changes in the range of terrestrial and aquatic species; and changes in the range of tree species and ecotypes. Turning to the human community dimension of climate change and forest resources, a few questions emerge:

- How do risks from the relationship between climate change and forest resources affect local communities?

- What are the impacts and risks from climate change and forest disturbance perceived by local residents?

- What is the range of community vulnerability and community capacity to respond to the effects of climate change on forest ecosystems?

Risk Assessment and Community Perceptions

There are a number of important considerations for communities when assessing climate change risks. Technical risk assessments often neglect risk perceptions or the more subjective interpretations, concerns, or anxieties about things that might go wrong (Crawford-Brown 1999). These risk perceptions often coalesce and are shared at the community level (Fitchen et al. 1987). Community risk perceptions can affect levels of local engagement and responses to environmental change and natural resource management. Kasperson et al. (1988) suggested that risk is often amplified or attenuated by regional or local 'stations' where communication plays a key role in how risk perceptions emerge and

The large gap between the scale of forecasting models and the scale where extreme conditions and climate change are actually experienced is deserving of more attention.

Community risk perceptions can affect levels of local engagement and responses to environmental change and natural resource management.

grow, whether they emerge at all, and how they fade away. Local opinion leaders and groups play key roles in shaping perception and motivating local response (Wondolleck and Yaffee 2000). Berkes and Jolly (2001: p1) suggested that, "The inevitable surprises of climate change will unfold on a regional and local stage." Therefore, if we are to accurately assess risk situations related to environmental change such as climate change and consequent forest disturbances, we need to more fully appreciate not only the biophysical characteristics of the local scale, but the human dimensions of the local scale as well.

Communities are at an important scale for risk analysis and management. Risk perceptions are shared at this level, thus filtering changing perceptions of individuals. Collective actions based on such perceptions can have consequences for natural resource management. Local actions can either facilitate or impede forest management decisions and strategies. For example, a community having lower risk perceptions than technical risk assessments may mobilize opposition to forest risk-mitigation treatments. On the other hand, a community with higher risk perceptions than technical risk assessments may take matters into their own hands to mitigate risks.

In forest-based communities, there is generally an intimate relationship between a changing environment and everyday life. Information is often gathered by direct personal experience rather than from information sources such as media or agency education efforts. This direct experience increases local knowledge of environmental processes and shapes decision-making by local individuals.

A critical problem in natural resource management is that there are often rampant assumptions of homogeneity when describing or dealing with forest-based communities. Communities are often treated as if they are all the same with the same vulnerabilities, histories, experiences, capacities, and characteristics. In fact, the relationship between communities and forests is very multi-faceted (Christensen and Donohue 1991). Timber and non-timber resources, scenic and aesthetic values, tourism and recreation interests, quality of life, and multiple ecological values are all part of how local communities interact with forest resources. Based on what we know about the heterogeneity in society and across communities, we can't continue to sweep even adjacent communities into the same category out of hand. How communities respond to changing forest conditions related to climate change depends on contextual factors that should be extensively assessed as part of regional or landscape risk assessments.

m li ati ns r mt e enai eninsula las a

Findings from research on the Kenai Peninsula, Alaska illustrate the important relationships between climate change, forest disturbance, and community response (Flint, in press; Flint 2004; Rapp 2005). On the Kenai Peninsula, spruce bark beetles have killed over 80-90 percent

if we are to accurately assess risk situations related to environmental change such as climate change and consequent forest disturbances, we need to more fully appreciate not only the biophysical characteristics of the local scale, but the human dimensions of the local scale as well.

How communities respond to changing forest conditions related to climate change depends on contextual factors that should be extensively assessed as part of regional or landscape risk assessments.

of spruce trees across over 1 million acres (Ross et al. 2001). Local community responses to the disturbance frustrated forest management and forest management strategies frustrated local community residents.

The spruce bark beetle (*Dendroctonus rufipennis*) is endemic or native to the area but the outbreak that peaked in the 1990s on the Kenai Peninsula was unprecedented. One of the most common hypotheses about why the current outbreak of these beetles are covering larger areas and causing greater mortality than usual is the warming trend in south-central Alaska. This warming trend is reducing host tree resistance and reducing beetle generation time (Berman et al. 1998). A locally based ecologist, Ed Berg, who works for the US Wildlife Refuge on the Kenai Peninsula, supports this hypothesis (Berg 2003). What is important about this from a community standpoint is that Ed Berg has become almost a household name on the Kenai Peninsula. Many local residents interviewed referred to him in their discussions of the spruce bark beetle outbreak and linked their understanding of the role of climate change in the Kenai Peninsula forest disturbance to Ed Berg and not to larger scale media exposure.

This supports the notion that key opinion leaders are important to how risks are 'amplified' across local and regional scales and how local understanding of environmental issues are framed. Interestingly, this particular expert is cited by environmentalists and timber industry supporters alike as well as those in the middle. He serves as a bridge between these disparate interests. This type of individual is a key resource for natural resource managers.

People pay close attention to environmental changes. One resident from Anchor Point, Alaska said, "The first year we were here it was 45 below in the winter. We haven't seen that in a long time." Another resident from Ninilchik, Alaska said,

> What caused the spruce beetle thing in my opinion? I'm no scientist, but it's global warming! The temperature has come up. Oh yes! When it gets to 67 degrees, these beetles come out and attack the trees.

It's an emotional response. The immediate experience with forest disturbance registers deeply with people who live, work, and play in and around forest-based communities. A resident from Homer, Alaska said,

> You work so hard to become comfortable and acclimated in your environment. When that changes around you, you feel so out of control with that change. It's one thing to decide, 'I'm going to cut down those trees or put a road in here.' But to have that imposed on you… It's totally out of your control and it was very emotionally upsetting for a lot of people. Very sad. A number of people just looked at their dead trees and just sobbed.

On the Kenai Peninsula, the type and level of risk perception varied from one community to another and was strongly influenced by experience and local factors (Flint 2004). Factor analysis of mail survey data from 1,088 local residents from six Kenai Peninsula communities

The immediate experience with forest disturbance registers deeply with people who live, work, and play in and around forest-based communities.

showed two distinct factors of risk perceptions that were correlated but not collinear. The first factor was immediate threats to personal safety and property including forest and grass fire and falling trees. The second factor was broader threats to community and ecological well-being. This factor included risk perceptions related to scenic and aesthetic qualities, local identity, watersheds, habitat, jobs and other economic factors (Flint, in press).

Multiple regression analysis of survey data revealed that broader threats had a strong relationship with participation in community action (Flint 2004). On the other hand, immediate threats did not affect community action participation despite that these concerns were typically higher than concerns about broader well-being. In other words, participation in some form of community action, such as attending a local meeting or opposition to a timber sale, was influenced by risk perceptions of broader threats to well-being rather than concerns about wildfire or falling trees. On the Kenai Peninsula, forest managers have focused on mitigating the risk of wildfire. Flint's research suggests that though people are generally concerned about fire, broader concerns about community and ecological well-being are more likely to motivate involvement in local community action.

> …though people are generally concerned about fire, broader concerns about community and ecological well-being are more likely to motivate involvement in local community action.

Implications and Conclusions

These findings have a number of implications for managing climate change and forest disturbances. First, we should assume heterogeneity across communities situated in changing landscapes, not homogeneity. Community assessments along biophysical, sociodemographic, cultural, and economic dimensions will help to systematically categorize and understand local community differences. Second, resource managers should tap into local capacities to motivate participation and involvement in decision-making. This includes identifying and involving local opinion leaders and recognizing local knowledge arising from lengthy direct experience with local environments. Third, risk analyses should incorporate local risk perceptions in addition to technical risk assessments. Integrating risk perceptions with risk assessments helps to highlight priority areas for risk mitigation as well as areas of disagreement where more sensitivity may be needed to avoid protracted conflict over natural resource management. Fourth, we should appreciate broader threats to community and ecological well-being, not just potential for catastrophic events and their economic costs. These efforts would help to engage the local scale over the long-term to deal with dynamic environmental and community change. Bringing local communities into natural resource management contributes to sound decision-making that is more likely to be broadly recognized and accepted from multiple perspectives.

> Community assessments along biophysical, sociodemographic, cultural, and economic dimensions will help to systematically categorize and understand local community differences.

e eren es

Berg, E. 2003. Refuge notebook of the Kenai National Wildlife Refuge. http://alaska.fws.gov/nwr0/kenai/notebook/2003. February 20, 2004.

Berman, M.; Juday, G.P.; Burnside, R. 1998. Climate change and Alaska's forests: people, problems, and policies. In: Weller, G.; Anderson, P.A., eds. Proceedings, Assessing the consequences of climate change for Alaska and the Bering Sea region. Fairbanks, AK: Center for Global Change and Arctic Systems Research, University of Alaska, Fairbanks: 21-42.

Berkes, F.; Jolly, D. 2001. Adapting to climate change: socio-ecological resilence in a Canadian Western Arctic community. Conservation Ecology. 5(2): 18. http://www.consecol.org/vol5/iss2/art18.

Christensen, H.H.; Donoghue, E.M. 2001. A research framework for natural resource-based communities in the Pacific Northwest. Gen. Tech. Rep. PNW-GTR-515. Portland, OR: U.S. Department of Agriculture, Forest Service, Pacific Northwest Research Station. 21 p.

Cohen, S.J. 1997. Scientist-stakeholder collaboration in integrated assessment of climate change: lessons from a case study of Northwest Canada. Environmental Modeling and Assessment. 2: 281-293.

Crawford-Brown, D. 1999. Risk based environmental decisions: methods and culture. Boston, MA: Kluwer Academic Publishers. 224 p.

Fitchen, J.M.; Heath, J.S.; Fessenden-Raden, J. 1987. Risk perception in community context: a case study. In: Johnson, B.B.; Covello, V.T., eds. The social and cultural construction of risk. Boston, MA: D. Reidel: 31-54.

Flint C.G. [In press]. Community perspectives on spruce beetle impacts on the Kenai Peninsula, Alaska. Forest Ecology and Management.

Flint, C.G. 2004. Community response to forest disturbance on Alaska's Kenai Peninsula. University Park, PA: The Pennsylvania State University. 297 p. Ph.D. dissertation.

Flint, C.G.; Luloff, A.E. 2005. Natural resource-based communities, risk, and disaster: an intersection of theories. Society and Natural Resources. 18(5): 399-412.

Haynes, R.W.; Cleaves, D. 1999. Uncertainty, risk, and ecosystem management. In: Sexton, W.T.; Malk, A.J.; Szaro, R.C.; Johnson, N.C., eds. Ecological stewardship: a common reference for ecosystem management. Kiddlington, Oxford, U.K.: Elsevier Science, Ltd.: 413-429. Vol. 3.

Kasperson, R.E.; Renn, O.; Slovic, P.; Brown, H.S.; Emel, J.; Goble, R.; Kasperson, J.X.; Ratick, S. 1988. The social amplification of risk: a conceptual framework. Risk Analysis. 8(2): 177-187.

Rapp, V. 2005. The Kenai experience: communities and forest health. Science Update 10. Portland, OR: U.S. Department of Agriculture, Forest Service, Pacific Northwest Research Station. 12 p.

Ross, D.W.; Daterman, G.E.; Boughton, J.L.; Quigley, T.M. 2001. Forest health restoration in South-Central Alaska: a problem analysis. Gen. Tech. Rep. PNW-GTR-523. Portland, OR: U.S. Department of Agriculture, Forest Service, Pacific Northwest Research Station. 38 p.

Wilbanks, T.J.; Kates, R.; Abler, R. 2003. Global change and local places: estimating, understanding, and reducing greenhouse gases. Cambridge, UK: Cambridge University Press. 24 p.

Wondolleck, J.M.; Yaffee, S.L. 2000. Making collaboration work: lessons from innovation in natural resource management. Washington, DC: Island Press. 277 p.

Climate Change and Community Resilience:
A Knowledge Management Exercise

Trista Patterson[1]

Tom Iraci, USDA Forest Service

[1] Research Social Scientist, USDA Forest Service, Pacific Northwest Research Station, 2770 Sherwood Ln. Suite 2A, Juneau AK, 99801.
Email: tmpatterson@fs.fed.us

Abstract

Northern renewable-resource based communities are vulnerable to climate change in many ways. Developing a strategy to deal with these vulnerabilities requires integration of information, both at multiple scales and among modes of inquiry. A number of factors have been identified in contributing to community resilience (social capital, human capital, resource security, economic diversity, participative democracy, appropriate infrastructure, etc). However, research which addresses human activity as a driver of climate is often juxtaposed against the findings of research which addresses climate change's impact on humans. While the former implies the need for mitigation, the latter stresses adaptation. This is problematic because public funds for problem solving are limited, and adaptation and mitigation can appear as mutually exclusive strategies. A systems perspective illustrates how both adaptive and mitigative capacities are necessary to bring climate into natural resource management. This paper presents a knowledge management exercise designed to challenge participants to consider the integrative value of their work. A conceptual model of the system allowed individual conference attendees to identify the locus and extent of their work with respect to eight disciplinary approaches and nine spatial scales. The poster was interactive, and designed to call attention to system feedbacks and drivers that would otherwise be obscured. The result was a collectively generated diagram which highlighted knowledge clusters and gaps. Participant discussion focused on linkages between studies, and the spatial and conceptual extensions of the identified works.

Keywords: Knowledge management, community response, climate change.

Organizing…information strategically can improve ability to examine linkages, compare among cases and spatial scales, and respond to new information…

Introduction

Addressing climate change vulnerabilities to Northern renewable-resource based communities means optimizing among costs and benefits of various interventions. Optimization is a technique best executed under linear conditions. It is less effective when applied to non-linear / emergent phenomena or multiple scales, but becomes intractable when an issue becomes demonstrably polarized.

Community stress and polarization often rises when groups must reorient around shifting resource bases (such as those affected directly or indirectly by climate change) (Tannen 1999). Many studies have speculated on the various contributors to community resilience (social capital, human capital, resource security, economic diversity, participative democracy, appropriate infrastructure, etc.), leading to a wide variety of perspectives on the same issue. Organizing this information strategically can improve ability to examine linkages, compare among cases and spatial scales, and respond to new information, while adding little cost to existing projects. This paper presents a knowledge management exercise designed to facilitate information sharing among those who work on "pieces of the puzzle" or to facilitate consensus on a "sense of the whole."

As applied to ecosystems, or to integrated systems of people and the natural environment, resilience has three defining characteristics: the amount of change the system can undergo and still retain the same controls on function and structure, the degree to which the system is capable of self-organization, and the ability to build and increase the capacity for learning and adaptation (Holling 1973, 2000) (Carpenter et al. 2001). Resilience in social systems also involves the human capacity for anticipating and planning for the future. Social resilience relates to community adaptive capacity, in that, in social systems, the existence of institutions and networks that learn and store knowledge and experience, create flexibility in problem solving and balance power among interest groups, playing an important role in adaptive capacity (Berkes et al. 2002, Scheffer et al. 2000).

Addressing how people respond to periods of change, how society reorganizes following change, is the most neglected and least understood aspect in conventional resource management and science (Gunderson and Holling 2002). Scalar and integrated investigations are necessary because climate is a global, not local phenomenon. However, little emphasis is placed on articulating a well-formed conceptual model, to which multiple contributors can reference their work (Adams et al. 2003). Effective knowledge management can make scarce resources go further by extracting tacit knowledge from contributors, encapsulating shared knowledge and structuring consensus, facilitating productive discourse, identifying knowledge gaps, defining shared goals and strategies, and informing others and extending knowledge applications.

Effective knowledge management can make scarce resources go further...

Method

The "bulls-eye" model has been used in a number of formats to address the complexity of climate change, both from disciplinary and spatial perspectives (Patterson et al., in press; Patterson 2004). A bulls-eye model was modified to reflect the content of the proposed conference content. As the conference presenters delivered their talks, the conceptual range and spatial extent of their talk was mapped on the diagram, and identified with letters. During the conference breakout sessions, the bulls-eye diagram was presented to conference participants, and they were invited to locate their primary area of interest on the diagram, and to indicate with whisker lines the extent of the conceptual and spatial application of their work. Each participant was assigned a number, so that other conference attendees could reference their work.

Diagram Description

The concentric circles on the diagram refer to the relevant **spatial scales** (concentric circles I-IX) of the work, with the most local work the subject of the smallest circle and work referencing global scales located at the outer circle (fig. 1). The boxes surrounding the outer circle represent research concerning **state functions** (labeled A-G) that in theory can be quantified and tracked over time. The numbered arrows represent research on **change functions** (labeled 1-8). A dynamic model would consider

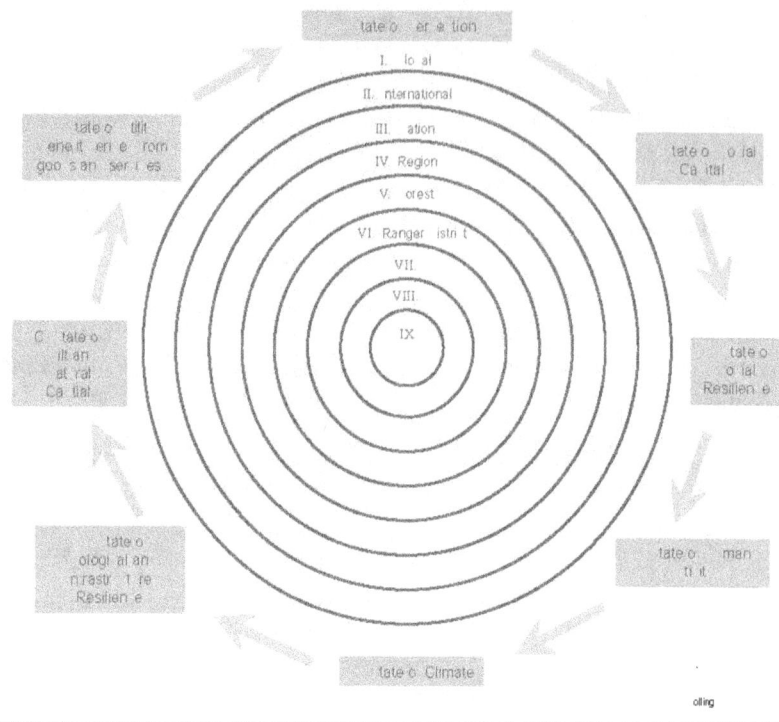

Figure 1—The knowledge management framework. Concentric circles I-IX represent increasing spatial scale. Letters A-H represent state variables, or data that can reflect a snapshot of the dynamic system at a given moment in time. Numbers 1-8 represent various disciplines and study of relations between variables.

these as "stock" versus "flow." These are explorations of relationships between two or more state functions, and their dynamics over time.

To understand the relationship between various components it is useful (though not necessary) to discuss them in a clock-wise fashion. Beginning with the bottom of the diagram, human activity and natural variability influence climate at local to global scales. Area (**A**) refers to attempts to document the State of Climate at each of these scales. Arrow (**1**) concerns the qualitative and dynamic relationship between climate variability and ecological and infrastructure resilience. Studies falling into region (**B**) are attempts to document the State of Ecological and Infrastructure Resilience by taking a more quantified approach. The amount of change these systems can undergo and still retain function and structure is the subject of area (**2**). Assessments of the State of Built or Natural Capital fall into section (**C**). The relationship between that capital and the way people derive satisfaction from consuming it, is the area of concern of arrow (**3**). Economics as a discipline is often concerned with maximizing the result: State of Utility (**D**). Studies of how people assess worth, fairness, risk, are all processes related to region (**4**). Social science surveys often document States of Perception (**E**). Much recent work has been done on how these perceptions are communicated and shared among stakeholders (**5**). The quantifications of networks, trusts and norms fall under documentation of the State of Social Capital and civic participation (**F**). Studies in area (**6**) examine the process by which as groups act in collective fashion, garnering resources and ultimately, maximizing net social benefit. Group capacity for self-organization, adaptation, mitigation

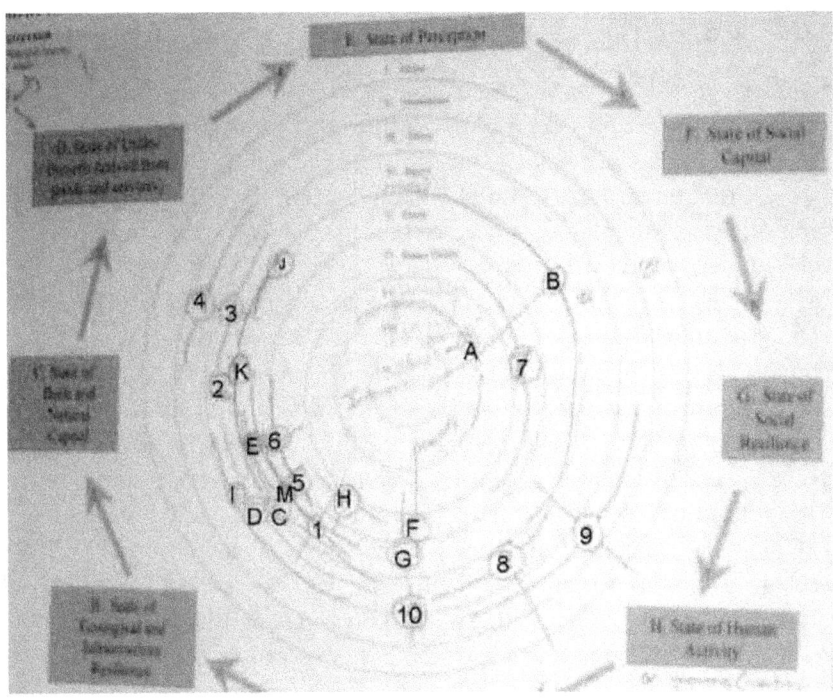

Figure 2—Participants drew their research interests upon the diagram, using whisker lines to express the disciplinary extent and spatial scale of their work. Numbers represent conference presentations, while letters represent conference audience members.

and continuing to maximize net social benefit in the face of change, falls under the category State of Social Resilience (**G**). The process by which this resilience is able to effect changes in human activity is the area of concern (**7**). Quantification of Human Activity, including economic structure and intervention such as taxes or incentives falls into area (**H**). In typical feedback form, this human activity mediates drivers responsible for climate change, the topic of investigations in region (**8**).

Results

The conference participants mapped their interests on the diagram, and used whisker lines to indicate when their work referenced more than one spatial scale. They drew whisker arcs around the circle from their 'data point' to refer to their work's disciplinary breadth, as illustrated below (fig. 2). A total of 10 conference presentations (represented by numbers), and thirteen attendees (represented by letters) were mapped on the diagram.

Presentations that were located on the diagram were sessions presented by (1) R.Nielson and J. Townsley; (2) L.Joyce and J. Morgan; (3) P.Mote, (4) B. Harding, K.Martin, S.Malloch; (5) L.Ziska; (6) J.Logan, (7) R.Rosenberger, D.Adams, C.Flint, D.Cox; (8) M.Delaney; (9) B. Carlson; (10) K. Redmond. Conference attendees who participated in mapping their interests on the diagram were (A) C. Flint, (B) B. Musik, (C) R. Rosenberger, (D) J.Lawler, (E) P.Bedlow, (F) A.Ray, (G) A.Kennedy, (H) C.Nitchke, (I) P.Glick, (J) S.Wall, (K) S.Wall, (L) E. Bella, and (M) D. Chew.

Discussion

This paper describes the use of a systems diagram, with which conference attendees were asked to consider conceptual pieces of the diagram in clockwise fashion. This depiction should not be taken to indicate that this is a linear process, the system components can be arranged in any number of ways. The benefits of knowledge layout in this manner, however, did confer a number of benefits. It counteracted the tendency to polarize between two concerns, namely how climate change is affecting communities versus how communities are driving climate change. First, the diagram helped facilitate dialog in common terms of how to maximize net social benefit, without making those concerns mutually exclusive. Second, it helped conference attendees to visually identify "knowledge clusters" and gaps. Most of the conference presentations and attendee interests were mapped to the lower left-hand corner of the diagram, namely the area associated with the state of ecological and infrastructural resilience. Many of the references to the economic discipline referred to the area between C and D, that is, the relationship between natural capital and the way people derive satisfaction from consuming it. The fewest references were made to work done on the state of benefit derived from goods and services (area D) and the state of social perception (area E), or how that might influence social function in the form of social capital (area F). Several participants noted that it might be interesting, (though challenging) to recruit presenters on this area (namely the social sciences) in the future.

A third product of the diagram was that it challenged exercise participants to consider the drivers of climate change, as well as climate change impacts. While conference participants noted that this was an important contributor to the system dynamics, many noted the challenge of encompassing such considerations in future conference events.

A final contribution of the diagram was that it allowed conference participants to explicitly address associations between scales and system components. While many researchers were collecting information at the forest or regional scale, very few referenced the global, or very site-specific scales. The lack of operative "community" at the global scale was noted to be a barrier to collective problem solving at this level. This is a notable gap, as climate change is a global, not localized problem, and as such studies which operate at a more localized scale but are unable to reference the broader global scale may have limited application to solving the serious challenges climate presents. Many commented on the proximity of other researchers to their own areas of interest, and remarked on the possibility of collaboration with other researchers in similar areas, but acting at different scales, or conversely researching at similar scales but on different system components.

These associations are critical for integrative studies in the future. This exercise was an interactive experiment with a conference audience that had expressed in the breakout discussions some tendency to view climate mitigation and adaptation as mutually exclusive strategies. The process of drawing individuals' research or interest areas on the diagram

...the diagram helped facilitate dialog in common terms of how to maximize net social benefit, without making those concerns mutually exclusive.

This exercise was an interactive experiment with a conference audience that had expressed in the breakout discussions some tendency to view climate mitigation and adaptation as mutually exclusive strategies.

helped identification of knowledge clusters and gaps at the conference. Facilitation of knowledge transfer both among disparate fields of research, and extending findings to other scales of inquiry can compound the value of existing studies with little added cost.

References

Adams, W.A.; Brockington, D.; Dyson, J.; Vira, B. 2003. Managing tragedies: understanding conflict over common pool resources. *Science*. 302(5652): 1915–1916.

Berkes, R.; Colding, J.; Folke, C. 2002. Introduction. In: Berkes, F.; Colding, J.; Folke, C., eds. Navigating social-ecological systems: building resilience for complexity and change. Cambridge, England: Cambridge University Press. 393 p.

Carpenter, S.; Walker, B.; Anderies, J.M.; Abel, N. 2001. From metaphor to measurement: Resilience of what to what? Ecosystems. 4: 765-781.

Gunderson, L.H.; Holling, C.S., eds. 2002. Panarchy: understanding transformations in human and natural systems. Washington, DC: Island Press. 503 p.

Holling, C.S. 1973. Resilience and stability of ecological systems. Annual Review of Ecology and Systematics. 4: 1-23.

Holling, C. S. 2000. Theories for sustainable futures. Conservation Ecology. 4(2): 7.

Patterson, T. 2004. Knowledge management for tourism, recreation and bioclimatology: Mapping the interactions. In: Matzarakis, A.; de Freitas, C.R.; Scott, D., eds. Advances in tourism climatology. Freiburg, Germany: Berlin Meteorlogical Institute, University of Freiburg. 12: 215-222.

Patterson, T.; Simpson, M.; Bastianoni, S. [In press]. Tourism and climate change: Two-way street or vicious/virtuous circle? Journal of Sustainable Tourism.

Scheffer, M.; Brock, W.A.; Westley, F. 2000. Mechanisms preventing optimum use of ecosystem services: an interdisciplinary theoretical analysis. Ecosystems. 3: 451-471.

Tannen, D. 1999. The argument culture. New York: Ballantine. 384 p .

Beedlow, P.

Rising Atmospheric CO^2 and Carbon Sequestration in Forests

Rising CO^2 concentrations in the atmosphere could alter Earth's climate system, but it is thought that higher concentrations may improve plant growth through a process known as the "fertilization effect." Forests are an important part of the planet's carbon cycle, and sequester a substantial amount of the CO^2 released into the atmosphere by human activities. Many people believe that the amount of carbon that forests sequester will increase as CO^2 concentrations rise. An increasing body of research suggests, however, that the fertilization effect is limited by nutrients and air pollution, in addition to the well documented limitations posed by temperature and precipitation. This review suggests that existing forests are not likely to increase sequestration as atmospheric CO^2 increases. Therefore, it is imperative that we manage forests to maximize carbon retention in above- and below-ground biomass and conserve soil carbon.

Peter Beedlow, US Environmental Protection Agency, Corvallis, OR. (541) 754-4634.
email: beedlow.peter@epamail.epa.gov

Bella, Elizabeth

Invasive Plant Expansion into Biogeoclimatic Envelopes under Current Climate and Global Climate Change Scenarios in Alaska

Alaska has long been considered immune to large-scale biological invasions due to its climate and its relative geographical isolation, but increased trade and travel to the state, as well as a changing climate, have begun to change this perception. A multi-agency approach of inventory, monitoring, education, and research is starting to define and plan for the complex problems of ecological, economic, and social effects of invasive plants on public lands in Alaska. This project aims to, over the next three years, increase our understanding of the biogeoclimatic mechanisms for invasive species range expansion in Alaska, and provide management recommendations for public lands agencies under a changing climate. We have determined a list of invasive species of concern for this study based on literature reviews of similar or identical species and their behavior in similar climates, and have started to model the current biogeoclimatic ranges of these higher-risk species using range envelope models and Alaska climate and GIS data. Range envelope models have previously have been applied to rare plant range reductions, but have great potential for application to invasive species range expansion determinations. We next plan to utilize Global Circulation Models (GCMs) to predict the same species ranges one hundred years in the future under different climate change scenarios, and to compare current and future ranges determine to changes in ranges, patterns of change, and rate of movement of species over the landscape. The results of this study will include the creation of detailed maps of current and future biogeoclimatic ranges of the selected invasion species in order to direct management efforts to control of higher-risk species, and to provide a template for predicting other species range expansions in Alaska and in similar northern climates.

Elizabeth Bella, Department of Environmental Science and Policy, University of California, Davis, 2101C Wickson Hall, One Shields Avenue, Davis, CA 95616
(530) 752-6003; email: ebella@fs.fed.us.

Professional Affiliation: Chugach National Forest, Seward Ranger District

---

Chew, J.; Bollenbacher, B.; and C. Stalling

Modeling Impacts On The Levels Of Sustainable Resources From Increased Wildfire Acres Associated With Potential Climate Changes

The impact that changing climates may have on the ability to sustain natural resource goals over a 300 year planning horizon for a national forest is examined by using a spatially explicit, stochastic, landscape-level simulation model. A national forest in the northern Rocky Mountains is simulated to examine different levels of wildfire, insect and disease activity that would result from warm and dry cycles and a higher probability of extreme fire events over the planning period. Differences in the long-term sustained yield for wood products, acres that have the potential to provide old growth conditions, the frequency of wildfire having a significant impact on water quality and the acres of wildfire in a wildland urban interface are compared. Two levels of fuel-reduction treatments

are examined for the scenario that results in the highest level of wildfire over the planning period.

Jimmie D. Chew, Forester, Rocky Mountain Research Station, USDA Forest Service, 800 E. Beckwith, Missoula, MT 59807
(406) 542-4171; email: jchew@fs.fed.us

Barry Bollenbacher, Regional Silviculturist Regional Office, Northern Region, USDA Forest Service, Missoula, MT
(406) 329-3297; email: bbollenbacher@fs.fed.us

Christine Stalling, Biologist, Rocky Mountain Research Station, USDA Forest Service
800 E. Beckwith, Missoula, MT 59807
(406) 542-4153; email: cstalling@fs.fed.us

Laskowski, M. and L.A. Joyce

Natural Resource Managers Respond to Climate Change: A Look at Actions, Challenges, and Trends

Natural resource managers in the Western U.S. are progressively responding to concerns about current and future climate change. Some of the catalysts include increases in impacts observed on climate-sensitive resources, increases in extreme weather events, heightened levels of public interest and concern, and extensive scientific evidence. We assessed the types of active measures western natural resource managers are taking in response to potential climate-change effects. The spectrum of responses was categorized as follows: awareness and discussion, assessment, monitoring, research, education and outreach, policy and planning, field-based activities, and mitigation. Activities ranged from holding informal meetings and specialized workshops within the institution to creating educational bulletins and exhibits for the public. Activities to develop a better information database included vulnerability assessments and initiating long-term monitoring. Further activities ranged from creating formal strategies, management plans, prescribed burning and grazing, to carbon sequestration and green house gas reduction. Challenges were associated with all active responses. Understanding current and future climate changes and deciphering their impact on the ecosystem as well as uncertainty about what and how much to do about it posed significant challenges. Other challenges include limited resources (human, financial, technological, and time) and lack of institutional interest. In general, managers responded to climate-change concerns when there were obvious incentives (e.g., improved grazing conditions, improved hydropower capacity). Those who oversee climate-sensitive resources, and/or who work in areas that have experienced extreme climate events or climate variability (e.g., droughts, landslides) have also responded with management actions. Additionally, managers receiving specific guidance on planning for climate change from partnerships with climate-focused organizations, extension staff, and/or scientists were more prepared to respond.

Michele Laskowski, Contractor, SI Inc, 240 West Prospect, Fort Collins, CO 80526
(970) 498-1123

Dr. Linda Joyce, Rocky Mountain Research Station 240 West Prospect, Fort Collins, CO 80526
(970) 498-2560; email: ljoyce@fs.fed.us

Upper Williamson River discharge (r = 0.73), Sprague River discharge (r = 0.65), net inflow to Upper Klamath Lake (r = 0.68), and moderately correlated with observed Crater Lake April 1st SWE (r = 0.52).

These results suggest that warm PDO phase equatorial sea-surface temperature gradients, as opposed to mean sea-surface temperature or sea-level pressure patterns, explain a large portion of hydrologic variability observed in the Upper Klamath basin. Furthermore, additional analysis indicated regional-scale correlations, which may extend the usefulness of the TNI outside of the Upper Klamath basin. Thus, the TNI may prove useful for long-lead stream flow forecast operations, ecosystem-scale modeling, and a variety of other environmental science applications.

Adam M. Kennedy, Environmental Sciences and Resources, Portland State University, PO Box 751 Portland, Oregon 97207, email: kenna@pdx.edu

Professional affiliation: Natural Resources Conservation Service (NRCS), Portland, Oregon

Kennedy, Adam M.

The Influence of El Niño-related Sea-Surface Temperature Gradients (Trans-Niño Index) on Upper Klamath Basin Stream Discharge

This research investigates large-scale climate variables affecting inter-annual hydrologic variability of streams flowing into Upper Klamath Lake, Oregon. Six indexes: the Pacific North American Pattern, Southern Oscillation Index, Pacific Decadal Oscillation (PDO), Multivariate ENSO Index, Niño 3.4, and a revised Trans-Niño Index (TNI) were evaluated independently for their ability to explain inter-annual variation of the Upper Williamson River, Sprague River, Upper Klamath Lake net inflow, and Crater Lake snow water equivalent (SWE). The TNI, which measures the sea-surface temperature gradient between region Niño 1+2 and region Niño 4, was the only index to show significant correlations during the current warm phase of the PDO. During the warm PDO phase (1978-present), the averaged October through December TNI was strongly correlated (α = 0.05) with the following April through Septeme

L. Kruger and T. Patterson

Knowledge Management for Climate Change in Northern Renewable-Resource Based Communities

Addressing climate change vulnerabilities to Northern Renewable-Resource Based Communities (NRRBCs) means optimizing among costs and benefits of various interventions. Optimization is a technique best executed under linear conditions. It is less effective when applied to non-linear/emergent phenomena or multiple scales, but becomes intractable when an issue becomes demonstrably polarized.

Polarization frequently occurs when groups are under stress. Community stress often rises when groups must reorient around shifting resource bases (such as those affected directly or indirectly by climate change). While many studies have speculated on the various contributors to community resilience (social capital, human capital, resource security, economic diversity, participative democracy, appropriate infrastructure, etc), organization of the resulting information has been less strategic. We suggest this as a leverage point that could improve a community's ability to examine linkages, compare among cases and spatial scales, and respond to new information, while adding little cost to existing projects. This poster explores one way complex information might be shared among those who work on "pieces of the puzzle," or how it might be presented to those who desire some "sense of the whole" before making policy decisions.

We present a conceptual model of the system, visually reorganizing factors affecting community resilience to call attention to system feedbacks and drivers that would otherwise be obscured. Ultimately, we aim to provide the basis for increased collaboration among disparate fields of research, identification of knowledge gaps and facilitation of knowledge transfer.

Linda Kruger and Trista Patterson, USDA Forest Service, Pacific Northwest Research Station, 2770 Sherwood Ln. Suite 2A, Juneau AK, 99801 Contact email: tmpatterson@fs.fed.us

---

Lawler, J.; White, D.; Neilson, R.; and A. Blaustein

Predicting Climate-induced Range Shifts for Mammals: How Good are the Models?

In order to manage wildlife and conserve biodiversity, it is critical that we understand the potential impacts of climate change on species distributions. Several different approaches to predicting climate-induced geographic range shifts have been proposed to address this problem. We investigated the potential implications of using these different approaches for conclusions drawn about future range shifts and extinctions. Using the current ranges of 100 mammal species found in the western hemisphere, we compared six methods for modeling their predicted future ranges. All approaches modeled current ranges as a function of current climate and current land cover. Future ranges were predicted using predicted future climatic conditions from a global circulation model and predicted future land cover from a process-based equilibrium vegetation model. Predicted future distributions differed markedly across the alternative modeling approaches, resulting in estimates of extinction rates that ranged between 0 and 7 percent, depending on which modeling

approach was used. Random forest predictors, a model-averaging approach, consistently outperformed the other techniques (correctly predicting > 99 percent of current absences and 86 percent of current presences). We conclude that the types of models used in a study can have dramatic effects on predicted range shifts and extinction rates; and that model-averaging approaches appear to have the greatest potential for predicting range shifts in the face of climate change.

Joshua J. Lawler, Department of Zoology, Oregon State University, c/o US Environmental Protection Agency, 200 SW 35th St., Corvallis, OR, 97333, USA. (541) 754-4834. email: lawler.joshua@epa.gov.

Denis White, US Environmental Protection Agency, 200 SW 35th St., Corvallis, OR, 97333, USA. (541) 754-4476. email: white.denis@epa.gov.

Ronald P. Neilson, US Forest Service, 3200 SW Jefferson Way, Corvallis, OR, 97331, USA. (541) 750-7303. email: rneilson@fs.fed.us

Andrew R. Blaustein, Department of Zoology, Oregon State University, Corvallis, OR, 97331, USA. (541) 737-5356.
email: blaustea@science.oregonstate.edu

Nitschke, Craig and J. L. Innes

Impact of Climate Change on Landscape-level Fire Severity Ratings in the North Okanagan, British Columbia, Canada

For forest managers, one of the most important aspects of climate change that need to be considered is how climate change will impact the effects of disturbances, including both natural disturbances and those induced by management activities. With global climate change models (GCMS) predicting increased warming of between 2 and 5°C with little or no change in precipitation in Western Canada, it seems likely that increased summer continental drying could result in an increased risk of drought and an increase in fire severity and frequency. To determine the affect of potential climate change on the fire severity ratings for a 145,000 ha landscape located in the North Okanagan region of British Columbia, Canada, an analysis was conducted using three GCMS, five weather stations, and the Canadian Forest Fire Danger

Rating System. The analysis compared the predictions of three GCMS: CGCM1, CGCM2, and Hadley CM3. Each GCM affected the fire severity ratings differently, with the Hadley model having the greatest and most divergent impact. The results suggest that by 2100, the mean fire season length may increase by 30 percent, with 90 percent of this increase occurring in the spring (Mar-May). By 2100, mean fire severity was found to increase by 42 percent in the spring, 95 percent in the summer (June-Aug), and 30 percent in the autumn (Sept-Nov). The preliminary results from this study suggest that climate change will have a significant influence on fire weather and severity in the North Okanagan. Increased fire season and severity could result in larger, more intense, and frequent fires that may significantly influence the ability of forest managers to maintain a sustainable timber supply and conserve biodiversity. An increased fire frequency could facilitate the migration of vegetation by creating opportunities for fire-tolerant species and limiting the regeneration of fire-intolerant species. Understanding the potential threat of climate change on fire severity can provide incentive for managers to design their forest landscapes as "fire-smart" and incorporate the impacts of climate change into sustainable forest management planning.

Keywords: Fire Severity, Climate Change, Okanagan, Sustainable Forest Management

Craig R. Nitschke and **John L. Innes**, Sustainable Forest Management Research Group, Department of Forest Resources Management, University of British Columbia, 2045-2424 Main Mall, Vancouver, BC, Canada V6T 1Z4
Correspondence to: nitschke@interchange.ubc.ca

Ray, Andrea J.

Linking Climate to Multi-purpose Reservoir Management in the Gunnison Basin

As in many other areas in the West, the Gunnison basin is increasingly sensitive to climate variability because new demands for water are being incorporated into the system, including in-stream flows for ecosystems and recreation. Some of the implications of climate variability and change for water management in the 21st century are:

- The effects of multi-year droughts, e.g., periods of 3-7 years of below average snow water equivalent (SWE) and inflows;

- The effects of decadal-scale periods in which average inflows are below normal, although there may be wet years interspersed;

- The potential impact of a long-term decrease in Aspinall inflows, due to decreases in precipitation and SWE;

- The potential impact of an earlier spring peak;

- The opportunity to take advantage of forecasting interannual climate variability to improve the efficiency of reservoir management, both in wet and dry years;

- The possibility of adaptive management with respect to the effects of climate on water as new understanding about the climate of the region becomes available.

The combination of increasing climate sensitivity and changing polices requires institutions that are able to be adaptive to cope with both anticipated changes and those which are difficult to predict. Characteristics of water management institutions that are likely to be able to cope with the changing policy and climate regimes will be discussed. Operations in this system have been adjusted for many reasons to benefit the basin, for example, managers have responded to both the flow recommendations for endangered fish and the severe drought of 2002 by increasing flexibility and finding new ways of operating to benefit a diverse set of water uses. Water management institutions in the Gunnison basin have significant adaptive capacity to respond to both policy changes and climate events, and also the capacity to respond to climate forecasts if the appropriate forecasts are available.

Andrea J. Ray, Ph.D., Research Scientist, NOAA/ Climate Diagnostics Center, 325 Broadway, Mailcode R/CD, Boulder, CO 80305-3328
http://www.cdc.noaa.gov/people/andrea.ray;
email: andrea.ray@noaa.gov

Speakers

Darius Adams
Department of Forest Resources
Oregon State University
Peavy Hall 210
Corvallis, OR 97331
541-737-5504
darius.adams@oregonstate.edu

Jamie Barbour
PNW Research Station
620 SW Main St., Suite 400
Portland, OR 97205
503-808-2542
jbarbour01@fs.fed.us

Bill Carlson
Carlson Small Power Consultants
13395 Tierra Heights Rd.
Redding, CA 96003
530-945-8876
cspc@shasta.com

Dave Cox
Mason, Bruce and Girard
707 SW Washington Ave., Suite 1300
Portland, OR 9705
503-224-3445
dcox@masonbruce.com

Matt Delaney
Delaney Forestry Services
1216 Calapooia St.
Albany, OR 97321
541-967-0576
mdelaney1@qwest.net

Angus Duncan
Bonneville Environmental Foundation
133 SW Second Ave., Suite 410
Portland, OR 97204
503-248-1905
angusduncan@b-e-f.org

Courtney Flint
Department of Natural Resources and
Environmental Sciences
W-503 Turner Hall
1102 S. Goodwin
University of Illinois
Urbana, IL 61802
217-333-2770
courtflint@yahoo.com

Benjamin Harding
Hydrosphere Consulting
1002 Walnut Suite 200
Boulder, CO 80304
303-443-7839
blh@hydrosphere.com

Richard Haynes
PNW Research Station
620 SW Main St., Suite 400
Portland, OR 97205
503-808-2002
rhaynes@fs.fed.us

Pete Holmberg
Washington Dept of Natural Resources
PO Box 47016
Olympia, WA 98504
360-902-1348
pete.holmberg@wadnr.gov

Linda Joyce
Rocky Mountain Research Station
240 W Prospect Ave
Ft. Collins, CO 80526
970-498-2560
ljoyce@fs.fed.us

Gary Lettman
OR Dept of Forestry
2600 State St.
Salem, OR 97310
503-945-7200
glettman@odf.state.or.us

Jesse Logan
Rocky Mountain Research Station
860 North 1200 East
Logan, UT 84321
435-755-3573
jlogan@fs.fed.us

Steve Malloch
Attorney
10212 Belgrove Ct. NW
Seattle, WA 98177
206-818-0482
smalloch@comcast.net

Kyle Martin
Columbia River Inter-Tribal Fish Commission
729 NE Oregon, Suite 200
Portland, OR 97232
503-238-0667
mark@critfc.org

Jack Morgan
USDA Agricultural Research Service
Crops Research Lab
1701 Centre Avenue
Fort Collins, CO 80526
970-492-7121
jack.morgan@ars.usda.gov

Phil Mote
Center for Science in the Earth System (CSES)
Joint Institute for the Study of the Atmosphere and
Ocean (JISAO)
University of Washington
PO Box 354235
Seattle, WA 98195
206-616-5346
philip@atmos.washington.edu

Ron Neilson
PNW Research Station
3200 Jefferson Way
Corvallis, OR 97331
541-750-7303
neilson@fs.fed.us

Michael Pellant
Bureau of Land Management
1387 S. Vinnell Way
Boise, ID 83709
208-373-3823
Mike_Pellant@blm.gov

Kelly Redmond
Western Regional Climate Center
2215 Raggio Pkwy
Reno, NV 89512
775-674-7011
krwrcc@dri.edu

Gordon Reeves
PNW Research Station
3200 Jefferson Way
Corvallis, OR 97331
541-750-7314
greeves@fs.fed.us

Randall Rosenberger
Department of Forest Resources
Oregon State University
109 Peavy Hall
Corvallis, OR 97331
541-737-4425
r.rosenberger@oregonstate.edu

Stephen Saunders
Rocky Mountain Climate Organization
PO Box 270444
Louisville, CO 80027
303-880-4598
saunders@rockymountainclimate.org

Joel Smith
Stratus Consulting
PO Box 4059
Boulder, CO 80306
303-381-8218
jsmith@stratusconsulting.com

Jim Stevens
The Campbell Group
One SW Columbia, Suite 1700
Portland, OR 97258
503-275-9675

John Townsley
USDA Forest Service
1240 South Second
Okanogan, WA 98840
509-826-3568
jtownsley@fs.fed.us

Lewis Ziska
USDA Agricultural Research Service
10300 Baltimore Ave.
Bldg 46A Barc West
Beltsville, MD 20705
301-504-6639
lziska@asrr.arsusda.gov

Metric Equivalents

When you know:	Multiply by:	To find:
Inches (in)	2.54	Centimeters
Feet (ft)	.3048	Meters
Miles	1.609	Kilometers (km)
Acres (ac)	.41	Hectares
Degrees Fahrenheit (°F)	(F-32)/1.8	Degrees Celsius (°C)

English Equivalents

When you know:	Multiply by:	To find:
Centimeters (cm)	.394	Inches (in)
Meters (m)	3.28	Feet (ft)
Kilometers (km)	.6215	Miles (mi)
Hectares (ha)	2.47	Acres
Degrees Celsius (°C)	1.8 C + 32	Degrees Fahrenheit (°F)